WINNING CARD PLAY

This is a comprehensive manual of card play destined to become a lifetime companion for many players. Every aspect of dummy play and defence is covered, and as each move and countermove comes under review, the secrets of winning play are revealed one by one. Throughout the book, the main emphasis is on the handling of those everyday situations that so often decide the result of a rubber or a match.

The reader is not burdened with sets of exercises at the end of each chapter. The exercises are, in fact, built in to the text so that, without realizing it, the reader is being tested all through the book. Sitting at the author's shoulder, often with only two hands on view, he shares in the planning of the play and defence on every deal. He is constantly 'learning by doing', and the logic of each situation is brought home to him in such a way that he is not likely to forget the lesson.

This is a book for reading over and over again. For those who already have some knowledge of card-play technique and for complete beginners, the author's message is the same. There is no limit to how far you can go if you learn to 'play your cards right'.

No one could be better qualified to write such a book than Hugh Kelsey, acknowledged to be one of the top authorities on the game and acclaimed throughout the world for the quality of his writings.

Also by Hugh Kelsey

Instant Guide to Bridge
Slam Bidding
Adventures in Card Play (with Géza Ottlik)

WINNING CARD PLAY

Hugh Kelsey

LONDON
VICTOR GOLLANCZ LTD
in association with Peter Crawley
1979

ISBN 0 575 02609 x

Printed in Great Britain by
Latimer Trend & Company Ltd Plymouth

Contents

Acknowledgments

I am grateful to Denis Young for giving my typescript the benefit of his usual careful scrutiny. A number of his helpful suggestions have been adopted in the final text.

H.W.K.

Introduction

In this manual of card play I have attempted to cover all the principal moves and countermoves in the continuing battle between the declarer and the defenders at the bridge table. Naturally there are some omissions, for a comprehensive work would run to several thousand pages, but I believe that the omissions are minor and relatively unimportant. With the aid of the techniques outlined in this book the reader will be able to deal competently with all the common card-play situations, and this will give him the confidence to tackle new problems as they arise.

No great originality can be claimed for the subject matter. The principles of winning card play are the same today as they were fifty years ago, and in the interval much has been written on the subject. However, a fresh approach can sometimes help to shed light on perplexing problems. I have tried to achieve clarity of exposition above all else.

Do not expect to find much space given to rare coups, exotic endings or spectacular deals. This is a textbook for practical players and the emphasis throughout is on ordinary hands of the type encountered every day. It is in the handling of these bread-and-butter situations that rubbers and matches are won or lost.

The book is divided into three sections. Part One deals with the simple principles of play and defence that provide the only sound basis for further study. I have been concerned not only to demonstrate the right play in each situation but also to explain why one play is superior to another. It is easier for a player to remember the correct action if he is aware of the reasoning behind it.

Since this is a graded course in card play, the level of instruction varies considerably. The reader must choose his point of entry to suit his own standard of play, and thereafter skip quickly over any pages that are too elementary for him. A player familiar with the basic principles, for instance, may elect to begin with Part Two, where certain aspects of technique, mainly in the field of tactics, are examined in greater depth. The purpose of this section is to extend the repertoire of the reader, training him to think along the right lines in many different situations and in general giving his game a keener edge.

Part Three crosses the barrier into the territory of advanced play, explaining the techniques of the end-game and giving a glimpse of the way in which the expert mind works. A study of this section will not turn the reader into a master player overnight, but it will at least demonstrate that expert status need not be beyond his grasp.

Part One
BASIC TECHNIQUE

I

Ways of Promoting Tricks

The principle of promotion – proper order – the positional factor – the finesse – postponing a finesse – double and combination finesses – two-way finesses – when to refuse a finesse – covering an honour – when not to cover – tricks from low cards – the hold-up – the duck

The secret of good play lies in exploiting the full potential of the partnership cards so as to win as many tricks as possible. It is as well to start with a clear idea of where the tricks may come from. Surprisingly, there are only three sources:

(1) High cards.
(2) Low cards in a long suit (once the high cards have gone).
(3) Trumps.

Every manoeuvre in the bridge-player's repertoire, from the simplest finesse to the most complex coup, has to draw its tricks from one of these three sources. In this chapter we shall concentrate on the first two, learning how to use high cards and long suits to the best advantage.

The Principle of Promotion

It is worth while reflecting for a moment on the hierarchy of rank and the way in which each card of a suit interacts with its neighbours. In the absence of trumps, an ace can always win the first trick. Hence the ace can be said to control the first round of a suit. When the ace has been played, the king becomes top dog, controlling the second round. Similarly, when the king has been played, the queen controls the third round. This is the principle of promotion in action. Whenever a high card in a suit is played, each lower card is promoted one step in rank.

Of course, in practical play it seldom happens that the first round of a suit is won by the ace, the second by the king and the third by the queen. For one thing the players are free agents and there is no compulsion on the holder of the ace to play it at the first opportunity. Furthermore, the ace is often used to capture an enemy king or queen, the king to capture a queen or jack, and so on.

How is promotion affected when two high cards are played on the same trick? Exactly as one would expect. Each lower card is promoted two positions in rank. Suppose, holding K Q J 10, you lead the king and lose to the enemy ace. Your queen is at once promoted from third to first rank and controls the next round. The jack and ten enjoy similar promotion and you make three tricks in the suit.

A four-step promotion is the maximum that can be achieved at one time. This can happen only when four high cards are played to the trick, as in the following example:

When you lead the jack from dummy it is covered by the queen, king and ace. Immediately your ten shoots up from fifth rank to first. The nine and the eight also receive four-step promotion, and you score three tricks.

```
            J 6 3

                  N
A 7 5 4      W         E      Q 2
                  S

            K 10 9 8
```

Proper Order

One situation in which rank loses its significance is where you have a solid sequence of high cards in one hand or the other. Holding A K Q J 10, for instance, there is no need to start with the ace. Since neither opponent has a higher card, the ten will win the first trick just as well. In effect your cards are equal and the order in which you play them is immaterial.

Rank reasserts itself, however, when the high cards are divided between your hand and the dummy.

```
    (a)         A K              (b)         A Q

                  N                            N
            W         E                  W         E
                  S                            S

            Q J 10                        K J 10
```

In diagram (a) you have no option but to win the first two tricks in dummy with the ace and king and, with the lead on the table, you may have no way of returning to hand to cash your third trick in the suit. A holding such as this, where the winners cannot be cashed without interruption, is known as a blocked suit. It is something to be avoided whenever possible.

The position in (b) is more flexible. You can win the first trick with any one of three cards – the ace, the king or the queen. If you win with the king or queen, however, you will block the suit and will be unable to enjoy your third trick unless you have a card of entry in another suit. The blockage can be avoided in this case by leading the jack or ten and winning the first trick with the ace. On the next round your king can exert its rank by overtaking the queen, and with the lead in your own hand you will be free to enjoy your third trick in the suit.

Let us add a few cards and make some minor changes in the diagrams.

(c)　　　A K 3　　　　(d)　　　A Q 3

```
   N                    N
 W   E                W   E
   S                    S
```

Q J 10 9　　　　　　　　　K J 4 2

In (c) you might win the first trick with any one of six cards. But if you win in your own hand (with the nine, for instance) you will be left with the undesirable blocked position of diagram (a). To avoid blocking the suit you must win the first two tricks with the ace and king. The lead of the three on the third round will then enable you to win two more tricks in your own hand.

Similarly, in (d), a blockage will develop if the first trick is won by the king or the jack. To be sure of running your four winners without interruption, win the first two tricks with the ace and queen (in either order).

From these examples we can extract an important rule of card play:

When high cards adjacent in rank are divided between the two hands, play first the high cards from the shorter holding.

The rule holds good whether the high cards are immediate winners or not.

(e)　　　K J 10 3　　　　(f)　　　K Q 5

```
   N                    N
 W   E                W   E
   S                    S
```

Q 2　　　　　　　　　　J 10 4 2

In these positions you need to drive out the ace in order to establish tricks in the suit. In (e) you should start with the queen from your own hand. There is then no risk of blocking the suit.

In (f) lead a low card to the king or queen. If this holds the trick, continue with the second honour card from dummy to force out the ace. There is a further point of interest in this diagram. If West plays the ace on the first round, you should 'unblock' by playing the king or queen under the ace. This costs nothing, for you still have three honour cards to take care of the next three tricks, and you retain the ability to run your tricks without interruption.

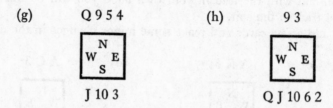

(g) Q 9 5 4

J 10 3

(h) 9 3

Q J 10 6 2

In these examples you have two honour cards to force out, but the principle is still the same. To avoid all risk of a blockage, first play the high cards from the shorter holding. Start with the jack or ten in (g), and by leading a low card to the nine in (h).

The Positional Factor

So far you have had an easy time of it with solid sequences of honour cards. What if your high cards are not in sequence or if the sequences are incomplete? Then you must take advantage of the positional factor, leading towards your high cards rather than playing away from them. The high cards are more likely to win tricks if one of the opponents has to play ahead of them.

(a) K Q 3

A 10 7   J 9 8 2

6 5 4

(b) K 6 4

10 9 8 5   A 3

Q J 7 2

Assume that you have plenty of outside entries and can lead from either hand. If you lead the king from dummy in diagram (a), you will make no more than one trick irrespective of the position of the ace. By leading from hand towards the high cards in dummy, however, you will make two tricks whenever the ace is favourably placed. West can do nothing to stop you, for he is forced to commit himself ahead of dummy. If he plays his ace 'on air', the king and queen are at once promoted to winning rank. And if West plays low, you win with dummy's queen, return to hand in another suit, and torment him again.

Diagram (b) shows a combination of cards that is often mishandled. Players tend to lead low towards the king, or to lead low from dummy to the jack and return a low card to the king. To be sure, it makes no difference when the suit breaks 3–3, but it costs a trick when the cards are divided as shown. For the maximum chance of three tricks in this situation you should lead twice towards the two honours; that is, lead the four to your jack, re-enter dummy in another suit, and lead the six towards your queen. You are rewarded when the ace tumbles down without capturing an honour card.

(c)   Q 5   (d)   J 4

K 9 6 4 | N | J 10 8 3   Q 10 6 2 | N | 9 8 5
          | W E | | W E |
          | S | | S |

        A 7 2   A K 7 3

In diagram (c) only one trick can be made if the first lead comes from dummy. But if you start by leading a low card towards dummy's queen, you make two tricks whenever West has the king.

Similarly, in (d), the limit is two tricks if the first lead is made from dummy. Three tricks can be made when West has the queen by starting with a low card towards the jack.

(e)   Q 8 6 5

J 10 3 | N | A 9
         | W E |
         | S |

       K 7 4 2

To make three tricks with the combination of cards shown opposite you need to find one of the defenders with a doubleton ace. The location of the ace may be a complete guess or there may be some indication from the bidding. In this case the winning line is to start with a low card from dummy towards your king. When this wins the trick you play low from both hands on the second round, leaving East with a severe attack of frustration.

The Finesse

The best-known stratagem in the play of the cards – the finesse – is one of the many plays that take advantage of the positional factor. By leading towards a tenace holding (a sequence of honours with a gap in it) you compel one of the defenders to play ahead of your high cards.

[15]

(a) A Q J   (b) A 7 4

K 8 7 [N W E S] 10 6 4 2   9 8 3 [N W E S] Q 10 6 2

       9 5 3   K J 5

Owing to the favourable position of the king in diagram (a), you can make three tricks by leading from the South hand. If West plays low you finesse the jack, return to hand in another suit, and lead low again for a finesse of the queen.

Likewise, in (b), three tricks can be made by leading the five to dummy's ace and finessing the jack on the way back.

Of course, a finesse is as likely to fail as it is to succeed. But if the missing honour card is badly placed you are sure to lose a trick in any case. You lose nothing extra by trying the finesse.

In most finessing situations it is correct to start by leading a low card. Otherwise you throw away part of your positional advantage.

(c) Q 6 5   (d) K J 9 4

10 7 4 [N W E S] K 9   Q 7 [N W E S] A 8 6 3

       A J 8 3 2   10 5 2

The best way to try for five tricks in diagram (c) is to lead a low card from dummy, finessing the jack when East plays the nine. The king drops under the ace on the second round and the queen picks up West's ten. Note the difference it makes if you lead the queen from dummy. This is covered by the king and ace, and there is no way of preventing West from scoring a trick with his ten.

In (d) you should start with a low card from hand, finessing dummy's nine if West plays the seven. On regaining the lead, play another low card from hand and you have three tricks when the queen appears. If you start by leading the ten, West will cover with the queen and you will make only two tricks.

(e) A J 10   (f) A J 10 3

K 9 8 3 [N W E S] 7 4 2   K 8 6 2 [N W E S] 7 4

       Q 6 5   Q 9 5

It is only when you have a strong sequence of honours that you can afford to lead a high card for a finesse. In (e) it is correct to lead the queen. If this is covered by the king and ace, you still have the jack and ten to take care of the next two rounds. And if West refuses to cover, the lead remains in your hand for a further finesse.

In (f) you can again afford to lead a high card, and the card that enables you to score four tricks without interruption is the nine. On the second round you can run the queen, retaining the lead in your hand for a third finesse. If you start with the queen, the second round will be won in dummy with the jack or ten, and you will need an outside entry in your hand if you are to take a third finesse.

Postponing a Finesse

There is sometimes an advantage in delaying your finesse until the second round.

(a)   A K J 10 5   (b)   A K J 10 8 3

```
(a)        A K J 10 5          (b)        A K J 10 8 3
                   N                              N
     8 7 6 3   W       E   Q        Q 6 5 4   W       E   9
                   S                              S
            9 4 2                          7 2
```

When you are missing five cards including the queen, the finesse gives a better chance than playing off the ace and king in the hope that the queen will drop. In diagram (a), however, there is no need to risk a finesse on the first round of the suit. First cash the ace or king just in case East has a singleton queen. If the queen fails to appear, return to hand in another suit and run the nine on the second round.

You should, however, avoid the mistake of cashing a high card when by so doing you will prevent yourself from finessing twice. In diagram (b) the correct play is a first-round finesse of the ten. When this succeeds, you can return to hand and repeat the finesse. Cashing a top card first would gain if East had a singleton queen, but the repeated finesse gains four times as often – when East has any low singleton.

Double and Combination Finesses

When finessing against two or more high cards, it is usually right to take the deep finesse first.

(a)　　　A Q 9 3　　　　　　　(b)　　　K J 9 3

K J 5　[W N E S]　8 7 6　　　Q 10 6　[W N E S]　A 8 4

　　　　1 0 4 2　　　　　　　　　　　7 5 2

The way to try for four tricks in diagram (a) is to lead low from the South hand, finessing the nine if West plays small. When this succeeds, return to hand and lead low again for a finesse of the queen. It would be a mistake to lead the ten on the first or second round. In the layout above it makes no difference, but it would if West had K J doubleton and East 8 7 6 5. By squandering the ten you would allow East to make a trick in the suit.

In diagram (b), when a low card appears from West on the first round, the best chance is to finesse dummy's nine.

(c)　　　　9 5 3　　　　　　　(d)　　　　9 5 3

Q 7　[W N E S]　K 6 4 2　　　K 7 4　[W N E S]　J 10 2

　　　A J 10 8　　　　　　　　　　A Q 8 6

In (c) you can expect to make three tricks as long as both missing honours are not with West. For optimum efficiency, lead low from dummy to your ten. When dummy gets in again run the nine, retaining the lead in the right place for a third finesse.

In (d) you must avoid a premature finesse against the king. First try the deep finesse against the jack and ten by leading a small card from dummy and inserting the eight if East plays low.

(e)　　　A J 9　　　　　　　(f)　　　K 10 9 4

Q 10 5　[W N E S]　K 8 6 2　　Q 8 6　[W N E S]　A J 5

　　　　7 4 3　　　　　　　　　　　7 3 2

Again, in (e), the deep finesse against the ten should be taken first, since West is more likely to hold K 10 or Q 10 than K Q. Only if the nine succeeds in driving out a high honour will there be a finesse to take on the second round.

In (f) you should start by leading low to dummy's nine. If this draws the queen or the jack, a finesse of the ten on the next round will give the best chance.

Two-Way Finesses

At times your cards will be such that you can finesse against a missing queen (or a jack) in either direction.

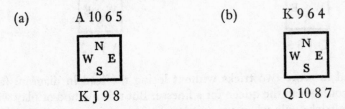

(a)   A 10 6 5

(b)   K 9 6 4

K J 9 8

Q 10 8 7

In (a) the location of the queen may be a fifty-fifty chance, but you can gain a slight advantage by leading the jack from your hand. If West has the queen he may be tempted to play it, thereby saving you a guess. If West plays low without apparent thought, you can play the ace from dummy and run the ten on the way back.

Likewise, in (b), you should start by leading the ten from hand. West may be trapped into covering with the jack.

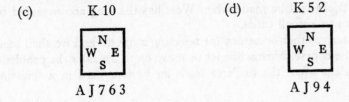

(c)   K 10

(d)   K 5 2

A J 7 6 3

A J 9 4

In (c) you can finesse against the queen in either direction, but this is not a case for flipping a coin. There is a sound reason for taking the finesse against West, leading low from hand and inserting the ten. This brings in five tricks when West has the queen doubleton as well as when he has the queen and two other cards. Five tricks cannot be made when East has the doubleton queen.

In (d) the natural thing is to play low to the king and finesse the jack on the way back. If you have reason to suspect that West has the queen, however, you can try a 'backward finesse' by leading the jack from hand. If this is covered by the queen and king, you have a finesse against the ten on the next round.

When to Refuse a Finesse

There are certain situations where the correct play depends on the number of tricks you need from a suit.

(a)	A 7 4	(b)	Q 5

```
        N                      N
    W       E              W       E
        S                      S
```

| Q J 6 3 | | A J 6 2 |

If you need to score two tricks without losing the lead in diagram (a), you must of course lead the queen for a finesse. But this method of play will produce three tricks only when the suit breaks 3–3, no matter who has the king. For the best chance of three tricks, lead low to the ace and then back towards your hand. If your jack wins the second trick, cross to dummy in another suit and lead again towards your queen. This line of play brings in three tricks whenever East has the king, when West has the singleton king, and when the suit breaks 3–3.

In diagram (b) you can never make more than two tricks by leading the queen for a finesse. To have a chance of three tricks, lead low from hand towards the queen. If it wins, return to the ace and continue with your low card. Three tricks will be made when West has the king accompanied by not more than two small cards.

There are many other occasions for rejecting a finesse and we shall meet them all in due course. Meanwhile let us move on to consider the problems of the defenders when the declarer leads an honour card in a finessing position.

Covering an Honour

When an honour card is led for a finesse, it is usually right for the next player to cover with a higher honour if he has one. The reason is found in the principle of promotion. By forcing the declarer to use two high cards on the one trick, you improve the chances of promoting your intermediate cards to winning rank.

Let us take the diagram we have just been looking at and fill in some cards for the defenders:

(a)   Q 5   (b)   Q 5

743 | N W E S | K 10 9 8   10 9 8 4 | N W E S | K 7 3

                 A J 6 2   A J 6 2

On the previous page it was stated that the declarer could never make more than two tricks by leading the queen for a finesse. That presupposed correct defence. It would clearly be losing technique for East to play low on the lead of the queen. After running the queen the declarer would be able to take a further finesse and make his three tricks. In diagram (a) it is easy enough for East to see that he can promote two tricks by covering the queen with his king. The ace wins the first round, the jack the second, but East takes the next two tricks with his ten and nine.

In (b) East holds no intermediate cards, but he should still cover the queen with his king in the hope of promoting tricks in his partner's hand. The play cannot lose and may gain handsomely.

The position is basically the same when the lead comes from the declarer.

(c)   A Q 8 5   (d)   A J 10 3

K 9 3 | N W E S | 10 6 4   K 6 5 | N W E S | 9 8 4 2

           J 7 2   Q 7

If South leads the jack in diagram (c), West must cover with the king to promote a trick for his partner's ten. If West fails to cover, the declarer makes four tricks in the suit.

Again, in (d), West should cover with the king when the queen is led. This time he must hope for his partner to have a fourth-round trick.

(e)   A J 8 5 4   (f)   10 5 3

Q 6 2 | N W E S | K 9 7   A 8 2 | N W E S | Q 9 4

           10 3   K J 7 6

In (e) if West does not cover the declarer's ten, the defenders will make only one trick. East is permitted to win the first round, but a subsequent finesse of the jack gives the declarer the rest.

Similarly, in (f), East must cover dummy's ten to promote two tricks for the defence.

When Not to Cover

Rules of thumb are no substitute for thinking at the bridge table, and there may be a good reason why you should not follow the normal practice. Remember that the sole purpose of covering an honour is to promote intermediate cards in your hand or your partner's. Do not cover when there can be nothing to promote.

(a)	A Q 10 9	(b)	A 5
K 8 6 3 W-E 7 5 4		K 9 6 2 W-E 8 7 3	
	J 2		Q J 10 4

If West covers the jack in diagram (a) he presents the declarer with four immediate winners. Looking at the wealth in dummy, West should play low. Then his king will be worth a trick on the fourth round.

Again, in (b), West should realize that there is no point in covering when the queen is led, since his king will always be good for a trick on the third round. If West covers, the declarer is able to score three tricks without loss.

(c)	Q J 10 8	(d)	J 10 9 4
9 5 W-E K 7 4 2		K 8 W-E Q 6 5 3	
	A 6 3		A 7 2

Looking at dummy's strong holding in diagram (c), East can see that there is nothing to be gained by covering when the queen is led. If he plays low, the declarer is held to three tricks.

In (d) East should not think of playing the queen when the jack is led. South makes three tricks if East covers, two if he plays low.

Now for some examples where the right play is not so obvious:

(e) Q J 9 2   (f) J 10 5

10 7 4 [N / W E / S] K 6 5   K 8 3 [N / W E / S] Q 9 2

A 8 3   A 7 6 4

Consider what will happen if East covers the lead of the queen in diagram (e). On winning with the ace, the declarer will be in a position to finesse against West's ten and will make all four tricks in the suit. To prevent this, East must play low on the first round. If the declarer continues with the jack from dummy, East can promote a trick for his partner by covering with the king.

That is usually the right procedure when an honour card is led from two honours in sequence. The defender should play low on the first honour but cover the second.

The position is similar in diagram (f). If East covers when the jack is led, South wins with the ace and returns a low card towards the ten, losing only one trick in the suit. East should play the two when the jack is led. West then wins with the king, and East cannot be denied a further trick in the suit.

10 9 3

A K 6 [N / W E / S] J 8 2

Q 7 5 4

Here is another example. The ten is led from dummy, and the defenders make only two tricks if East is foolish enough to cover with the jack. If East plays low, however, the declarer cannot establish the suit without conceding three tricks.

When you are in doubt about whether or not to cover an honour, follow this general rule: cover when you can see two enemy honours on your left or one on your right; play low when you can see one honour on your left or two on your right.

However, you should remember that there are exceptions to every rule. Nothing should induce you to cover in situations like the following when the declarer is marked with length in the suit.

Q 6 4   J 9 5

A [N / W E / S] K 5 3   K [N / W E / S] Q 7 2

J 10 9 8 7 2   A 10 8 6 4 3

In each case this is the trump suit, which has been rebid by the declarer. If you cover when the honour card is led from dummy it may cause some amusement round the table, but partner will not be smiling.

Again this is the trump suit and the declarer leads the jack from hand. Sitting West, you realize that there can be nothing to promote, for the declarer would not lead the jack unless he had the ten as well. He is trying to locate the queen and hoping for some help from you. Naturally you should play low without batting an eye and let him find it for himself – if he can.

A 8 6 4

Q 5   N W E S   7 3 2

K J 10 9

Tricks From Low Cards

Even with good finessing technique, you will seldom make enough tricks for your contract with high cards alone. At no trumps, the only other source of tricks is a long suit. Suppose you have a holding like the following.

K Q J 4 2

10 5   N W E S   A 9 6

8 7 3

This is the sort of suit that can usually be persuaded to yield some low card tricks. The honours in dummy serve to drive out the ace and to draw the rest of the enemy cards, and you are left with two extra winners on the table. Altogether the suit is worth four tricks to you, two won with high cards and two with low cards. Of course, the enemy cards do not have to be divided 3–2. That is the most likely division, but they could be split 4–1 or even 5–0, in which case you would not do so well.

If the suit breaks 3–2, you may still need an outside entry in dummy in order to enjoy your four tricks. Do you see why?

The Hold-Up

The reason is that you are not in full control when the ace of a suit is held by the defenders. The ace is the most flexible of stoppers since it enables its owner to take a trick at the time of his choosing. There is no compulsion for East, in the above example, to take his ace on the first or second round of the suit. He may elect to 'hold up' his ace, allowing the king to win the first trick and the queen the second. He has to take his ace on the third round, but he has achieved his purpose of cutting you adrift from dummy. Unless there is an outside entry, you will have no means of reaching the extra winners established in dummy. By refusing to take his ace too soon, East has succeeded in killing your low-card tricks.

Naturally, hold-up technique is available to both sides. The defenders normally attack in a long suit against no trumps in an effort to establish extra winners for themselves. The declarer should not allow his stoppers to be forced out too easily.

Suppose that West leads a low card and East plays the queen. Usually it will pay to hold up the ace for two rounds, playing the seven under the queen and the ten when East continues. The ace wins the third round, but the line of communication has

6 2

K J 9 5 3   W   E   Q 8 4

A 10 7

been cut and West will be unable to cash his established winners unless he has an outside entry.

Let us now consider another type of suit in which you can hope to develop extra tricks.

A K 8 7 6 3

Q 10 5   W   E   J 9

4 2

Again we assume that dummy has no outside entry. If you cash the ace and king and then concede the third round to the defenders, you will establish no fewer than three extra winners in dummy. But extra winners are valueless without an entry to cash them. What went wrong?

The Duck

In effect, you permitted the opponents to hold up their stopper until the third round of the suit. Owning the top cards, you were in a position to choose when the defenders should take their trick. You should have preserved communication with dummy by 'ducking', playing low from both hands and letting the opponents have their trick on the first round.

This play has nothing to lose, since the defenders are bound to win a trick in the suit at some stage. The advantage of letting them have it on the first round is that you can later draw all the remaining cards by leading to the ace and cashing the king. The lead is then in the right place for you to enjoy the three extra low-card tricks that have been established.

The duck is one of the commonest plays in the game, invaluable when there is a shortage of entries. In the next example dummy again has no outside entry.

You lead the queen for a finesse and West covers with the king. What should you do?

	A 7 6 5 2	
K 8	N W E S	10 9 3
	Q J 4	

Well, you could win with the ace and score a second trick with the jack, but that would be the end of the road. The defenders would win the third round, and your two low-card winners would be stranded in dummy.

The only way to make four tricks in the suit is to duck the first trick, allowing West's king to win. Then you can win the second round with your jack, the third with dummy's ace, and continue with the established small cards. Note, once again, that the duck costs nothing. It is just a matter of letting the defenders have their trick at a time convenient to you.

The technique of conceding an early trick to the enemy can also be used effectively in defence.

Leading against no trumps, West should start with a low card, not the ace or the king. This gives the declarer the first trick in the suit, but when East gains the lead he still has a card of his partner's suit to return.

	10 6 3	
A K 8 4 2	N W E S	9 5
	Q J 7	

	K 7	
8 3	N W E S	A Q 9 6 5 4
	J 10 2	

Against no trumps, West leads the eight of his partner's suit and the king is played from dummy. Unless East has an outside entry he should duck, preserving communication with his partner.

The techniques that we have been looking at – unblocking, finessing, covering honours, holding up high cards, and ducking – comprise the basic tools of card play. So far we have studied them within the context of a single suit. Now it is time to take a wider view and apply them to the play of a complete hand.

2

Planning the Play at No Trumps

Bypassing the long suit – the hold-up – the danger hand – when
not to hold up – guidelines for holding up an ace – attacking the
right entry – finessing for safety – the duck – duck thwarts hold-up

When the opening lead has been made and dummy goes down on the table,
train yourself not to touch a card until you have formed a plan of campaign.
The success of the contract will often depend on your play to the first trick,
so avoid hasty action. Sit back and think. At trick two it may be too late.

Your first task is to count the number of immediate winners in the combined hands – the tricks you can win without giving up the lead. If these
are enough for your contract you will obviously have no problems. But
more often there will not be enough immediate winners and you will have
to look at ways of developing extra tricks in one suit or another. This may
involve giving up the lead, and you must consider carefully what damage
the defenders may be able to inflict on you. When there are several possible
ways of trying for extra tricks, look for the safest line of play.

The defenders will normally launch an attack in their longest suit and
you will have to rely on your high cards to control the situation. Often you
will counter-attack in *your* longest suit, trying to drive out an ace or a king
before the enemy suit becomes established. The play of many no trump
hands develops into a race against time, with each side trying to establish
its long suit first. The defenders start with the advantage of the opening
lead, which lets them get in the first blow and puts them a tempo (time-
unit) ahead. Your compensating advantage as declarer is that you normally
have more in the way of high cards to stop the run of the enemy suit.

When you have made your plan, and not before, you can play to the first
trick.

Here is an example of an everyday situation:

♠ A 6
♡ 6 4
◇ Q J 4 3
♣ K J 10 9 2

```
    N
 W     E
    S
```

♠ K 5
♡ A K Q 8 3
◇ K 7 6 2
♣ Q 5

You play in three no trumps on the lead of the queen of spades. Counting your quick winners, you see that you have only five – two spades and three hearts. Four extra winners must therefore be developed for your contract.

Of course, you will make a couple of extra tricks in hearts if the suit breaks 3–3. But you cannot count on this and you still need tricks elsewhere. Looking further afield, you see the possibility of developing extra tricks in both diamonds and clubs. But you will not have time to establish both suits. When you give up the lead the defenders will knock out your second spade stopper, and they will be able to take at least three spade tricks to defeat the contract if they ever get in again. The enemy will win the race, in other words, unless you can develop the four extra tricks you need in one suit.

Diamonds will provide, at most, three extra tricks, but clubs will be good for four tricks once the ace has been knocked out. So you correctly decide to lead a club at trick two.

Your planning is not yet complete, however. You have still to make a decision about where to win the first trick – in dummy with the ace or in your own hand with the king. Does it matter? Well, it may do. If you win in dummy and lead clubs, an awkward defender may hold up his ace on the first round. He will win the second club and return a spade, and you will have no quick entry to those established clubs on the table. And if you switch to diamonds after winning the first club you may run into a 4–1 break and again be held to eight tricks.

The sure way of making three no trumps is to win the first spade in hand with the king, preserving the ace in dummy as an entry, and lead the queen of clubs (first the high card from the shorter holding to avoid any possible blockage). Continue clubs to knock out the ace, and you cannot be prevented from making your game with two spades, four clubs, and at least three hearts.

The point about preserving an entry can be set down as a general rule:

When you can win a trick in either hand, preserve the winner in the hand most likely to need a card of entry later in the play.

Bypassing the Long Suit

Although it is customary for the declarer to look for his extra tricks in the longest combined suit, this is not always a practical course of action. For one thing, the time element may not permit it.

Again you play in three no trumps on a spade lead. This time you can count seven immediate winners – two spades, one heart and four clubs – leaving two extra tricks to be developed.

♠ 5
♡ A J 10 3
◇ Q 9 6 5
♣ A K Q 5

```
      N
   W     E
      S
```

♠ A K
♡ 9 5 2
◇ J 10 8 3 2
♣ J 8 3

Three extra tricks might be developed in diamonds, the longest holding in the combined hands. Unfortunately you lack the time to establish tricks in diamonds, for that would involve giving up the lead twice. The defenders would win the first diamond and force out your second spade stopper, and as soon as they came in with the next diamond they would run enough spade tricks to defeat the contract.

You must therefore look to the heart suit, where it may be possible to establish the two extra tricks you need in time. Lead a low heart (not the nine, for West may have a singleton or doubleton honour) at trick two and finesse dummy's ten. When in with the second spade (on which, of course, you discard a diamond from dummy), lead your second small heart for a finesse of the jack. On this line of play you will make nine tricks whenever West has both heart honours, when hearts are 3–3 with the honours divided, and when West has a singleton or doubleton honour.

An excellent reason for refusing to play on your longest suit is when the suit does not guarantee enough tricks for the contract. It is easy to go wrong on the following hand if you take your eye off the ball.

♠ K 6 4
♡ 8 5
◇ A Q J 5
♣ K 8 7 6

```
      N
   W     E
      S
```

♠ Q J 8
♡ A Q
◇ 9 7 4 3
♣ A Q J 3

West leads a low heart against your contract of three no trumps. East plays the jack and you win with the queen.

Two hearts, a diamond and four clubs give you a total of seven immediate winners, leaving two extra tricks to be developed. The longest suit in the combined hands is diamonds, and you would certainly be unlikely to go down if you led a diamond for a finesse of the jack at trick two. But it could happen. East might have a singleton king, for instance, or king, ten and two others, and then you would have some explaining to do to your partner.

There is no need to court bad luck on this hand. The sure way to establish the tricks you need is to play on spades, even though there are only six cards in the suit between the two hands. If you are allowed to score one spade trick, you can, of course, try the diamond finesse without any risk at all.

From the lesson of this hand we can extract another general rule:

Never take a risky finesse when you can make sure of your contract without it.

The Hold-Up

The declarer's most useful counter to the threat of a long enemy suit is found in hold-up play. By refusing to release a stopper (usually an ace) until such time as one defender is exhausted in the suit, he severs the link between the enemy hands.

Here is a straightforward example.

♠ A 4 3
♡ Q 2
◇ K Q J 6 3
♣ Q 7 4

```
      N
  W   E
      S
```

♠ K 9 5 2
♡ A 8 5
◇ 8 2
♣ A K J 2

West leads the jack of hearts against your contract of three no trumps. Going through the proper motions, you see that you have two quick winners in spades, four in clubs and at least one in hearts. The extra tricks you need can be established in diamonds.

The only potential danger lies in the heart position, and you do not know how real the problem is until you see what happens on the first trick. When you play the queen of hearts from dummy East covers with the king. Now, unless hearts break 4–4, you are in danger of defeat.

Suppose the hearts are 5–3. Needing tricks in diamonds, you have no chance if the ace of diamonds is in the same hand as the long hearts. But if the ace of diamonds is in the short heart hand you can succeed with the aid of a hold-up. Refuse to take the ace of hearts at the first trick. Play low again on the second heart, keeping your ace for the third round. Your contract is now secure if the player with the ace of diamonds is out of hearts. A look at the full hand shows the distribution you are guarding against.

Note that if the ace of hearts is played on the first or second round the defenders have no trouble in making five tricks.

♠ A 4 3
♡ Q 2
◇ K Q J 6 3
♣ Q 7 4

♠ Q 8 6
♡ J 10 9 6 3
◇ 9 4
♣ 10 5 3

```
      N
  W   E
      S
```

♠ J 10 7
♡ K 7 4
◇ A 10 7 5
♣ 9 8 6

♠ K 9 5 2
♡ A 8 5
◇ 8 2
♣ A K J 2

One specialized form of hold-up is known as the Bath Coup.

```
              864
                ┌──────┐
                │  N   │
K Q 10 9 5      │W   E │      7 3
                │  S   │
                └──────┘
              A J 2
```

When the king is led South plays the two, allowing West to hold the trick. This is a highly effective move, for West is unable to continue the attack without allowing South to make two tricks in the suit.

It is not only when you have the ace of the enemy suit that a hold-up may be a wise precaution.

Against your contract of three no trumps West leads a low spade and East plays the queen. For immediate winners you can count one spade, three hearts, one diamond and one club. Three more tricks must be developed, and the club suit will yield them even if the finesse is wrong.

♠ 7 6 4
♡ K 8 2
◇ J 7
♣ A Q J 9 3

```
┌──────┐
│  N   │
│W   E │
│  S   │
└──────┘
```

♠ K J 2
♡ A Q 6
◇ A Q 5 4
♣ 10 6 5

The danger in winning the first trick is that West may have started with A 10 x x x in spades. If the club finesse loses, East will return his remaining spade and West will score four tricks in the suit.

This danger is averted quite easily by holding up in spades, playing the two under East's queen. Now if East continues spades he will cut the link between the defenders' hands in the dangerous case where West has five. If West has fewer than five spades the contract is always safe, provided that if East switches to a diamond at trick two you go straight up with the ace and run the ten of clubs. The most you can lose are two spades, a diamond and a club.

The Danger Hand

The last deal introduces a concept that greatly influences the declarer's play of the cards – that of the 'danger hand'. It often happens that it is dangerous to lose the lead to one opponent but not to the other. In the above example it would have been dangerous to win the first spade and take a losing finesse in clubs, because East was in a position to make a damaging lead. The remedy, as we saw, was a hold-up. But suppose that you had to take your finesse into the West rather than the East hand. Then it would be a mistake to hold up, for with West on lead the jack of spades would constitute a second stopper. Let us change a few cards in the last example to clarify this point.

♠ 7 6 4
♡ K 8 2
◇ J 9 7
♣ A Q J 9

```
    N
  W   E
    S
```

♠ K J 2
♡ A Q 6
◇ A Q 10 5 4
♣ 10 6

dangerous, for it may give the defenders a chance to establish the spades while West still holds a diamond stopper. Opposite is one possible layout:

To sum up, with this sort of holding your decision on whether to hold up or not must depend on whether you expect to lose the lead to East or to West.

There are times when it is right to hold up even

♠ K J 4
♡ A 7 2
◇ 7 5 4
♣ Q 10 9 2

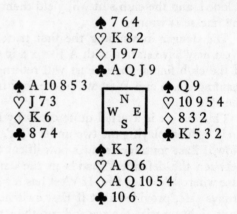

♠ 9 5
♡ 10 4 3
◇ J 9 6 3 2
♣ K 8 4

♠ Q 10 8 6 2
♡ J 9 6 5
◇ K 10
♣ A 6

♠ A 7 3
♡ K Q 8
◇ A Q 8
♣ J 7 5 3

Again West leads a low spade and East plays the queen. This time you should not dream of holding up. Win with the king, cross to the king of hearts, and run the nine of diamonds.

The difference in approach is due to the fact that you can be sure of establishing the three extra tricks you need without allowing East to gain the lead. The hold-up is therefore unnecessary, since you have a second spade stopper if West is on lead.

The hold-up is, in fact, highly

♠ 7 6 4
♡ K 8 2
◇ J 9 7
♣ A Q J 9

♠ A 10 8 5 3
♡ J 7 3
◇ K 6
♣ 8 7 4

♠ Q 9
♡ 10 9 5 4
◇ 8 3 2
♣ K 5 3 2

♠ K J 2
♡ A Q 6
◇ A Q 10 5 4
♣ 10 6

though you have two stoppers in the enemy suit. For a change let us see the full hand from the start.

West leads the three of diamonds against your contract of three no trumps and East plays the king.

You have seven top winners and need to establish two more. The extra tricks can come only from clubs, and it may seem natural to win the first trick and lead a club straight away. Do you see what will happen if you do? East will win the first club and return his diamond, and even if you play low West will overtake with the jack and play another diamond to knock out your queen. When West subsequently gains the lead with the king of clubs he will be able to cash two more diamonds to defeat the contract.

The way to cater for this dangerous 5–2 diamond break is to hold up the ace of diamonds at the first trick. When you win the diamond continuation and play a club East may win with the ace, but your hold-up has put the defenders out of touch with each other. East has no diamond to return, and you are able to establish the clubs in peace.

This hold-up guarantees the success of the contract unless West started with both top clubs, and in that case the defence was destined to prevail from the start.

When Not to Hold Up

We have already noted one situation where a hold-up would be a mistake – where you could be sure of a second stopper in the suit by losing the lead to the safe opponent.

Sometimes the cards will be such that you can be sure of a second stopper no matter which opponent gains the lead.

(a)	J 5	(b)	9 2

```
        N                      N
    W       E              W       E
        S                      S
```

K 10 3		A 10 8 4

In diagram (a) if West leads a low card and East plays the queen, you can make sure of a second stopper by winning with the king. To hold up would restrict you to one trick in the suit.

Similarly in (b) you should capture any honour card at once with the ace. The ten, nine and eight between them will be worth a second trick to you.

Guidelines for Holding Up an Ace

With five cards of the enemy suit in the combined hands, hold up twice, with six cards hold up once, and with seven cards win the ace immediately.

3 2	6 3 2	7 6 3 2
N W E S	N W E S	N W E S
A 5 4	A 5 4	A 5 4
Hold-up twice	*Hold-up once*	*No need to hold-up*

The purpose of the hold-up is to guard against the possibility of one defender having five or more cards in the suit, and you can see that these rules are designed to achieve just that. When you have five cards, you need to hold up twice to cut communications when the suit breaks 5–3. When you have six cards the dangerous break is 5–2, and one hold-up is enough to cut the link. When you have seven cards, if one defender has five the other must have a singleton, in which case no hold-up is needed.

Rules of thumb can be helpful if applied with discretion but they must not be regarded as a substitute for common sense. One good time to reject a hold-up is when it would give the defenders the opportunity to make a damaging switch.

♠ 7 4
♡ 8 5
◇ Q J 6 4
♣ A K 10 4 3

♠ A Q 6
♡ A 9 3
◇ K 7 5 3
♣ Q J 7

Once again your contract is three no trumps. West leads the two of hearts and East plays the queen. How should you play?

With seven top tricks, you need to develop two more in diamonds, and you may be tempted to hold up the ace of hearts in case the suit breaks 5–3.

However, when leading from a suit that is not headed by a sequence of honours, players tend to lead their fourth-highest card. West's lead of the two of hearts therefore gives a good indication that the suit will break 4–4, in which case you can make sure of your contract by winning the first trick with the ace of hearts and playing on diamonds.

The danger in holding up is that East, having scored a heart trick, may switch to spades and establish three more tricks in that suit before you have knocked out the ace of diamonds.

The capacity of the defenders to hurt you with a sudden switch is a factor that should always be borne in mind, not only when you are considering a hold-up but when you are contemplating any play that may involve giving up the lead.

Here is a case in point.

♠ A Q J 7
♡ 9 8 3
◇ A 10 6 5
♣ K 5

```
      N
  W       E
      S
```

♠ 6 4
♡ A 7 4
◇ J 3 2
♣ Q J 10 9 3

This time your contract is one no trump and West leads the three of spades. Plan the play.

For top winners you have three aces, and there are possibilities of extra tricks in both spades and clubs.

If West has led away from the king of spades, as seems likely, you could make three tricks in spades by finessing twice and establish four tricks in clubs to bring your total up to nine.

But you contracted for seven tricks, not for nine, and you should look for the safest possible way of making your contract. Think of what might happen if the spade finesse lost at trick one.

East would no doubt switch to hearts, attacking the only entry to your hand before you had a chance to get the clubs going. The defenders would subsequently hold up the ace of clubs for one round, and you could well be held to five tricks.

There is no reason to take the risk. The safe way of making your contract is to play the ace of spades at the first trick and lead the king of clubs, continuing clubs for as long as it takes to drive out the enemy ace. That way you cannot be denied four club tricks and your three aces.

Attacking the Right Entry

When you may have to lose the lead twice in developing the extra tricks needed for your contract, give some thought to the question of which stopper should be knocked out first. Usually this will be the entry in the hand that contains the long suit.

You play in three no trumps on the lead of the queen of hearts. There are five quick winners and you need to develop four extra tricks. A successful finesse in clubs will see you home, but if the club finesse is wrong you will need a trick from spades as well.

Now take note of the dangers. The big threat to the safety of the contract is the possibility of a five-card heart suit with West. If you win the first heart and take a losing finesse in clubs, a heart will come back, knocking out your second stopper in

♠ 10 6 5 4
♡ 7 3
◇ 9 3
♣ A J 10 5 2

```
      N
  W       E
      S
```

♠ K Q
♡ A K 5 2
◇ A K 7
♣ Q 9 6 3

the suit before you have established your spade trick. And if West has the ace of spades you will duly go one down.

You might consider a hold-up as a way of overcoming this difficulty. The trouble is that this would merely substitute one danger for another. West would no longer be able to establish his hearts, but he would have the opportunity to switch to diamonds (or even to spades) at trick two, and again you might be held to eight tricks.

Hold-up play is not the answer. On this type of hand you must give top priority to knocking out the entry that may lie in the hand that contains the long suit. Win the first heart and lead the king of spades at trick two. If a defender takes the ace and plays another heart, you can win and take the club finesse in perfect safety. If East produces the king of clubs and a third heart, it means that the suit breaks 4–3, and you can lose no more than two hearts, a spade and a club.

Note that there is no risk attached to your spade lead, even if the king is allowed to win. There is no distribution of the cards on which the defenders can take more than three spade tricks, and you can still afford to lose a trick to the king of clubs.

Finessing for Safety

There are some hands on which a finesse should be taken, not with a view to developing the maximum number of extra tricks but in order to steer the lead away from the dangerous defender.

♠ Q 6 3
♡ A 8 5
◇ K 4
♣ A 9 8 4 3

	N	
W		E
	S	

♠ K 8
♡ K Q J 2
◇ A J 10 5
♣ 7 6 2

You play in three no trumps after East has overcalled in spades. West leads the nine of spades which is allowed to run to your king.

With eight immediate winners you need to establish only one extra trick. Any attempt to establish the club suit would be hazardous, but you can easily establish an extra trick in diamonds even after a losing finesse. The normal way to tackle the diamond suit would be to play low to the king and finesse the ten on the way back. This would give you the optimum chance of making four tricks in the suit. But here you do not need four tricks from the diamonds, and it would be highly dangerous to lose a finesse to West, who would be only too eager to shoot another spade through dummy's queen.

East is harmless on lead, and you should therefore play the diamonds the other way round. Lead the jack from hand at trick two and let it run if West plays low. It is a matter of indifference to you whether this finesse wins or loses. The spades are immune to attack when East is on lead since the queen provides a second stopper. Whatever happens you will make your nine tricks.

The Duck

When entries are short in one hand or the other, you may be less concerned with preventing the establishment of the enemy suit than with finding a way of harvesting the tricks in your own long suit.

Here is a situation of the sort that you will meet again and again at the bridge table.

♠ 7 6 3
♡ Q 7 5
◇ A 10 8 5 2
♣ 7 2

```
   N
W     E
   S
```

♠ A K Q
♡ J 10 4
◇ 7 6 4
♣ A K 8 3

You play in two no trumps on the lead of a low heart. East takes the ace and returns a heart to his partner's king, and West continues with a third heart to which East follows.

In dummy with the queen of hearts, you can count seven immediate winners. There is no chance of making an extra trick in either of the black suits, so you have to turn to diamonds for for your eighth trick.

On a normal 3–2 division of the outstanding diamonds you can expect, eventually, to establish two extra winners in the suit. But you will not be able to cash those winners if the ace of diamonds is played at an early stage, for dummy has no other card of entry.

The solution is to let the defenders have their diamond tricks first, retaining the ace in dummy as a third-round entry. Lead a low diamond from the table at trick four. If the defenders cash the thirteenth heart at this stage, you must be careful to discard a club, not a diamond, from your hand. When you regain the lead in one of the black suits, lead another diamond and repeat the duck, playing low again from dummy.

If both defenders follow to two rounds of diamonds your contract is safe. On the third round the ace of diamonds will extract the defenders' last card in the suit, and you can cash an established diamond winner as your eighth trick.

Ducking plays can be surprisingly effective even when the first round of the suit is controlled by the defenders.

Duck Thwarts Hold-Up

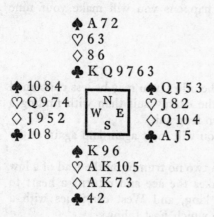

♠ A 7 2
♡ 6 3
◇ 8 6
♣ K Q 9 7 6 3

♠ 10 8 4
♡ Q 9 7 4
◇ J 9 5 2
♣ 10 8

♠ Q J 5 3
♡ J 8 2
◇ Q 10 4
♣ A J 5

♠ K 9 6
♡ A K 10 5
◇ A K 7 3
♣ 4 2

The contract is three no trumps and West leads the four of hearts to his partner's jack. You can count six top winners and you must hope to establish three extra tricks in clubs, which you need to find breaking 3–2.

First try playing the hand in straightforward fashion. Win the first trick with the king of hearts (there is no point in holding up since your ten will serve as a third stopper if West has five hearts) and lead a club to the king and ace. When East returns a heart to your ace, you play a second club to the queen and concede a third club to establish the suit. The defenders may now cash two heart tricks but you have the remainder, making two spades, two hearts, two diamonds and three clubs for a total of nine tricks. So you make your contract. What's wrong with that?

What is wrong is that an experienced defender in the East seat will not make the mistake of taking his ace of clubs on the first round of the suit. He will hold up his ace, allowing dummy's king to score. Now try and establish the club suit! East wins the second round and leads a heart, and you have nowhere to go for tricks. With only one entry, the ace of spades, in dummy, you may set up the clubs but you will never get back to dummy to enjoy them. By holding up his ace of clubs, East has restricted you to one trick in the suit, and your contract has to go two down.

Let us now counter the experienced defender by putting an experienced declarer in the South seat. He sees that he can afford to lose two club tricks, and he makes sure of retaining a link with dummy by ducking a club at trick two, playing low from both hands. East wins and returns a heart as before, but on winning this trick South still has a club to lead. The king of clubs forces out the ace on the second round, and the rest of the clubs are South's to cash as soon as he enters dummy with the ace of spades.

The effect of the duck is to prevent East from holding up in clubs, compelling him to use up one of his stoppers on the first round. Duck thwarts hold-up – it might almost be the title of a Disney cartoon.

3

Defending Against No Trumps

The opening lead – leading partner's suit – passive leads – third
hand play – lowest of touching cards – finessing against dummy –
the rule of eleven – returning partner's suit – the high-low signal –
unblocking – the duck – second hand low – the defensive hold-up
– the distributional echo – counting the tricks

Only on rare occasions will the defenders have enough immediate winners
to defeat the contract out of hand. In most cases it will be necessary to
develop extra tricks in one suit or another, and the best place to look for
them will normally be in the longest combined suit held by the partnership.
If the declarer's stoppers can be knocked out quickly enough, the established small cards in the long suit may provide the extra winners that are
needed to sink the contract.

The Opening Lead

The privilege of making the opening lead confers a big advantage, but it is
one that can easily be dissipated. It is vital to make the first blow a telling
one. There will often be no second chance if the initial attack is launched in
the wrong direction.

The defender on lead has to ask himself two questions:

(a) Which suit offers the best chance of defeating the contract?
(b) Which card should be led from that suit?

In choosing the suit to lead you will often receive some guidance from
the bidding. When partner has bid a suit, for instance, it will usually be
right to lead it. When an opponent has bid your best suit, it may be as well
to think of something else. In the absence of any such indications, it is
generally best to attack in your own long suit in the hope of establishing
extra tricks.

There is scope for judgement in choosing the suit, but not so much in
selecting the card to lead from that suit. Opening leads are largely standard-

ized. It is conventional to lead a particular card from a particular combination. If you stick to these standardized leads your partner will have a good idea of what you are leading from.

When you are lucky enough to have a suit headed by three or more honour cards in sequence, you have an ideal aggressive lead against a no trump contract. Lead the top card of the sequence.

K Q J 9 3	lead the king
Q J 10 9 5	queen
J 10 9 4	jack

The top card is still the right choice from a broken sequence, where the third card in line is missing.

K Q 10 6 5	lead the king
Q J 9 8	queen
J 10 8 7 2	jack

An exception arises when your sequence is headed by the ace and king. Now the king is the normal card to lead.

A K Q 7 4	lead the king
A K J 6	king

From an interior sequence, where the second card in line is missing (or the second and third cards), lead the honour card immediately below the gap.

A Q J 9 3	lead the queen
A J 10 7 5	jack
A 10 9 8 4	ten
K J 10 8 2	jack
K 10 9 7 6	ten
Q 10 9 6	ten

From a suit headed by no more than two high cards, lead the fourth-highest card.

A K 8 5 4	lead the five
K Q 8 3 2	three
Q J 7 4	four
K 10 6 4 3	four
Q 7 6 5 3	five
A 9 7 6 4 3	six

This conventional lead helps partner to judge how many cards you have in the suit. When you lead the two, for instance, partner knows at once that you have led from a four-card suit. Similarly, if you lead the three and play the two on the next round, he knows that you started with five cards. Such information can be very helpful to the defence.

When you have four small cards, the fourth-highest is not the right choice. Lead the top card, which makes it clear to partner that you have no honour in the suit.

9 8 6 3	lead the nine
7 6 5 2	seven

Leading Partner's Suit

When partner has been active in the bidding, it is usually right to lead his suit rather than try to establish a suit of your own.

Lead the top card in partner's suit when you have two honour cards in sequence, three small cards, or any doubleton.

Q J 5	lead the queen
J 10 2	jack
8 5 3	eight
9 4	nine
K 5	king

In leading an honour card from a short holding in partner's suit you are following the familiar principle of playing the high cards from the shorter hand first.

Here the lead of the king allows the suit to be developed with the minimum of fuss. A lead of the five would result in a deplorable blockage.

When you have three or four cards headed by an honour in partner's suit, lead the lowest card.

```
            8 3
      ┌─────────┐
      │    N    │
K 5   │ W     E │  Q J 9 6 4 2
      │    S    │
      └─────────┘
          A 10 7
```

A 7 6	lead the six
K 10 2	two
Q 5 3	three
J 8 5 2	two

The idea is to trap an intermediate honour card in the declarer's hand.

When you lead the two, partner will play the ace and return the nine, trapping the declarer's ten and restricting him to one trick in the suit. South makes two tricks if you start with the jack.

```
              6
          ┌─────────┐
          │    N    │
  J 7 2   │ W     E │  A Q 9 8 4
          │    S    │
          └─────────┘
             K 10 5 3
```

Passive Leads

When you have no attractive lead to make, choose the lead that is least likely to give away a trick.

♠ K 10 4 2	*S*	*N*
♡ 8 7 2	1 ◇	1 ♠
◇ A J 9 5	1 NT	3 NT
♣ Q 3		

Here both your suits have been bid by the opponents, and your safest lead is the passive one of the eight of hearts.

Third Hand Play

The opening leader operates largely in the dark, but a little light has usually dawned by the time his partner has to play. There are inferences to be drawn from the rank of the card led, for instance, and the sight of dummy is often helpful. Nevertheless, the defenders labour under the constant handicap of being able to see only part of their combined resources, and this can make it difficult for them to co-ordinate their efforts.

When partner leads a low card, your first duty is to try to help establish his suit. If dummy has only small cards in the suit, play your highest card in an effort to win the trick. Even if you do not succeed, you will at least force a high card from the declarer and thus promote your partner's cards.

When West leads the four East should play his highest card, the king. On the return of the jack the declarer's queen is trapped and the defenders run five tricks. If East fails to play the king, the declarer makes an unexpected trick with his queen.

8 6

A 10 7 4 2   W E   K J 3

Q 9 5

5 3

K 9 7 6 4   W E   Q 10 2

A J 8

When West leads the six East should play the queen. This forces out the ace, and when East regains the lead he can return the ten, trapping the jack and restricting the declarer to one trick in the suit. South makes two tricks if East refuses to play the queen on the first round.

Again, East must play the ace when
the five is led. Otherwise South makes
two tricks in the suit.

```
                    7 4
                  ┌───────┐
                  │   N   │
        Q 9 6 5 3 │ W   E │ A 10 2
                  │   S   │
                  └───────┘
                    K J 8
```

Lowest of Touching Cards

We have seen that in leading from a sequence of honour cards the highest
card is chosen. This guarantees possession of the next lower card in rank.

In following to partner's lead we convey equally valuable information by
playing the other way round. Holding two or more high cards in sequence,
we play the lowest of the sequence.

```
              7 5
            ┌───────┐
            │   N   │
  K 9 8 6 2 │ W   E │ Q J 3
            │   S   │
            └───────┘
            A 10 4
```

When West leads the six East must,
of course, play high in an effort to
win the trick. But his touching cards
are equals, in effect, and the jack is
the right card to play.

This helps to clarify the position
for West when South wins the trick
with the ace. West knows that his part-
ner must have the queen, since South would not have squandered the ace if
he could have won the trick more cheaply. Consequently, when West regains the lead he can confidently continue with a low card to his partner's
queen.

When East plays the queen on the first round, the inference that the
declarer has the jack is equally sure.

The six is led to the queen and ace.
West knows that his partner would
have played the jack if he had held it,
so he is not tempted to continue the
suit when he regains the lead. He
switches to another suit and waits for
his partner to lead through the jack.

```
                  7 5
                ┌───────┐
                │   N   │
      K 9 8 6 2 │ W   E │ Q 10 3
                │   S   │
                └───────┘
                  A J 4
```

Finessing Against Dummy

Bridge slogans such as 'third hand high' should not be followed blindly. It
is normally correct to play high when there are only low cards on the table,
but when dummy contains honour cards the winning policy is to finesse
against them, playing only as high as is necessary to win the trick or to force
a stopper from the declarer.

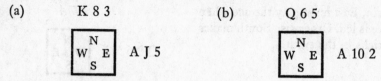

(a)   K 8 3   (b)   Q 6 5

A J 5   A 10 2

In diagram (a) when West leads a low card and dummy plays low, East should put in the jack. If the declarer has the queen he cannot be prevented from making a trick in the suit, and he will make two tricks if East goes up with the ace. It is possible, however, that West has both queen and ten, in which case the declarer need not make a trick at all.

Similarly, in (b) East should insert the ten when West leads a low card and dummy plays low. The finesse stands to gain when West has led from the king and jack, and it can never lose.

(c)   J 7 2   (d)   Q 6 4

K 10 5   A 9 3

Two further finesses are shown above. In (c) the play of the ten gains when West has led from the queen and can never cost.

In (d) the play of the nine gains when West has led from the jack and ten. Again it can give the declarer nothing that is not his for the taking.

The Rule of Eleven

We have already seen that the conventional lead of the fourth-highest card yields valuable information about the distribution of the suit. But that is not all it does. The lead also enables you to work out the number of higher cards in the suit that are held by the declarer. This is found by applying the 'Rule of Eleven'.

Just subtract the value of partner's card from eleven. The answer is the number of higher cards in the suit held by dummy, declarer and yourself. You can see some of these cards in your hand and in dummy, and the balance must be held by the declarer.

There is nothing mysterious about the working of this rule. The number of cards in a suit higher than any particular spot-card is found by subtracting the value of that card from fourteen (it would be thirteen but for the fact that the ace ranks high). Check it for yourself. When the opening leader is known to have three cards higher than the card led, the number of higher cards in the other three hands must be obtained by subtracting from eleven.

The application of this rule will sometimes enable you to take even deeper finesses against dummy's high cards.

```
              K 6 5
                    N
       Q J 8 7    W   E    A 10 9 4
                    S
               3 2
```

West leads the seven, the five is is played from dummy, and you start doing your sums. Well, what do you know? You can see all four cards higher than the seven in your own hand and in dummy. Knowing that the declarer cannot beat the seven, you play the four, leaving partner on play for another lead through dummy's king.

The Rule of Eleven does not always indicate that a finesse is required, as the next diagram shows.

West leads the six and the eight is played from the table. It may seem natural to finesse against the jack by inserting your ten, but the application of the Rule of Eleven will keep you straight. Of the five cards higher than the six, four are visible. The declarer

```
                      J 8
                           N
       A 9 7 6 5 4       W   E    K 10 3
                           S
                      Q 2
```

can have only one, in that case, and it cannot cost to play your king.

Sometimes the Rule of Eleven will indicate that a switch to another suit might be a good move. Let us have a look at a complete hand.

```
                    ♠ 10 4
                    ♡ 10 6 5
                    ◊ A Q J 8 2
                    ♣ Q 9 5
    ♠ Q 9 6 5 3                   ♠ A 2
    ♡ A 7 2          N            ♡ K J 9 4
    ◊ 10 4         W   E          ◊ 7 6 3
    ♣ 10 6 2         S            ♣ J 8 7 4
                    ♠ K J 8 7
                    ♡ Q 8 3
                    ◊ K 9 5
                    ♣ A K 3
```

South opens one no trump (15–17), North raises to three no trumps, and West leads the five of spades to your ace.

The Rule of Eleven tells you that South has four cards higher than the five, and at least one of them must be an honour card because with an honour sequence your partner would have led the top card. At best, West's suit may be headed by K Q 9 or K J 9, but even then South will have a stopper. And if West establishes his suit he will be unable to cash it, for on the bidding he is marked with no more than seven high-card points and therefore no outside entry.

Since a spade continuation offers no hope, you should try another suit. The heart suit looks promising, and the best shot is to lead the jack in the hope that partner has the ace. This is the 'backward finesse' situation which we noted in Chapter 1. Whether South covers the jack with his queen or not, the defenders can take four heart tricks to defeat the contract. The backward finesse is often used by defenders, for the sight of one of the enemy hands makes it easier to spot the possibilities.

This hand introduces another important aid to defence – the counting of declarer's points. By totting up the points shown by declarer in the bidding, East was able to deduce that his partner could not have a good spade suit *and* an outside entry. Such counting is the life-blood of good defence, and we shall examine the subject in greater detail in a later chapter.

Returning Partner's Suit

The last hand showed that it is sometimes right for East to try a new suit, but this is the exception rather than the rule. When partner leads his long suit against a no trump contract he will normally expect you to return it when you gain the lead. Most of the time it will be right to do so rather than launch a new attack of your own. Defence is a co-operative venture and little can be achieved by pulling in opposite directions.

The question of which card to return is a vital one. It is conventional to return the highest remaining card from an original holding of three cards, and the fourth-highest card from an original holding of four or more.

(a)   4   (b)   4

K 10 8 5 2   [N W E S]   Q 7 6 3   K 10 8 5 2   [N W E S]   Q 7 3

A J 9   A J 9 6

In each case the five is led to the queen and ace. In diagram (a) you return the three when you gain the lead. This assures West that you started with four cards in the suit, and after capturing the declarer's nine with his ten, he will continue with the king to drop the jack.

In diagram (b) your return of the seven gives equally valuable information. Knowing you to have started with only three cards in the suit, West can place South with four. On winning the nine with his ten, therefore, he will switch to another suit and wait for you to make a further lead through South's jack.

Let us see how information gleaned from the return of suit can be applied in practical defence.

South plays in three no trumps and West leads the three of diamonds to his partner's ace. East returns the ten of diamonds and South covers with the queen.

At this point West has a complete blueprint of the diamond distribution. From the return of the ten he knows that his partner began with ace, ten and another and South with queen, jack and two others. Do you see what will happen if West wins the second trick and continues the suit? He will

```
              ♠ K 8 6 5
              ♡ A 9 4
              ◇ 6 4
              ♣ A Q 9 5
♠ 10 7 2                    ♠ A 9 4
♡ J 8 3 2       N          ♡ 10 6 5
◇ K 9 8 3    W   E         ◇ A 10 5
♣ 8 4           S          ♣ K 7 6 3
              ♠ Q J 3
              ♡ K Q 7
              ◇ Q J 7 2
              ♣ J 10 2
```

establish a further diamond winner but, lacking any card of entry, he will never get in to cash it.

The defence can win three diamond tricks only if West ducks on the second round, playing the eight under the queen. The duck maintains communication, and when East regains the lead he is able to give his partner two more diamond tricks. The defenders score three diamonds, the ace of spades and the king of clubs to put the contract one down.

In an ideal world there would be no need for exceptions to rules, but at the bridge table it is not always possible for East to stick to the principle of returning his lowest card from an original holding of four. Consider this situation:

```
              6
A 9 5 4 2      N      K J 10 3
             W   E
              S
             Q 8 7
```

West leads the four and East wins with the king. If he returns the three a blockage will result (no matter which card South plays) and the defenders will be unable to run their five tricks.

To give the defence a chance, East must return the jack at trick two and hope that his partner can read the situation. There is the further point that South's second spade might be the nine, in which case the return of the jack is needed to prevent South from scoring a trick in the suit.

The High-Low Signal

In addition to the information exchanged by the rank of the cards led or played in attempting to win a trick, defenders can pass vital messages across the table by the rank of the cards they play when merely 'following suit' (i.e. when not trying to win the trick).

The general principle is that a high card is encouraging, a low card discouraging. To show a liking for partner's lead, play a higher card than is strictly necessary when following suit. The message is confirmed when you follow with a lower card on the second round. This high-low signal or 'echo' is one of the commonest defensive tools and one of the most useful. Here are some examples:

	(a)	A 3			(b)	7 6 4	
		N				N	
Q J 8 6 5	W E	K 4 2	Q J 9 3	W E	K 8 2
		S				S	
		10 9 7				A 10 5	

In (a) West leads the six and the ace is played from dummy. East should play the four in an attempt to encourage his partner to continue the suit when he regains the lead. To be sure, the four is not a particularly high card, but if West is paying attention he may notice that the two is missing and draw the right conclusions.

In (b) East should play the eight on his partner's lead of the queen. If he plays the two and South wins with the ace, West is likely to switch when next on lead for fear that South holds A K 10.

	(c)	7 6 4			(d)	10 5 3	
		N				N	
Q J 9 3	W E	8 5 2	A K J 8	W E	9 4 2
		S				S	
		A K 10				Q 7 6	

In (c) East should discourage with the two when West leads the queen. It costs a trick for West to lead the suit again.

Again, in (d) East should discourage with the two on his partner's lead of the king. West will switch to another suit, and East may later have a chance to lead through South's queen.

	(e)	6 4			(f)	A Q	
		N				N	
K Q 10 5 2	W E	A 9 3	J 10 9 6 4	W E	8 7 3 2
		S				S	
		J 8 7				K 5	

In (e) East should display enthusiasm by playing the nine on his partner's lead of the king. If he plays the three West may switch, fearing that South is preparing a Bath Coup for him with A J 7.

It is usually right to encourage when holding four cards in partner's suit. Hence in (f) East should play the eight on the first round.

(g)   8 6 4

A K J 10 5   N W E S   Q 2

9 7 3

The lead of an ace against a no trump contract is a special lead calling for partner's highest card. Thus when West leads the ace in diagram (g) East is expected to drop the queen. Then it is clear to West that he can run the suit.

Unblocking

When you hold a doubleton honour in partner's suit it is important to avoid a blockage. Get rid of the honour card on the first round.

(a)   8 7 4

K Q 10 9 6   N W E S   A 2

J 5 3

(b)   7 6 3

Q J 10 8 2   N W E S   K 4

A 9 5

When West leads the king in diagram (a) East must overtake with the ace and return the two. The way is then clear to take five tricks in the suit. If East plays low, the suit will be dead unless West has an outside entry.

Again, in (b) East should play the king on his partner's lead of the queen. Otherwise South may prevent the establishment of the suit, either by taking his ace on the first round and attacking West's entry or by holding up his ace for two rounds.

It is not only when partner leads an honour card that you may have to unblock. Consider these examples:

(c)   A 5

10 8 6 4 3   N W E S   Q J 7

K 9 2

(d)   K 7

A 9 6 5 2   N W E S   J 10 8

Q 4 3

In (c) West leads the four and the ace is played from dummy. Unless East plays one of his honour cards, South will be able to block the suit by winning the king on the second round and the defenders may be restricted to one trick in the suit. When signalling or unblocking with honour cards it is conventional to play the highest of equals. Thus East should play the queen under the ace, denying possession of the king.

In (d) when West leads the five and the king is played from dummy, East should unblock by playing the jack. When he gains the lead he can return the ten to wrap up four tricks in the suit. Note that the play of the eight on the first round would permit South to block the suit by rising with the queen on the second round.

Here is a more complex unblocking situation.

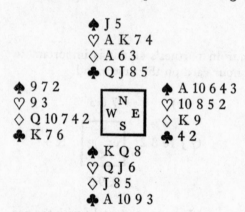

♠ J 5
♡ A K 7 4
◇ A 6 3
♣ Q J 8 5

♠ 9 7 2
♡ 9 3
◇ Q 10 7 4 2
♣ K 7 6

♠ A 10 6 4 3
♡ 10 8 5 2
◇ K 9
♣ 4 2

♠ K Q 8
♡ Q J 6
◇ J 8 5
♣ A 10 9 3

West leads the four of diamonds against three no trumps and the ace is played from dummy. First see what happens if East follows meekly with the nine. South continues with a losing club finesse. West can now lead a diamond to his partner's king, but East has no way of putting West back on lead to enjoy the rest of the suit.

To defeat the contract East must unblock at trick one, dropping his king of diamonds under the ace. On winning the king of clubs, West will switch, and when East comes in with the ace of spades he can lead his second diamond to give his partner four tricks in the suit.

Note that South played well in putting up the ace of diamonds, judging that East was likely to have one of the top honours. There is no point in holding up in diamonds since the club finesse has to be taken into the danger hand. Playing the ace of diamonds at trick one stands to gain when there is a genuine blockage in the suit (K 10 or Q 10 doubleton with East), and there is always the chance of misdefence.

The Duck

We have already seen one example of a defensive duck. Here are some other situations where it is right for a defender to play low on the first round in order to preserve contact with his partner.

[50]

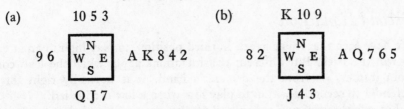

(a) 10 5 3

(b) K 10 9

9 6 | N W E S | A K 8 4 2

8 2 | N W E S | A Q 7 6 5

Q J 7

J 4 3

In (a) West leads the nine. Lacking an outside entry, East should duck on the first round, playing the eight to encourage a continuation. If West has an entry, East later makes four tricks in the suit.

The position in (b) is similar when West leads the eight. With no outside entry of his own, East should play the seven no matter which card is played from dummy. As before, he hopes for West to be able to lead the suit again.

Here is a more advanced example:

♠ A 10
♡ K J 5
◇ A K J
♣ Q J 8 7 4

♠ 7 2　　　　　　♠ K Q 9 6 4
♡ 10 9 6 4 2　| N W E S |　♡ 8 7 3
◇ 10 7 6 4　　　　◇ 9 3 2
♣ K 2　　　　　　♣ A 5

♠ J 8 5 3
♡ A Q
◇ Q 8 5
♣ 10 9 6 3

North-South game
Dealer North

W	N	E	S
	1 ♣	1 ♠	1 NT
pass	3 NT	all pass	

West leads the seven of spades and the ten is played from dummy. It seems natural for East to win with the queen and return a low spade to the ace, but if he does so it is the end of the defence. No matter which defender wins the first club, there will be no way of establishing and cashing a third spade trick.

Placing South with four spades for his bid of one no trump, East should duck the first spade, playing the nine under dummy's ten to encourage a continuation. The difference is that when West wins the first round of clubs with the king he still has a spade to lead. This knocks out the ace, and when East comes in with the ace of clubs he is able to cash three spade tricks to defeat the contract.

Second Hand Low

We have seen that it is correct, in third position, to play high in an attempt to win the trick. But different considerations apply when the lead comes from dummy or from the declarer's hand. It is normally right for the defender in second position to play low when a low card is led.

For one thing, if you are second to play your partner is last to play, and he may well be able to win the trick more economically than you can. Furthermore, it is seldom right to waste the power of your high cards 'on air'. Aces are best kept for the task of capturing enemy kings and queens, for in so doing they help to promote your intermediate cards.

(a)	K 8 3		(b)	J 7 6	
A 10 5	N W E S	J 9 6 2	Q 8 4	N W E S	K 9 5 2
	Q 7 4			A 10 3	

When South leads the four in diagram (a) it would clearly be wasteful for West to play the ace. That would present the declarer with two tricks in the suit, one more than his rightful quota. West should play low on the first round, keeping his ace to deal with the queen.

It is perhaps easier to go wrong in diagram (b), but again West should play low when South leads the three. East is able to deal with the jack and the declarer is held to one trick in the suit. If West goes up with the queen on the first round, South may score two tricks by taking a later finesse against the king.

Another sound reason for playing low is to force the declarer to guess.

If East charges in with the ace when this suit is led from dummy, he takes all the pressure off declarer. He should play low, of course, to give South a chance to go wrong. South may finesse the jack or even the nine, and he may finish up without a trick in the suit.

	7 5	
Q 10 4	N W E S	A 8 6 3
	K J 9 2	

The Defensive Hold-Up

Hold-up play can be just as profitable for the defending side as for declarer, and defenders should be reluctant to part with their stoppers. When the hand with the long suit is short of entries it will often be possible to cut the declarer adrift from his winners.

A Q J 8 5

10 6 3 | N W E S | K 7 2

9 4

South leads from hand and finesses the jack in a situation where North has no outside entries. If East takes his king, he leaves South with easy access to the four winners on the table. If East allows the jack to win, however, he restricts South to two tricks in the suit. An element of deception is also present, for if East plays low smoothly enough South may assume that the finesse is working and try it again. In that case he will make only one trick in the suit.

The next example also has deceptive overtones.

South leads from hand to dummy's king. If East takes his ace, he leaves declarer with no option on the second round but the winning one of finessing the ten. If East plays low without batting an eye, however, South may well go wrong on the next round, putting up the queen in the hope that

K Q 10 7 2

J 9 4 | N W E S | A 8 3

6 5

the ace is with West. South has only to misguess and the suit is dead, even if dummy has an outside entry.

At times it is right to hold up with a double stopper.

♠ A 7 3
♡ 6 4
◇ K J 10 9 4
♣ 10 7 2

♠ 10 2
♡ Q J 10 8 5
◇ 7 6 3
♣ K 9 5

| N W E S |

♠ J 9 5 4
♡ 9 3 2
◇ A Q 2
♣ Q 6 4

♠ K Q 8 6
♡ A K 7
◇ 8 5
♣ A J 8 3

South plays in three no trumps on the lead of the queen of hearts. He holds up once, wins the second heart and runs the eight of diamonds.

The fate of the contract rests with East. If he takes the first diamond the defence is finished. South wins the heart return and leads a second diamond to knock out the ace. East may switch to a club, but South goes up with the ace and runs for home, scoring three spades, three diamonds, two hearts and a club.

It is a different story if East holds up his queen on the first round of diamonds. He wins the second diamond and returns a heart and, with no more diamonds in hand, South has to play on the black suits. He is unlikely to make more than seven tricks.

The Distributional Echo

To achieve an effective defence, it is often necessary for a defender to take his ace at the precise moment when the declarer (or dummy) is exhausted of the suit. Holding up too often can be just as fatal as not holding up at all. Consider this hand.

West leads the jack of spades against South's contract of three no trumps. East encourages with the eight and South wins with the king. The jack of diamonds is allowed to win the next trick, and South continues with the four of diamonds to dummy's ten.

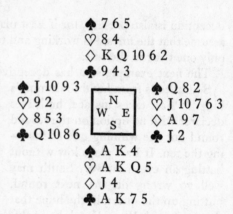

It is apparent that if the declarer is allowed to steal a second trick in diamonds he will make his contract. But how can East tell that he must take his ace on the second round? How can he be sure that South has only two diamonds?

The answer is that West must tell him by the order in which he plays his cards. When the declarer tackles a suit in which dummy has length, it is conventional for defenders to play high-low with an even number of cards (two or four) and low-high with an odd number. This distributional echo is one of the most useful of defensive signals.

In the above case, having three diamonds, West plays his lowest card, the three, on the first round. Since the two of diamonds is in dummy, East immediately knows that the declarer has only two cards in the suit and that he must take his ace on the second round.

Suppose that we exchange West's three of diamonds for South's queen of hearts. Now, with only two diamonds, West plays the eight on the first round. This is clearly the beginning of an echo, and East knows that he must hold up his ace until the third round to exhaust declarer of the suit.

Counting the Tricks

A certain flexibility is needed in defence, and this can be achieved only by thinking along the right lines. Defenders should constantly ask themselves two questions: How many immediate winners does the declarer appear to have? and, Where might the defensive tricks to defeat the contract come from?

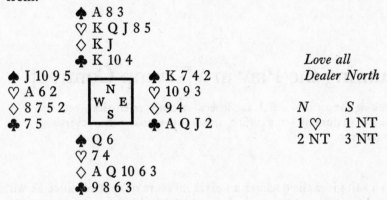

♠ A 8 3
♡ K Q J 8 5
◇ K J
♣ K 10 4

Love all
Dealer North

♠ J 10 9 5
♡ A 6 2
◇ 8 7 5 2
♣ 7 5

♠ K 7 4 2
♡ 10 9 3
◇ 9 4
♣ A Q J 2

♠ Q 6
♡ 7 4
◇ A Q 10 6 3
♣ 9 8 6 3

N	S
1 ♡	1 NT
2 NT	3 NT

West leads the jack of spades, the three is played from dummy and East wins with the king. Let us follow East's thought-processes as he works out his defence.

The first point to register is that the queen of spades is marked in the South hand by the opening lead. Secondly, South is unlikely to have both red aces, for with ten points he would be rather strong for his response of one no trump. The point is academic anyway, for if South *does* have both red aces he has nine straight winners. East therefore bases his defence on the assumption that his partner has one of the missing aces.

The next thing to consider is the most promising source of defensive tricks. A second spade trick can no doubt be developed, but the trouble is that it will come too late. If South has only one ace he will certainly have the queen of diamonds, and he will be able to develop the extra tricks he needs for his contract before the defenders can set up their second spade trick.

The other possible source of defensive tricks is the club suit. A switch to the small club at trick two, and a further club lead from West when in with his ace will produce five tricks for the defence. That looks all right, but let's check once more. Could this club switch give the declarer his contract? No, for if declarer has eight immediate winners at this moment the contract is unbeatable. In practice, South is unlikely to have more than seven immediate winners, two spades plus five tricks in one of the red suits. The club switch may give him an eighth trick but not a ninth.

Clear thinking thus points the way to the winning defence. East switches to his small club at trick two, and when West comes in with the ace of hearts he leads his second club to give East three tricks in the suit.

4

Planning the Play in a Trump Contract

Working for a ruff – watch the losers – trumps as entries – setting
up a suit in dummy – the ruffing finesse – the cross-ruff – reversing
the dummy

Playing in a suit gives the declarer an extra measure of control, since he will
presumably have selected a trump suit in which his side has a clear numerical
superiority. There is not the same need to rely on high cards to stop the run
on an enemy suit, for the small trumps will do the job just as well.

But if the declarer can put his small trumps to good use so can the
defenders. While they remain at large, the enemy trumps represent a serious
threat to the declarer's high cards in the side suits. That is why, on many
hands, it is right to give top priority to 'drawing' the opposing trumps before
they can do any damage.

However, the trump suit may have a purpose to serve quite apart from its
function of providing a number of extra controlling cards. It may prove in
itself to be a fruitful source of extra tricks. This is the third source of tricks
mentioned in the first chapter. By ruffing (another word for trumping) losing
cards in the short trump hand, it is often possible to increase the total
number of tricks available. Indeed, the prospect of extra tricks from the
trump suit is usually the main reason for electing to play in a suit rather than
in no trumps. Obviously, when tricks of this sort are needed it may be necessary to postpone for a while the drawing of the enemy trumps.

There are many other factors that may make it unprofitable to draw
trumps immediately. In fact, so much of this chapter is concerned with
exceptions that it may be as well to emphasize at the beginning this general
rule.

**Always draw trumps immediately if this will leave you with
enough winners for your contract.**

Here is a straightforward example:

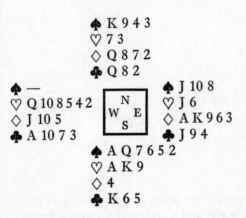

♠ K 9 4 3
♡ 7 3
◇ Q 8 7 2
♣ Q 8 2

♠ —
♡ Q 10 8 5 4 2
◇ J 10 5
♣ A 10 7 3

♠ J 10 8
♡ J 6
◇ A K 9 6 3
♣ J 9 4

♠ A Q 7 6 5 2
♡ A K 9
◇ 4
♣ K 6 5

West leads the jack of diamonds against your contract of four spades. You play low from dummy and ruff the diamond continuation.

As always, the first thing to do is to count your winners. Here you have six winning trumps plus two top hearts, and a ninth trick can be established in clubs. What about the tenth trick?

Well, in view of the convenient shortage on the table, it should be possible after cashing the ace and king of hearts to ruff your losing heart with one of dummy's trumps. This creates an extra trick in trumps, bringing your total up to ten.

The next question is whether you can afford to draw trumps before ruffing your heart loser in dummy. In this case you can. The defenders have only three trumps between them. Even if these are all in the one hand, you will still have a trump left in dummy to deal with the losing heart after trumps have been drawn.

There is no need to take risks. Draw trumps with the ace, king and queen, then play off the top hearts and ruff your third heart in dummy. Subsequently you can establish a club trick for your contract.

It is worth noting that any attempt to ruff the heart before drawing trumps is bound to fail on the lie of the cards. If you ruff with a low spade East will over-ruff, while if you ruff high with the king of spades East must make a trump trick.

Working for a Ruff

There are times when you have some work to do before you can hope to ruff a loser in dummy.

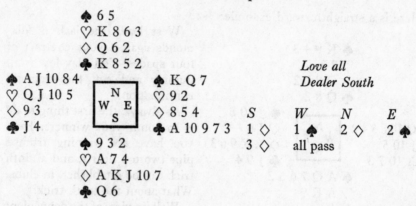

♠ 6 5
♡ K 8 6 3
◇ Q 6 2
♣ K 8 5 2

Love all
Dealer South

♠ A J 10 8 4   ♠ K Q 7
♡ Q J 10 5   ♡ 9 2
◇ 9 3   ◇ 8 5 4
♣ J 4   ♣ A 10 9 7 3

♠ 9 3 2
♡ A 7 4
◇ A K J 10 7
♣ Q 6

S	W	N	E
1 ◇	1 ♠	2 ◇	2 ♠
3 ◇	all pass		

West leads the queen of hearts, and when dummy goes down you pause to take stock. Five diamonds, two hearts and a club add up to eight tricks, leaving you with an additional winner to find.

Hearts are not likely to break evenly, and the only other possibility is to ruff your third spade in dummy. Clearly you cannot afford to draw trumps, for that would leave dummy with no trump to ruff the spade. You must win the first trick (in either hand) and lead a spade at once. When you regain the lead play another spade. The next time you are in you will be able to play your third spade and ruff in dummy (with the queen of diamonds for safety). Then you can draw trumps and establish your ninth trick in clubs.

Note that it would be fatal to draw even one round of trumps before playing a spade. That would put the defenders a tempo ahead, enabling them to extract dummy's trumps and prevent the ruff of your third spade. An initial trump lead, in fact, would have defeated the contract.

All the basic techniques that apply to no trumps can also be used in the play of trump contracts. In the next hand you have to be careful to avoid blocking the trump suit.

You play in five diamonds on the lead of the jack of hearts. Going through the correct motions, you see that you have nine top tricks – five trumps, three hearts and a club. The two extra tricks that you need can be found by ruffing your two losing clubs with dummy's trumps.

A little care is needed over the entry position. Suppose that you win the first trick in hand, cash the ace of clubs, ruff a club with a low trump, play the ace of diamonds and a diamond to your queen, and ruff the remaining club with the king of diamonds. You will then have to return to hand with a heart,

♠ 9 8 6 3
♡ Q 8 7 3
◇ A K 7 4
♣ 2

♠ 5 2
♡ A K 6
◇ Q J 10 9 2
♣ A 9 5

but that will not be completely safe if there is an enemy trump outstanding.

The exercise of a little foresight eliminates all risk. The need to ruff clubs in dummy can be reconciled with the need to draw trumps if you unblock the trump suit by ruffing your clubs with the ace and king of diamonds. You can afford to do this since the diamonds in your hand are adequate for the job of drawing trumps. The correct sequence of play is the ace of hearts, the ace of clubs, a club ruff with the ace of diamonds, a diamond to the queen, a club ruff with the king of diamonds and a diamond to the jack. You are then in a position to draw any trumps that are still outstanding and score at least two further heart tricks for your contract.

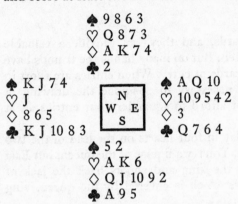

Always ruff high when you can afford to do so. For one thing, this will guard against a possible over-ruff by an opponent. In the above case you are not so much concerned with an over-ruff, since it is most unlikely that East has only two clubs, as with preserving the small trumps in dummy as safe cards of re-entry to your hand. Ruffing a club with a low diamond results in defeat if the full hand is something like the one shown opposite.

Watch the Losers

As well as counting winners, it is important, when playing in a trump contract, to keep an eye on the loser situation. When the defenders are threatening to establish too many tricks, you may have to delay the drawing of trumps until you have taken steps to reduce the number of your potential losers.

Your contract is four hearts, and West leads the three of spades to the jack and king. Although you have only four immediate winners, you can expect to establish four more in trumps and two in diamonds to bring your total up to ten.

The position does not look so healthy when you check losers, however. You cannot avoid losing two trumps and the ace of diamonds, and the enemy are threatening to establish a fourth defensive trick in spades.

♠ 7 6 2
♡ J 9 6
♢ K 7 4
♣ A K 8 5

```
      N
   W     E
      S
```

♠ A K 5
♡ Q 10 8 7 4 3
♢ Q J
♣ 7 3

Clearly you cannot afford to play trumps straight away. You must give top priority to finding a way of disposing of your losing spade.

A glance at the diamond suit provides the solution. Your small spade can be discarded on dummy's king of diamonds, provided that you knock out the ace of diamonds immediately while you still have the spade situation under control. Play the queen of diamonds at trick two. Win the spade return, cash the jack of diamonds, cross to dummy in clubs and discard your five of spades on the king of diamonds. Only then is it safe to tackle the trumps.

Trumps as Entries

Trumps can act as controlling cards, and they can provide a valuable source of extra tricks, as we have seen. But on many hands the trumps have to serve an additional function as cards of entry. When entries are short in the long trump hand, it may be necessary to postpone the drawing of trumps simply because you cannot afford to squander your entries all at once.

♠ A Q 5
♡ J 3
◇ A 7 6
♣ K Q 8 4 2

```
    N
  W   E
    S
```

♠ 8 6 3
♡ A Q 10 9 7 4
◇ Q 4
♣ 6 3

You play in four hearts on the lead of the two of spades. You try a finesse of the queen, but East produces the king and shoots back the jack of diamonds, which is covered by the queen, king and ace.

No luck so far, and if you are to make the contract you need everything to lie favourably from now on. Your ten tricks will have to consist of six trumps, two clubs, and the aces of spades and diamonds. That means you need a reasonable heart split with the finesse working, and you must find the ace of clubs with West.

The normal method of tackling a trump suit like this is to lead the jack and run it if East does not cover. The lead thus remains in dummy, enabling you to repeat the finesse and draw the outstanding trumps. However, you will not be likely to make your contract if you play like that. The point is that you have no entries outside the trump suit, and you will probably need to lead clubs twice from your hand in order to make two tricks in the suit. You must therefore make the most of your trump entries.

Lead the jack of hearts from dummy by all means, but when East plays low you must overtake with the queen. Then abandon trumps for the moment and lead a club towards dummy. If West has the ace he will probably play low, allowing dummy's queen to win. You can then make use of your second trump entry, leading the three from dummy and finessing the nine. When West follows suit you can continue with the ace of trumps to draw East's king. Then lead your second club towards dummy. This time West will no doubt take his ace and return a diamond or a spade, but the king of clubs in dummy will eventually provide a parking place for your losing spade.

    The distribution that you have to play for is something like the hand opposite.

    It is clear that the contract cannot be made if three rounds of trumps are drawn at once.

```
                    ♠ A Q 5
                    ♡ J 3
                    ◇ A 7 6
                    ♣ K Q 8 4 2
  ♠ J 9 7 2                      ♠ K 10 4
  ♡ 6 2            N             ♡ K 8 5
  ◇ K 9 5      W       E         ◇ J 10 8 3 2
  ♣ A J 9 7        S             ♣ 10 5
                    ♠ 8 6 3
                    ♡ A Q 10 9 7 4
                    ◇ Q 4
                    ♣ 6 3
```

Setting Up a Suit in Dummy

Extra tricks in the trump suit can normally be created only by ruffing in the short trump hand. Ruffing in the long trump hand does not increase the trick total, since the declarer expects to make his long trumps anyway.

    There are occasions, however, when the declarer's long trumps can be used to help establish a suit in dummy. And if dummy's trumps are needed as entries, it will again be necessary to delay the drawing of the enemy trumps.

```
  ♠ K 10 4
  ♡ 8 6 2
  ◇ A K Q 7 2
  ♣ J 5
        N
     W     E
        S
  ♠ A Q J 7 2
  ♡ 9 4 3
  ◇ 8 3
  ♣ A 7 6
```

North opens one diamond, East overcalls one heart, and you eventually become the declarer in four spades.

    When West leads the queen of hearts, East overtakes with the king and continues with the ace and the jack. West discards the ten of clubs on the third heart, and East switches to the two of clubs which you win with the ace.

    You have nine immediate winners and must rely on the diamond suit to provide the tenth trick. Your first move should be to test the trump position. Lead a small spade to dummy's ten and return the four of spades to your jack. If either defender shows out on the second round of trumps, you will have to draw the remaining trumps with the ace and queen and rely on a 3–3 diamond break.

If both opponents follow to two rounds of trumps, however, you can succeed when the diamonds are either 3–3 or 4–2. Since you need the king of spades as an entry to dummy, you should not draw the last trump at this point. Instead play two rounds of diamonds, then ruff a small diamond with a high trump in your hand. Return to dummy with the king of spades, drawing the last trump in the process, and discard your two losing clubs on the queen and seven of diamonds.

There is no real risk attached to playing diamonds before drawing the last trump. If the diamonds are divided 5–1 you are not going to make the contract however you play.

The Ruffing Finesse

The presence of a trump suit makes possible a new type of finesse known as the ruffing finesse, where a trump performs the function of an extra ace in the suit. Consider the possibilities of the following hand.

You play in five clubs after East and West have contested strongly in spades. The opening lead of the ace of spades is ruffed in dummy, and a club to your ace draws the opposing trumps. How should you continue?

♠ —
♡ A Q J 10 3
◇ 10 7 3
♣ Q 10 7 6 4

Counting three spade ruffs in dummy, you have ten winners and the eleventh trick could come from either hearts or diamonds. If you tackle diamonds you might lose three tricks straight away, so you should attempt to establish your eleventh trick in hearts.

```
    N
 W     E
    S
```

♠ Q 8 4
♡ 6
◇ K 5 2
♣ A K J 9 5 2

At no trumps there would be only one way of trying for a second trick in hearts – by leading the six and taking an immediate finesse.

Playing in clubs, however, you have a choice. You can either take the natural finesse, or you can lead to the ace of hearts and return the queen, ruffing if East plays the king and discarding a diamond if he plays low. The power of your trump suit prevents East from making a trick with the king if he has it. Playing in clubs, you can take the finesse whichever way suits you best.

In this case it would be risky to finesse naturally, for if the finesse lost, a diamond switch might defeat the contract. East is the danger hand, in fact, and you must keep him off lead by taking the ruffing finesse. If East plays low when the queen is led on the second round of hearts, discard a diamond from hand and your contract is safe whatever happens. If West produces the king of hearts and attacks diamonds, the defenders can take no more than one trick in the suit. If West leads anything else, you will eventually discard both remaining diamonds on dummy's hearts and finish up with twelve tricks.

Suppose that the diamond holdings were reversed, North having K x x and South 10 x x. How would this affect your play? Now West would be the danger hand, and you would make sure of keeping him off lead by taking a natural heart finesse into the East hand. Again your contract would be safe whether East returned a diamond or not.

A K J 10

A ruffing finesse against the queen is possible when a side suit is distributed as shown opposite.

According to the needs of the situation, South can elect to play either defender for the queen. He can take two natural finesses against West, or he can cash the ace and king and run the jack through East.

6 2

The Cross-Ruff

There is one type of hand on which trumps are not drawn at all. Instead, the declarer plans to score the trumps in both hands separately by ruffing. Here is an example of the cross-ruff:

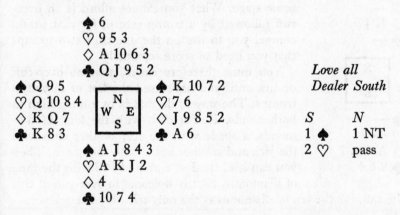

	♠ 6	
	♡ 9 5 3	
	◇ A 10 6 3	
	♣ Q J 9 5 2	*Love all*
♠ Q 9 5	♠ K 10 7 2	*Dealer South*
♡ Q 10 8 4	♡ 7 6	
◇ K Q 7	◇ J 9 8 5 2	
♣ K 8 3	♣ A 6	
	♠ A J 8 4 3	
	♡ A K J 2	
	◇ 4	
	♣ 10 7 4	

S	N
1 ♠	1 NT
2 ♡	pass

West leads the king of diamonds to dummy's ace. Clearly you would need to be lucky to make eight tricks by drawing trumps, even if you manage to ruff a couple of spades in dummy.

The right way to try for the contract is by ruffing in both hands, aiming to score six trump tricks plus two aces. Ruff a diamond with the two of hearts, cash the ace of spades and ruff a spade, ruff a diamond with the jack of hearts and ruff another spade in dummy. When that stands up you have six tricks, with the ace and king of trumps to come.

When planning a cross-ruff it is as well to cash your tricks in the side suits at an early stage. Otherwise the opponents may discard while you are ruffing and may eventually ruff your side winners.

Also, you may have to take precautions against the possibility of an over-ruff.

♠ A J 7 6 4 3
♡ A 5
◇ K J 9 3
♣ 5

Your contract is six diamonds, and West leads the ten of spades to dummy's ace. With nine top tricks you need to establish three more in one hand or the other. An attempt to set up either clubs or spades may fail if you run into a bad break.

```
    N
 W     E
    S
```

The safest method of playing the hand is on a cross-ruff, hoping to score five tricks in the side suits and seven of your eight trumps. Start by playing ace, king and another heart, ruffing in dummy with the three of diamonds. Then cash the

♠ 5
♡ K 7 4
◇ A Q 8 7
♣ A K 9 6 4

ace and king of clubs. If all has gone well your contract is secure, but there is still room for carelessness. The following cards are left.

♠ J 7 6 4
♡ —
◇ K J 9
♣ —

```
    N
 W     E
    S
```

♠ —
♡ —
◇ A Q 8 7
♣ 9 6 4

You need six of the remaining seven tricks and you can therefore afford to be over-ruffed at some stage. What you cannot afford is an over-ruff followed by a trump return, for that would compel you to use on the one trick two trumps that you need to score separately.

You must therefore ensure that no over-ruff occurs until you have used the last of dummy's trumps. The way to do that is by ruffing high in both hands. Ruff a club with the king of diamonds, a spade with the ace, another club with the jack and another spade with the queen. Then you can lead the last club and ruff with the nine of diamonds. East is welcome to over-ruff at this stage if he can, for the ten of diamonds is the only trick for the defence.

Reversing the Dummy

It was noted on page 61 that extra tricks could not be created by ruffing in the long trump hand. That is usually the case, but on certain exceptional hands it may be possible to conjure up an extra trick by ruffing several times in the long trump hand so that it eventually becomes the short trump hand. This process is known as reversing the dummy.

You arrive in a contract of six spades, and West leads the queen of hearts to dummy's ace. A count of quick winners reveals five spades, one heart, four diamonds and one club, making a total of eleven. There is no possibility of ruffing anything on the table since dummy has no shortage, and at first glance it appears that you will have to rely on the club finesse for your twelfth trick.

You dislike banking on anything as uncertain as a finesse? All right, try transposing yourself mentally across the table. Imagine that dummy is the master trump hand and look at your problems from a different angle. Suppose that you can ruff three losing hearts in the South hand and use the North cards to draw trumps. The effect is to increase the number of trump tricks from five to six, and you are no longer dependent on the club finesse.

♠ K J 4
♡ A 8 7 2
◇ Q 6 4
♣ A Q 7

```
  N
W   E
  S
```

♠ A Q 10 7 5
♡ 5
◇ A K J 3
♣ 8 6 5

The dummy reversal will work only if the trumps break 3–2 since North is required to draw the opposing trumps, and it needs careful timing. The key move is to ruff a heart in your hand at trick two. Continue with the ten of spades, then a small spade to dummy's jack. If either defender shows out on this trick, you will have to draw the remaining trumps and fall back on the club finesse.

But if both opponents follow to the second round of trumps you can continue with the dummy reversal. Ruff another heart with the queen of spades, cross to the queen of diamonds, and ruff the last heart with the ace of spades. Finally, lead a club to the ace (no risky finessing at this stage), draw the last trump with the king of spades, discarding a club from hand, and claim three more diamond tricks for your contract.

The full hand could be as shown opposite.

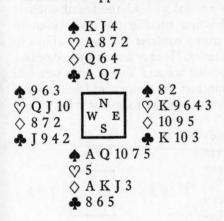

♠ K J 4
♡ A 8 7 2
◇ Q 6 4
♣ A Q 7

♠ 9 6 3
♡ Q J 10
◇ 8 7 2
♣ J 9 4 2

♠ 8 2
♡ K 9 6 4 3
◇ 10 9 5
♣ K 10 3

♠ A Q 10 7 5
♡ 5
◇ A K J 3
♣ 8 6 5

5

Defending Against Trump Contracts

Leading partner's suit – dangerous leads – passive leads – encouraging with an honour – counting declarer's tricks – preventing a ruff in dummy – when to lead trumps – singleton leads – the suit-preference signal – count your tricks – the trump echo – doubleton leads – MUD leads – when not to ruff – trump promotion – the uppercut – the forcing game

A shift of emphasis is needed when defending against suit contracts and techniques have to be slightly modified. The defenders can no longer expect to score tricks by establishing low cards, for the declarer will normally have enough trumps to stop the run of the suit. The aim of the defenders is therefore limited to scoring tricks with their high cards and tricks in the trump suit itself.

The changed approach is often apparent in the choice of opening lead. Holding A K x x x, for example, it is normal to lead the fourth-highest card against no trumps, conceding the first trick in the expectation of making four later tricks. But against a trump contract you cannot afford to give the declarer a cheap trick in this manner. He may have only one or two cards in the suit, and unless you make your ace and king at once you will not make them at all. Against a suit contract the proper lead is the king. This gives nothing away, and you will have a chance to look at dummy and decide on the best continuation.

Safety is a prime consideration in leading against a suit contract, for a trick given away on the opening lead usually turns out to be a trick lost for ever.

In the diagram shown here the declarer's queen is destined to be a loser, but it becomes a winner if the suit is led from the West hand. At no trumps it may be worth West's while to concede an extra trick for the sake of establishing the long suit, but in a trump contract all that the lead achieves is to throw away West's natural trick.

```
              7 6
           ┌───────┐
           │   N   │
K 10 8 5 2 │ W   E │ J 9 3
           │   S   │
           └───────┘
              A Q 4
```

A lead from a sequence of three honour cards is ideal, combining safety and aggression. The card to lead from each sequence below is underlined.

A K̲ Q   K̲ Q J   Q̲ J 10   J̲ 10 9

When you have a broken sequence, or only two honours in sequence, a certain amount of risk is involved, but such leads are still preferable to a lead from an unsupported honour card.

A K̲ 5   K̲ Q 10   Q̲ J 9   J̲ 10 6

You will notice that the king is the standard lead from both K Q x and A K x. This may occasionally create a little confusion for partner, but at least he will know that your king has the backing of either the ace or the queen, and all ambiguity will disappear if he can see one of these cards in dummy or in his own hand. One further point – when holding A K alone it is customary to reverse the order by leading the ace and continuing with the king. This tells partner that you have a doubleton, and if you can find an entry to his hand he will be able to give you a ruff.

Leading Partner's Suit

When partner has bid a suit you have a good indication of the best defence. Lead your highest card from a sequence, from three small cards, or from any doubleton, and lead your lowest card from three or four cards headed by any honour except the ace. If you have the ace of partner's suit, lead it. After all, you would feel foolish if you allowed the declarer to score a trick with a singleton king.

Dangerous Leads

In general it does not pay to lead a low card from any suit that is headed by the ace. The risk of presenting declarer with a trick that he cannot otherwise make is too great. Try to avoid leading from such holdings as A 7 6, A J 8 3 or A Q 4 2, but if you decide that you must do so lead the ace.

Leading away from lower honour cards can also prove to be expensive at times. Any lead from an unsupported king, queen or jack may present the declarer with an extra trick. Nevertheless, there are occasions when you have no option but to lead from an unsupported honour. The fourth-highest card (or the lowest from three cards) is then the right choice.

Careful attention to the bidding will usually tell you when you must risk an attacking lead from an honour card. One obvious occasion is when dummy is known to have a strong side suit on which declarer will obtain discards as soon as he has drawn trumps.

♠ 7 4	*N*	*S*
♡ K 7 3	1 ◇	1 ♠
◇ 8 5	3 ◇	3 ♠
♣ Q 10 7 6 4 2	4 ♠	pass

Given time, South will be able to discard most of his losers on dummy's diamonds. Clearly you must attack at once in order to take such tricks as you can in the other suits. Lead the three of hearts. It is a dangerous lead, of course, but danger is a relative matter. On this hand and this bidding it is much more dangerous *not* to lead a heart.

Why a heart and not a club? This illustrates a further difference in tactics when defending against a suit contract. Against no trumps you would lead your longest suit, clubs, but length is not an asset in defence against a trump contract. The fact that you have six clubs indicates that either declarer or dummy is likely to be short in the suit, so it can hardly be a fruitful source of tricks for the defence. The heart suit offers by far the better prospects.

Passive Leads

The alternative to trying to grab your tricks at once is to sit back and let the declarer do his own work. This policy may be indicated (a) when you have no attractive attacking lead and (b) when it appears likely from the bidding that the contract will be a close affair.

♠ 8 7 2	*N*	*S*
♡ K J 4		1 ♡
◇ A J 9 2	1 NT	2 ♣
♣ Q 7 3	2 ♡	3 ♡
	4 ♡	pass

There is no long suit in dummy to worry about, and it sounds as though both opponents have stretched to the limit to reach game. The lead least likely to give away a trick is the eight of spades.

Encouraging With an Honour

The partner of the opening leader is sometimes in a position to indicate the right defence by the card he plays to the first trick.

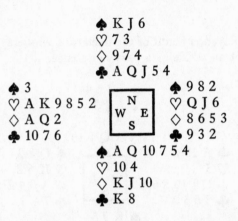

♠ K J 6
♡ 7 3
◊ 9 7 4
♣ A Q J 5 4

♠ 3
♡ A K 9 8 5 2
◊ A Q 2
♣ 10 7 6

♠ 9 8 2
♡ Q J 6
◊ 8 6 5 3
♣ 9 3 2

♠ A Q 10 7 5 4
♡ 10 4
◊ K J 10
♣ K 8

South plays in four spades after West has overcalled in hearts. The opening lead is the king of hearts and it is up to East to guide the defence.

Defenders employ normal high-low signals (high to encourage, low to discourage) against suit contracts as well as against no trumps. One refinement that is of particular value in suit play is the convention that the play of an honour card under partner's honour at the first trick guarantees possession of the next lower card. Hence in this example East should signal with the queen of hearts, affirming possession of the jack as well.

Now West knows how to proceed. He continues with a small heart to his partner's jack. East switches to a diamond (what else?) and the defenders take their four tricks before the declarer can get going. Note that the contract cannot be defeated without an early diamond lead from East. The declarer is in a position to run six spades and five clubs as soon as he gains the lead.

The main difference in signalling against a suit contract is that defenders do not start an echo with four small cards when an honour card is led. With such a holding there is no reason to encourage a continuation. Defenders do start an echo with a doubleton, however, to indicate their ability to ruff on the third round.

This is a situation that crops up frequently. When West leads the king East should encourage with the eight. West continues with the ace and leads a third round for East to ruff.

Q 10 4

A K 9 6 5

N
W   E
S

8 3

J 7 2

The corollary is that when East plays his lowest card on the first round West will not be tempted to continue the suit.

When East plays the two on his partner's king, West realizes that he must look for tricks elsewhere before the declarer can establish the queen of this suit for a discard.

Q 10 4

A K 9 6 5

N
W   E
S

8 3 2

J 7

Counting Declarer's Tricks

After one or two tricks have been played, a count of the declarer's winners will often tell you whether to adopt an active or a passive defence.

South plays in four hearts on the lead of the queen of diamonds. The five is played from dummy and East encourages with the nine. South ruffs the second diamond and runs the ten of hearts to East's king.

Looking at the menacing clubs in dummy, East may be tempted to lead a small spade in the hope of winning two quick tricks in the suit. But if he goes through the proper motions and counts declarer's tricks he will realize that

```
            ♠ J 7 6 4
            ♡ A J 3
            ◇ K 5
            ♣ A Q J 10
♠ A 10 2                ♠ Q 8 3
♡ 5          N          ♡ K 6 2
◇ Q J 10 8 6 3  W   E   ◇ A 9 4 2
♣ 8 6 5         S       ♣ 7 4 3
            ♠ K 9 5
            ♡ Q 10 9 8 7 4
            ◇ 7
            ♣ K 9 2
```

there is no need to risk a spade lead. South has at the most five trump tricks and four clubs, and he therefore needs at least one trick from spades to make his contract. South will have to tackle spades himself, so East should adopt the passive course of returning a trump and leaving declarer to do his own work.

Preventing a Ruff in Dummy

Defenders should look out for opportunities of thwarting the declarer's plans to ruff losers in dummy. This often calls for alert defence and the proper use of entry cards.

West leads the king of hearts against South's contract of two spades. If he is allowed to hold the trick he may wonder what to do next, but it will not greatly matter for the chance to defeat the contract will have come and gone.

In order to beat two spades the defenders must make haste to remove dummy's trumps, denying declarer the chance to ruff a heart on the table.

```
            ♠ Q 10 4
            ♡ 8 3
            ◇ K 7 6 4
            ♣ Q 8 3 2
♠ K 7 5                 ♠ 6 3
♡ K Q 10 2   N          ♡ A J 7 4
◇ J 9 3     W   E       ◇ Q 10 5 2
♣ J 10 6       S        ♣ K 9 5
            ♠ A J 9 8 2
            ♡ 9 6 5
            ◇ A 8
            ♣ A 7 4
```

West cannot profitably switch to trumps at trick two, but East can! He should overtake his partner's king of hearts with the ace and return a trump. When declarer plays low, West wins with the king and plays a second round of trumps. Subsequently West wins a heart trick and plays his third trump, removing the last trump from dummy and leaving the declarer with six losers.

When to Lead Trumps

Some readers may have noticed that an initial trump lead by West on the last hand would have served equally well to defeat the contract of two spades. East can win the first heart and lead his remaining trump, and West is in a position to clear the trumps when he gets in with the second heart.

A trump lead is often a good idea when the bidding suggests that dummy's trumps may be used for ruffing. It can be particularly effective when you have the declarer's side suit well stopped.

		S	N
♠	9 2		
♡	A 6 3	1 ♡	1 ♠
◇	A J 10 7	2 ◇	3 ♡
♣	Q 10 6 3	4 ♡	pass

Your diamonds appear to be well placed over the declarer and could be worth three tricks. North is likely to be short in diamonds, however, and there is a danger that some of your diamond tricks may be ruffed away. You should plan to remove dummy's trumps, starting with a lead of the three of hearts. When you regain the lead in diamonds you can continue with the ace and another heart to wipe out dummy's ruffing power.

The complete hand may be as follows.

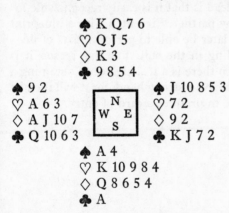

♠ K Q 7 6
♡ Q J 5
◇ K 3
♣ 9 8 5 4

♠ 9 2
♡ A 6 3
◇ A J 10 7
♣ Q 10 6 3

♠ J 10 8 5 3
♡ 7 2
◇ 9 2
♣ K J 7 2

♠ A 4
♡ K 10 9 8 4
◇ Q 8 6 5 4
♣ A

Any lead except a trump permits the declarer to score the one diamond ruff in dummy that is all he needs for his contract. As it happens, the lead of the ace and another trump works equally well on this hand, but the initial lead of the three gives greater flexibility. After all, partner might have had a singleton king!

The other situations that suggest a trump lead can be summarized as follows:

1. When the opponents bid three suits and finally settle in the fourth.
2. When declarer, after receiving support in his suit, bids no trumps and is put back into his suit.

3. When your side has general strength in three suits and the opponents sacrifice at a high level.

4. When your take-out double is passed for penalties.

In general a trump lead is likely to prove satisfactory only when you have two or three cards in the trump suit. Do not lead trumps when you have a singleton (except in situations 3 and 4 above) or when you have four trumps. Then a different type of defence is required, as we shall see.

Lead the lowest card from three trumps, even when you have two honours in sequence. It would be embarrassing if your side failed to make a trump trick from three honour cards, which is what could happen if you led the jack in the situation shown here.

Do not be afraid of leading away from an honour card. A trump trick given away by a lead from Q x x or J x x will often come back with interest.

```
                Q 9 5 4

               ┌───────┐
               │   N   │
        J 10 3 │ W   E │  K
               │   S   │
               └───────┘

                A 8 7 6 2
```

Singleton Leads

The most direct way of trying for tricks in the trump suit is by leading a singleton to prepare the way for a ruff. This can be a dynamic form of defence when the conditions are right. If partner has the ace of the suit he will be able to give you a ruff straight away, and you may achieve more than one ruff if you find partner with a further entry.

One disadvantage of the singleton lead is that it is easily recognizable for what it is by the declarer as well as by partner. Presented with a blueprint of the distribution, the declarer may later be able to perform feats of deep finessing against your partner's holding in the suit. For this reason it is advisable to lead a singleton only when there is a real chance of obtaining a ruff. Do not lead a singleton when you have a strong hand, for it will then be unlikely that your partner will be able to produce a card of entry.

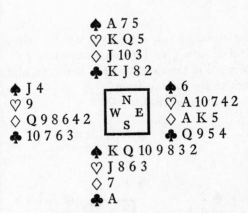

♠ A 7 5
♡ K Q 5
◇ J 10 3
♣ K J 8 2

♠ J 4
♡ 9
◇ Q 9 8 6 4 2
♣ 10 7 6 3

♠ 6
♡ A 10 7 4 2
◇ A K 5
♣ Q 9 5 4

♠ K Q 10 9 8 3 2
♡ J 8 6 3
◇ 7
♣ A

It is when your own hand is weak that a singleton lead has the best chance of success. Partner is then marked with some strength, and there is every likelihood that you will be able to obtain at least one ruff.

South plays in four spades and West leads the nine of hearts to the king and ace. East recognizes that there can be little chance of defeating the contract unless the nine of hearts is a singleton, so he plans to give his partner a ruff.

Before returning a heart, East might think of cashing the king of diamonds to indicate where his entry lies, but if he does so it will no longer be possible to defeat the contract. After ruffing the heart at trick three West will lead a second diamond, but the declarer will ruff, draw trumps and claim the rest.

If the defenders are to negotiate the two ruffs needed to beat the contract, it is essential for East to return a heart at trick two. But how can he tell his partner to switch to diamonds rather than clubs?

The Suit-Preference Signal

East can indicate where his entry lies by means of a special signal. In situations like this when one defender leads a card for his partner to ruff, there are always two side suits to consider. It is conventional to show preference between these two suits by the size of the card that is led for partner to ruff. The lead of a high card indicates preference for the higher-ranking side suit, the lead of a low card for the lower-ranking.

In this particular example East should return the ten of hearts at trick two, showing a liking for diamonds, the higher-ranking of the two remaining suits. West ruffs the heart, leads a diamond back to his partner's king, and ruffs another heart to put the contract one down.

If East had held the ace of clubs instead of the top diamonds, he would have returned the two of hearts at trick two, implying preference for the lower-ranking side suit.

This suit-preference signal is a highly effective weapon that deserves a place in the armoury of every defender. Opportunities for its use are fairly frequent.

Count Your Tricks

When partner leads an obvious singleton and you are able to win the trick, it does not follow that you should always give him an immediate ruff. Remember that your ultimate objective is the defeat of the contract, and ask yourself where the defensive tricks are coming from.

Imagine that you are East on the following hand.

South is in four hearts and West leads the two of spades to the king and ace. Clearly, you could give partner a spade ruff at trick two, but that would not be a very bright defence. You need four tricks to defeat the game and, since partner is not likely to have both missing aces, two of those tricks will have to come from diamonds.

You need to find partner with the ace of diamonds, and you must attack the suit at once since

```
                  ♠ K Q 10 8 7 3
                  ♡ A Q 8 3
                  ◇ 6 4
                  ♣ 9
  ♠ 2                          ♠ A J 9 5
  ♡ 7 4           N            ♡ 9 2
  ◇ A 9 8 5 2   W   E          ◇ Q J 7
  ♣ K 8 6 5 3     S            ♣ Q 10 4 2
                  ♠ 6 4
                  ♡ K J 10 6 5
                  ◇ K 10 3
                  ♣ A J 7
```

you will never have another opportunity. The lead of the queen of diamonds at trick two gets the timing right. This will probably be covered by the king and ace, and partner will return a diamond to your jack. Now, with two diamond tricks in the bag, you can lead a spade for partner to ruff as the setting trick.

Note that if you had returned a spade at trick two, West would have had no good move to make after taking his ruff. The best he can do is to cash the ace of diamonds, holding the declarer to ten tricks. If West fails to cash out, South will eventually discard all his diamonds on dummy's spades to make an overtrick.

This deal illustrates an important principle of defence. **When the contract can be defeated only if partner has a particular card, assume that he has that card and defend accordingly.**

A singleton does not always have to be led at the first opportunity, of course. A switch at a later stage may prove to be equally effective.

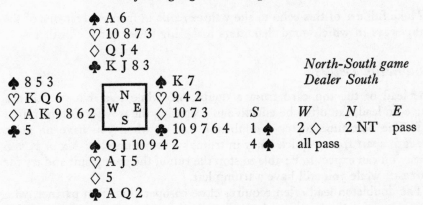

♠ A 6
♡ 10 8 7 3
◇ Q J 4
♣ K J 8 3

North-South game
Dealer South

♠ 8 5 3
♡ K Q 6
◇ A K 9 8 6 2
♣ 5

♠ K 7
♡ 9 4 2
◇ 10 7 3
♣ 10 9 7 6 4

♠ Q J 10 9 4 2
♡ A J 5
◇ 5
♣ A Q 2

S	W	N	E
1 ♠	2 ◇	2 NT	pass
4 ♠	all pass		

West is likely to start with the king of diamonds, on which East will discourage with the three. In view of his partner's failure to start an echo, West realizes that there is likely to be only the one diamond trick for the defence. He must therefore hope to find East with one of the missing high cards – either an ace or the king of spades. A heart switch will be right when partner has that ace, but it is dangerous to put all the defensive eggs in the one basket. The club switch is more promising, for it is likely to defeat the contract when East has either the ace of clubs or the king of spades.

West therefore switches to his singleton club at the second trick. South wins with the ace and, fearing a club ruff, properly refuses the spade finesse, playing the ace and another spade instead.

In with the king of spades, East has a bit of a problem. If his partner has another trump he should return a club for West to ruff. If West is out of trumps, however, the only chance is to switch to hearts in the hope that West has the ace and queen. How can East tell what to do?

The Trump Echo

As always, the answer is that his partner should tell him what to do. West imparts the vital message by the order in which he plays his trumps. The trump echo is used in the opposite sense to the echo in a plain suit. It is conventional to play low-high in trumps when holding two (or four) and high-low with three.

In this example West should therefore play the five of trumps on the first round and the three on the second round. The echo promises a third trump and hints strongly at the ability to ruff something. Thus East is in no doubt about how to continue when he wins the king of spades. He returns a club for his partner to ruff, and West switches to the king of hearts to establish a fourth trick for the defence.

Make full use of this echo to show three cards in trumps. It is one of the many ways in which good defenders make life easier for each other.

Doubleton Leads

The lead of the top card from a doubleton, while less dynamic than a singleton lead, can often be effective in preparing the way for a third round ruff. The best time to try a doubleton lead is when you have no great strength apart from a quick entry in trumps – something like A x or K x x. Then you can expect to be able to stop the run of the trump suit and try for your ruff while you still have a trump left.

The doubleton lead often requires close co-operation from partner, who must recognize the lead for what it is and take appropriate measures, holding up an ace when necessary.

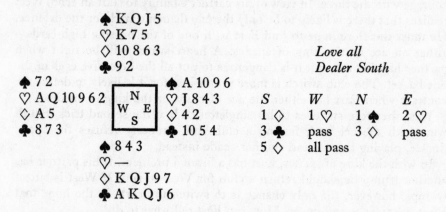

```
                    ♠ K Q J 5
                    ♡ K 7 5
                    ◊ 10 8 6 3          Love all
                    ♣ 9 2               Dealer South
  ♠ 7 2                     ♠ A 10 9 6
  ♡ A Q 10 9 6 2    N       ♡ J 8 4 3        S      W      N      E
  ◊ A 5          W     E    ◊ 4 2            1 ◊    1 ♡    1 ♠    2 ♡
  ♣ 8 7 3           S       ♣ 10 5 4         3 ♣    pass   3 ◊    pass
                    ♠ 8 4 3                  5 ◊    all pass
                    ♡ —
                    ◊ K Q J 9 7
                    ♣ A K Q J 6
```

From West's point of view a spade lead is the only one that holds out any prospect of developing extra tricks for the defence. West therefore leads the seven of spades, the king is played from dummy, and it is up to East to diagnose the situation.

Is the seven of spades a singleton? If so, East should win and return a spade for his partner to ruff. But if the lead is from a doubleton, as is actually the case, East must hold up his ace, signalling encouragement with the ten of spades. West subsequently wins the first round of trumps, leads the two of spades to his partner's ace, and scores a spade ruff as the setting trick.

Sometimes it is far from easy to tell whether the lead is a singleton or a doubleton, but in this case East should reach the right conclusion. If West has a singleton spade South must have four, but with four spades South would surely have supported his partner who bid the suit. East should therefore play the ten of spades at trick one.

MUD Leads

At times the problem is to distinguish, not between a singleton and a doubleton but between a doubleton and a trebleton lead. We have seen that a lead from three small cards is sometimes chosen as a passive lead when nothing else is attractive. If you lead the top card from three and follow with a lower card on the second round, there is a danger that partner will put you with a doubleton and try to give you a ruff on the third round. For that reason many players prefer to lead the middle card from three and play the top card on the next round. Thus from a holding of 9 7 3 the seven would be led, the nine played on the second round and the three on the third round. This sequence of plays (middle, up, down – or MUD for short) is generally used only in defence against suit contracts. The big advantage is that when you lead the seven and follow with the three on the next round, there is no ambiguity. Partner *knows* you must have a doubleton.

This method of leading can be thoroughly recommended, but make sure you have a clear understanding with your partner about it.

When Not to Ruff

So far we have been having a merry time ruffing at every opportunity, but it is important to realize that there are times when it does not pay to ruff in defence. One obvious occasion is when you would be ruffing with a natural trump trick.

On this hand there is no point in seeking a ruff by leading the singleton heart, for you are virtually certain of making a trump trick in any case. The heart lead cannot gain and may well

		S	N
♠ Q J 5			
♡ 4		1 ♠	2 ♠
◇ A J 8 7 3		4 ♠	pass
♣ 10 9 8 2			

lose by ruining partner's holding in the suit. Try to develop tricks elsewhere by leading the ten of clubs.

When you have nothing but small trumps it is generally right to ruff when you have the chance to kill one of the declarer's winners. But be wary of ruffing when declarer can play a loser on the trick, even if your trump holding appears to have little value. Like aces, trumps should not be wasted 'on air'.

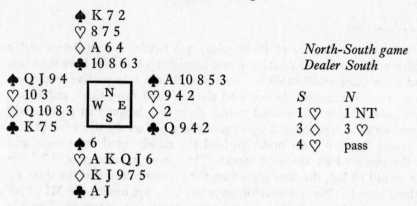

♠ K 7 2
♡ 8 7 5
◇ A 6 4
♣ 10 8 6 3

| | North-South game |
| | Dealer South |

♠ Q J 9 4   ♠ A 10 8 5 3
♡ 10 3   ♡ 9 4 2
◇ Q 10 8 3   ◇ 2
♣ K 7 5   ♣ Q 9 4 2

♠ 6
♡ A K Q J 6
◇ K J 9 7 5
♣ A J

S	N
1 ♡	1 NT
3 ◇	3 ♡
4 ♡	pass

West attacks with the queen of spades and South has to ruff the second round. He continues with a diamond to the ace and a diamond back, and the fate of the contract hinges on East's action at this point. If East ruffs with a 'useless' trump, the contract cannot be defeated; if he discards, it cannot be made.

A ruff by East does not gain a trick, because South follows with a low diamond which would have been a loser anyway. The ruff loses a trick because it weakens East's trump holding. On regaining the lead South is able to draw the remaining trumps in two rounds, and he still has a trump in dummy with which to ruff the fourth round of diamonds. He makes his contract for the loss of a spade, a trump and a club.

Note the difference if East treats his trumps with proper respect and refuses to waste one on the second diamond. South wins with the king and concedes the third diamond to West. He wins the return, draws two rounds of trumps, and plays a fourth diamond, ruffing in dummy. But East is able to over-ruff with the nine, and the defenders cannot be denied a club as the setting trick.

It is an instructive hand, worth replaying a few times until the principle sinks in. Basically, the defenders are destined to win four tricks – a spade, a club, a diamond and a trump (by over-ruffing dummy). If East ruffs a losing diamond, however, two defensive tricks – the trump and the diamond – are telescoped into one.

Trump Promotion

When the declarer ruffs with a small trump it will usually pay to over-ruff if you are able to do so.

The position is different when the declarer ruffs with an honour card, for now the principle of promotion comes into operation. The fact that declarer has played a high trump promotes every lower trump in the defenders' hands by one step in rank, and the defence may end up with an extra trump trick.

This advantage is dissipated if you over-ruff with an honour card of your own. It is normally correct to refuse to over-ruff when declarer ruffs high. Opposite is a standard position.

Hearts are trumps, and South would have no difficulty in making two tricks if he had the lead. The lead is in dummy, however, so South leads a diamond and ruffs with the queen of hearts. It is easy to see that West will make two tricks if he discards his spade, for his jack of hearts has been promoted to third rank. If West commits the folly of over-ruffing he will make only one trick.

Other well-known positions where refusing to over-ruff an honour gains an extra trump trick are when a defender has K 10 x over A Q J x x, or Q 9 x x over A K J 10 x.

At times it may be less clear where the extra trump trick may come from, but it is still good technique to refuse to over-ruff.

```
                ♠ —
                ♡ —
                ◇ J 5
                ♣ 4
    ♠ 7                     ♠ 6
    ♡ A J      N            ♡ 5
    ◇ —      W   E          ◇ Q
    ♣ —        S            ♣ —
                ♠ —
                ♡ K Q 10
                ◇ —
                ♣ —
```

South opens with a bid of three spades and plays there. West leads the ace of hearts, receives a heavy signal, and continues with the three. East wins the second heart with the nine and returns the queen of hearts (clearly a suit preference signal for clubs, although hardly necessary in view of the dummy).

South ruffs the third heart with the queen of spades and the ball is back in West's court. If West over-ruffs with the king, the only other trick for the defence will be the ace of clubs.

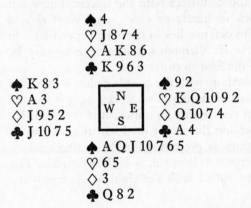

```
              ♠ 4
              ♡ J 8 7 4
              ◇ A K 8 6
              ♣ K 9 6 3
  ♠ K 8 3                   ♠ 9 2
  ♡ A 3        N            ♡ K Q 10 9 2
  ◇ J 9 5 2  W   E          ◇ Q 10 7 4
  ♣ J 10 7 5   S            ♣ A 4
              ♠ A Q J 10 7 6 5
              ♡ 6 5
              ◇ 3
              ♣ Q 8 2
```

Although West cannot tell whether a second trump trick can be promoted or not, he certainly has nothing to gain by over-ruffing. As a matter of normal technique he should discard on the third heart. South will continue with the ace of spades and then the jack. Now West takes his king and leads a club to his partner's ace, and a further heart lead promotes a trick for the eight of spades.

The Uppercut

Another form of trump promotion is aptly named the uppercut. This occurs when a defender ruffs as high as possible ahead of the declarer, the idea being to force a high trump from declarer's hand and thus promote a trump trick for partner.

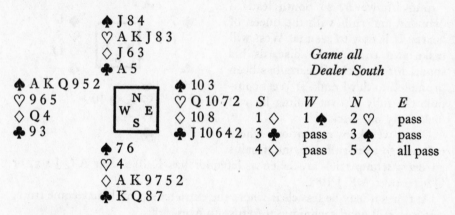

West leads the king of spades and continues with the queen. There can be little hope of a defensive trick in hearts or clubs, and West should realize that the only chance for the defence lies in the trump position. On the bidding South is likely to have six diamonds, but something may be achieved by leading a third spade for East to ruff.

West should be careful not to continue with the ace of spades, on which a sleepy partner might discard instead of ruffing. The correct play is a small spade at trick three. East will then realize that an uppercut is required. He ruffs with the ten of diamonds, forcing the ace or the king from declarer's hand, and West's queen of diamonds is promoted for the setting trick.

Note that the technique of the uppercut is to ruff as high as possible. The punch would be ineffectual if East ruffed with the eight of diamonds instead of the ten.

The Forcing Game

Many contracts are played in a 5–3 trump fit, and a 4–1 division of the opposing trumps can cause severe embarrassment to the declarer. It was mentioned earlier that a trump lead is not a good idea when you have four of them. With four trumps, forget about passive leads and attack in your long suit. The idea is to force the declarer to weaken his trump holding by ruffing in his own hand. If he has to ruff just once, he may be unable to draw your trumps without losing control of the hand.

The same reasoning applies when you have a singleton trump, for there is then every chance that your partner will have four. Again you should try to shorten declarer's trump holding.

Often this forcing defence has to be combined with hold-up play in the trump suit, denying declarer any chance of taking the force in the short trump hand.

South plays in four spades after East and West have contested in hearts. West leads the two of hearts and South ruffs the second round. Then comes a spade to dummy's queen and a spade back to the jack.

If West, thinking he has declarer on the hook, takes his ace and continues with the king of hearts, South can counter neatly by discarding a diamond instead of ruffing. Now the defence collapses, for dummy is in a position to ruff a

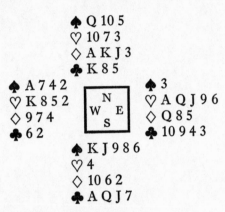

♠ Q 10 5
♡ 10 7 3
◇ A K J 3
♣ K 8 5

♠ A 7 4 2
♡ K 8 5 2
◇ 9 7 4
♣ 6 2

♠ 3
♡ A Q J 9 6
◇ Q 8 5
♣ 10 9 4 3

♠ K J 9 8 6
♡ 4
◇ 10 6 2
♣ A Q J 7

fourth heart and the declarer cannot be prevented from making ten tricks.

West should, of course, hold up his ace of trumps once more. If South plays a third trump, West can take his ace and continue hearts and the defence must make at least four tricks. More likely, South will switch to clubs after two rounds of trumps, but West can ruff the third club and cash the ace of trumps, leaving South with only nine tricks. When the diamond finesse fails, so does the contract.

Part Two
SHARPENING THE TOOLS

6

The Care of Entries

Unblocking – the duck – overtaking – hidden entries – defence – unblocking discards – the Deschapelles Coup

When there are plenty of entries in both hands the declarer seldom has much difficulty in making his contract. Unfortunately these ideal conditions are hardly ever obtained. Usually there is a scarcity of entries in one hand or the other, and the declarer has problems of communication to take into account when planning his overall strategy.

Foresight is a prime factor in the proper handling of entries. When faced with an early choice of winning a trick in either hand, the declarer must look ahead, consider all possible snags, and take care to preserve the entry in the hand most likely to need it in the later play. It would be easy to go wrong on the following hand.

You play in four hearts on the lead of the ten of spades. You can count two spades, five trumps and two diamonds for nine tricks, and a diamond ruff in dummy should bring the total up to ten.

♠ A 8 4 3
♡ K 9 6 2
◇ K 5
♣ 9 8 4

```
    N
W       E
    S
```

♠ K 7
♡ A Q 10 8 3
◇ A 9 4
♣ 10 6 3

What could go wrong? Well, if Destiny is in a fickle mood an opponent may be void in trumps. This need not worry you unduly, for you will naturally play the ace or the queen of trumps at trick two, thereby retaining the option of finessing either way against the jack. If West is void in trumps you can continue with three rounds of diamonds, ruffing in dummy with the king. Then run the nine of trumps, finessing twice against the jack to bring in ten tricks.

If East is void in trumps, you can finesse the nine of trumps on the second round, play three rounds of diamonds, ruffing in dummy with the six, and cash the king of trumps. You will then need to find a safe way back to hand in order to draw the last trump. A third-round spade ruff is not altogether safe, for if West began with only two spades he will be able to over-ruff.

So our preview of possible dangers and our forecast of the course of play finally tells us how to play to the first trick. The ace of spades should be played at trick one, preserving the king as a card of re-entry to our hand at trick eight.

Unblocking

A good way of creating extra entries in one hand is by unblocking the high cards from the other. There is often an element of gambit in these plays, the unblocking play creating an immediate trick for the defenders in exchange for an entry that may be worth several tricks.

♠ Q J 2
♡ 7 4
◇ Q J 10 8 5
♣ 8 4 3

You play in three no trumps on a spade lead. There appear to be nine tricks all right, counting two spades, two hearts, four diamonds and a club, but a little care is required.

♠ A 10 3
♡ A K J 6
◇ K 9
♣ A J 9 5

The first trap to avoid is that of playing a high spade from dummy. The queen and jack of spades are needed to ensure access to the table after the diamond ace has been knocked out. Furthermore, if East plays a low card on dummy's two of spades, you must resist the temptation to win a 'cheap' trick with the ten. It would turn out to be far from cheap, for the defenders would hold up the ace of diamonds until the second round and you would be left with no means of reaching the established diamonds.

To make sure of your nine tricks you must unblock in spades by winning the first trick with the ace. Then play the king of diamonds and continue the suit to force out the ace, and the queen and jack of spades will ensure that you can get back to dummy to enjoy the established diamonds.

There are several other situations in which declarer can create an entry to dummy in the suit led by the defenders.

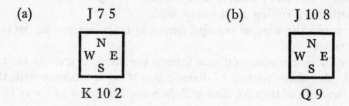

(a)   J 7 5   (b)   J 10 8

         K 10 2   Q 9

Defending against your no trump contract, West leads a low card in diagram (a) and East plays the ace. Needing a quick entry to dummy, perhaps to take a finesse, you should drop your king under the ace. With any luck the jack will now provide your entry.

In diagram (b) when West leads a low card, you should play an honour card from the table just in case East allows you to win the first trick. If East plays the ace or the king, unblock by playing your queen. The defenders are unable to press home their attack in the suit without allowing dummy to gain the lead.

It will usually pay to unblock in situations like the following:

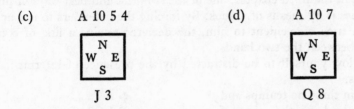

(c)   A 10 5 4   (d)   A 10 7

J 3   Q 8

In (c) when West leads a low card and East plays an honour, drop the jack to prepare the way for a later finesse of the ten. If you block the suit by retaining the jack, you will need an outside entry in dummy if you are to enjoy two tricks in the suit.

Similarly, in (d) drop the queen under East's king if dummy has no outside entry. Later you can finesse the ten, making two tricks if, as expected, West has led from the jack.

There are many situations in which problems of communication between the two hands can be eased by the routine unblocking of intermediate cards.

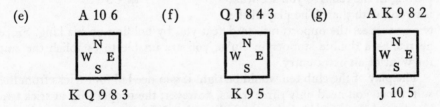

(e)   A 10 6   (f)   Q J 8 4 3   (g)   A K 9 8 2

KQ 9 8 3   K 9 5   J 10 5

Having no side entry in diagram (e), South should lead the king and unblock the ten from dummy. The second round is won by the ace, and if West shows out the way is clear to finesse against East's jack on the third round.

Needing four tricks in diagram (f) and with only one side entry to the table, South should start by leading the nine to dummy's jack. A low card is returned to the king, and if East shows out South is poised to take a third-round finesse against the ten.

If South needs all five tricks in diagram (g), it is correct to play the ace on the first round to guard against the possibility of a singleton queen with East. But if dummy has no outside entry South must be careful to unblock the jack (or the ten) from his own hand. If the queen does not drop, South returns to hand and leads his remaining honour card for a finesse. Failure to play an honour card on the first round will result in a blockage when West has Q x, Q x x or Q x x x.

The Duck

As we noted in the third chapter, one of the simplest and best ways of preserving entries is by means of a duck. By forcing the defenders to use up a stopper at a time convenient to him, the declarer retains a line of communication between the two hands.

Do not allow yourself to be distracted by the presence of intermediate honour cards.

You play in three no trumps and receive the lead of the nine of hearts. There are seven immediate winners, and you therefore need to develop two extra tricks in clubs for your contract. At trick two you lead the four of clubs on which West plays the seven. What do you play from dummy?

At first sight it may seem reasonable to try the double finesse by putting in the ten. Do you see what is wrong with that? The play of the

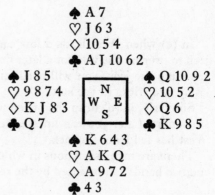

♠ A 7
♡ J 6 3
◇ 10 5 4
♣ A J 10 6 2

♠ J 8 5
♡ 9 8 7 4
◇ K J 8 3
♣ Q 7

♠ Q 10 9 2
♡ 10 5 2
◇ Q 6
♣ K 9 8 5

♠ K 6 4 3
♡ A K Q
◇ A 9 7 2
♣ 4 3

ten gives East the opportunity to defeat you by holding up his king. Since he retains a double stopper in clubs, you are unable to establish the suit for want of an extra entry.

The play of the club ten would be right if you needed four tricks from the suit. Since you need only three tricks, however, the proper play at trick two is a low club from dummy, compelling the defenders to use one of their stoppers on the first round. When you regain the lead you play a club to the ace and continue with the jack of clubs to drive out the king. This line of play assures you of three club tricks when the suit breaks 3–3 and also when either defender has a doubleton honour.

Note that it is still vital to duck in dummy if West plays the queen on the first round of clubs.

When entries are short it is always as well to give some thought to the best method of forcing the defenders to part with a stopper on the first round of a suit.

♠ 8 6 5
♡ A 9 3
◇ K J 7 6 4
♣ 5 3

♠ A K 4
♡ K 7 2
◇ Q 5 2
♣ A K 9 4

You are in three no trumps and West leads the four of hearts. Naturally you preserve dummy's entry by playing low, and when East produces the jack you win the trick with the king.

Having six tricks in the other suits, you need three from diamonds. If the suit breaks 3–2 you will make an overtrick, so you turn your attention to the possibility of a 4–1 break. If the opening lead is an honest card the defenders can establish no more than two tricks in hearts, which means that you can afford to lose two diamonds. But on this hand a first-round duck in diamonds will do you no good, for the defenders will immediately knock out the ace of hearts and subsequently shut out the diamonds by holding up the ace until the third round.

In fact you are not going to succeed in this contract if East has four diamonds headed by the ace. But if West has four diamonds, you can force him to take his ace on the first round by leading the queen of diamonds at trick two. Win the heart return with dummy's ace, and the time is ripe to make your duck by leading a low diamond from dummy. This gives up the chance of an overtrick, but at this stage ensures your contract against a 4–1 diamond break. This duck is a form of safety play, a term applied to a wide range of plays designed to improve the declarer's chances, sometimes at the cost of a trick. We shall be looking at safety plays in detail in a later chapter.

Many of these ducking plays have the purpose of combating the possible hold-up of an enemy stopper. The next hand continues the theme with a slight variation.

West leads the queen of clubs against your contract of three no trumps. It is always amusing when the defenders lead your best suit, but your smile fades when East discards the three of hearts. So there is no chance of establishing extra tricks in clubs, and you will have to look to the diamonds for the two tricks that you need. After winning the first club how should you play?

♠ K 9 8
♡ 10 9 6
◇ K 10 9 8
♣ 6 5 3

♠ A 6 3
♡ A K Q
◇ Q 3
♣ A K 7 4 2

The normal method of tackling the diamonds is to lead the queen from hand (first the high card from the shorter holding to avoid blocking the suit). However, every rule has its exceptions. The danger here is that East may have both the ace and the jack of diamonds. If you lead the queen you give him the opportunity to hold up his ace. He will win the next diamond whether you play the nine or the king from dummy, and you will lack the entries to set up a second trick in the suit.

As always, your aim must be to force out one of the enemy stoppers on the first round, and to that end you should lead the three of diamonds at trick two for a finesse of the eight. Now your contract is completely safe. If the eight of diamonds wins, you return a diamond to your queen to establish a second trick in the suit. And if East captures the eight of diamonds with the jack, you win any return in hand and lead the queen of diamonds, over-taking with dummy's king and continuing with the ten if necessary to drive out the ace.

Overtaking

Overtaking an honour card is often the right solution to a problem of communication. It may cost a trick, but the trick will come back with interest if you are able to establish an otherwise unreachable suit.

<table>
<tr>
<td>(a)</td>
<td>A Q 10 9 4 3</td>
<td>(b)</td>
<td>K 9 8 6 2</td>
<td>(c)</td>
<td>K J 10 8 3</td>
</tr>
<tr>
<td></td>
<td>N
W E
S</td>
<td></td>
<td>N
W E
S</td>
<td></td>
<td>N
W E
S</td>
</tr>
<tr>
<td></td>
<td>K</td>
<td></td>
<td>A Q</td>
<td></td>
<td>Q</td>
</tr>
</table>

Suppose, in each of these diagrams, that you can afford to lose a trick in the suit but have only one side entry in dummy.

In (a) if you cash the king and then cross to the outside entry, you will make six tricks in the suit if you find a 3–3 break or a doubleton jack. But the better method is to overtake the king with the ace and continue with the queen and ten. You will then have five tricks whenever the suit breaks 3–3 or 4–2.

In (b), needing four tricks, cash the ace, overtake the queen with the king, and continue with the nine. You will succeed when the suit breaks 3–3 and also when either defender has J x or 10 x.

In (c) the only real chance of four tricks is to overtake the queen with the king and continue with the jack, hoping for the nine to drop in three rounds.

Try your hand at this slam contract.

♠ 5 3
♡ 10 9 5
◇ A J 9 4 3
♣ 8 7 2

♠ K Q
♡ A Q J 8 4
◇ K Q 7
♣ A K 5

Pressing for points, you arrive in a contract of six hearts. West leads the jack of spades to his partner's ace and East returns a spade.

Naturally you must cross to dummy in order to take a heart finesse. The question is how? If you lead the seven of diamonds to dummy's jack, the diamond suit will be blocked. This will not matter if the suit divides 3–2, but it will be fatal if the division is 4–1. After a successful heart finesse you will have no way of disposing of your club loser and defeat will be your portion.

There is nothing to be done if East has four diamonds headed by the ten, but correct play protects you against four diamonds in the West hand. Lead the king of diamonds at trick three and overtake with dummy's ace. After finessing against the king of hearts and drawing all the outstanding trumps, continue with the queen of diamonds. If East shows out, you have a marked finesse against the ten of diamonds to provide a parking place for your losing club.

Hidden Entries

Potential cards of entry may be hard to recognize as such simply because they are low cards. Yet there is no reason why a low card should not act as an entry once the high cards have gone.

Many combinations of cards can be manipulated by means of small unblocking plays to provide an extra entry in the hand that needs it.

(a)   A Q 4 3

N
W E
S

K 6 5 2

(b)   K J 6 4

N
W E
S

A Q 8 3

In diagram (a), assuming a normal 3–2 break, the fourth round can be won in either hand, depending on which cards are played by South under the ace and queen. Needing a third entry to dummy, South should unblock the six and the five under the ace and queen. The king draws the last enemy card in the suit, and South can reach dummy again by leading his two to the four. If South needs two entries to his own hand, of course, he retains the six or the five to take command of the fourth round.

The position is similar in diagram (b). Needing three entries to dummy, South should cash the ace and then lead the eight to dummy's jack. If the expected 3–2 break materializes, he can subsequently enter dummy twice more – by overtaking his queen with the king, and finally by leading his three to the six. Again, according to the needs of the situation, South can equally well ensure three entries to his own hand by retaining his eight for the fourth round of the suit.

A player's expertise, or the lack of it, is usually apparent in the way he handles his small cards. Take the North seat in the next hand and watch your partner put a game on the floor (you will have to do that often enough).

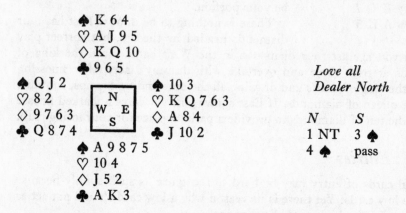

Love all
Dealer North

N	S
1 NT	3 ♠
4 ♠	pass

Three no trumps is easier, but South plays in four spades and is lucky to escape the killing club lead. West leads the eight of hearts and East's queen is allowed to win the first trick. Winning the club switch, South leads the five of spades to the king, returns a spade to his ace, plays his ten of hearts to the ace and continues with the nine of hearts, intending to discard his club loser if East plays low.

But East covers with the king of hearts and South has to ruff. West over-ruffs and leads a club to South's king, leaving the position shown opposite.

Your partner is stuck in the wrong hand, unable to reach dummy's jack of hearts in time for a club discard.

You see where he went wrong, of course. If he had not squandered his five of spades, he would now have been able

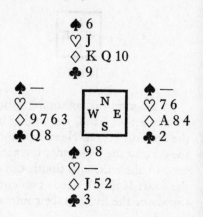

to cross to the six of spades, discard his club on the jack of hearts, knock out the ace of diamonds and claim ten tricks.

At times the problem is to determine the best way of reaching an isolated winner in dummy.

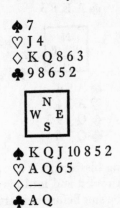

♠ 7
♡ J 4
◇ K Q 8 6 3
♣ 9 8 6 5 2

♠ K Q J 10 8 5 2
♡ A Q 6 5
◇ —
♣ A Q

West leads the jack of diamonds against your contract of four spades. You play the queen from dummy and ruff East's ace.

You can count six trump tricks plus two side aces, and it will always be possible to establish a ninth trick in hearts. The king of diamonds will supply the tenth trick if you can find a way of reaching it. One idea is to lead a low heart towards dummy's jack. That will ensure success when West has the king of hearts – a fifty-fifty chance.

But there is a better plan which succeeds whenever hearts break no worse than 4–3. Lead the queen of hearts from hand at trick two. If either defender wins with the king, dummy's jack will serve as a later entry, enabling you to discard one of your losers on the king of diamonds. If the queen of hearts is allowed to win, there are good chances of at least one overtrick. Continue with the ace of hearts and a heart ruff, discard your fourth heart on the diamond king, and try the club finesse.

This is a case where you have to delay the drawing of trumps in order to avail yourself of the ruffing power of dummy's lone trump.

DEFENCE

So far we have been considering the care of entries from the declarer's point of view. It is perhaps even more important for the defenders to look after *their* entries, which are likely to be thin on the ground anyway.

All the standard ducking, unblocking and overtaking plays are available to the defenders. Plays designed to preserve entries are less easy to spot in defence, however. It often takes a high degree of defensive co-operation to ensure that the entry of the defender who owns the long suit is not taken out too soon. Here is a common situation.

South plays in three no trumps on the lead of the six of hearts. He allows East to win the first trick with the jack, wins the heart continuation with dummy's king, and leads the two of diamonds from the table.

This is the critical moment, for if East plays low the defence is dead. West's only card of entry, the king of diamonds, is forced out prematurely, and the defenders are held to three tricks.

♠ K 10 5
♡ K 5
◇ 10 8 4 2
♣ A K 8 3

♠ J 8 3
♡ Q 10 8 6 3
◇ K 7
♣ J 9 4

N
W E
S

♠ Q 7 6 2
♡ J 9 2
◇ A 6 5
♣ 10 5 2

♠ A 9 4
♡ A 7 4
◇ Q J 9 3
♣ Q 7 6

In this sort of situation East should be on the alert for any chance of protecting his partner's entry. He must go up with his ace of diamonds on the first round and lead his third heart, knocking out the declarer's last stopper in the suit before his partner's entry can be removed.

Suppose, in the above diagram, that the ace and king of diamonds are interchanged. Now it is more difficult for East, but the position is basically the same. To defeat the contract he must play the king of diamonds on the first round and return his third heart.

It may be possible to create an entry for partner out of thin air.

♠ K 10 4
♡ J 10 2
◇ K Q 10 6 3
♣ A 3

N
W E
S

♠ Q J 8 3
♡ A 7 6 4
◇ A 5
♣ K J 6

South opens a weak (12–14 point) no trump, North raises to three no trumps, and West leads the four of clubs on which the three is played from dummy. Over to you in the East seat.

There are twenty-eight high-card points in view, and you can place all the remaining honour cards with South. The only asset that West may possess is a five-card club suit headed by the ten. It is not hard to see that if you win the first trick with the king of clubs there will be no further defence. South will win the club continuation, knock out your red aces and finish up with ten tricks. You must therefore try to persuade South to take his queen of clubs on the first round by playing your jack. The full hand:

As the cards lie, South can still make his contract by allowing the jack of clubs to win the first trick, but he would need to be gifted with second sight to make such a play. In practice he is sure to win with the queen of clubs and try to steal a heart trick, intending if successful to switch to diamonds. If he failed to slip past the ace of hearts he could still hope for a 4–4 club break.

As it happens, you win the first heart and lead the king of clubs to dummy's ace, conjuring up five tricks for the defence.

```
                 ♠ K 10 4
                 ♡ J 10 2
                 ◇ K Q 10 6 3
                 ♣ A 3
 ♠ 7 5                        ♠ Q J 8 3
 ♡ 8 5          N             ♡ A 7 6 4
 ◇ 9 7 4 2    W   E           ◇ A 5
 ♣ 10 8 7 4 2    S            ♣ K J 6
                 ♠ A 9 6 2
                 ♡ K Q 9 3
                 ◇ J 8
                 ♣ Q 9 5
```

```
          8 5
              N
 J 9 7 4 3  W   E   A Q 2
              S
          K 10 6
```

A similar coup is possible in the situation opposite.

West leads the four, and if East suspects that his partner has no side entry he should play the queen rather than the ace. South dare not hold up, since for all he knows the ace and jack may be with West, and when East gains the lead the defenders can run four tricks in the suit. Note the difference if East plays the ace on the first trick. Now it is easy for South to shut out the suit by holding up his king until the third round.

Unblocking Discards

The need to create an entry in the hand of one defender may call for far-sighted unblocking on the part of the other.

South plays in three no trumps and the defenders begin with four rounds of diamonds, declarer discarding two clubs and a spade from the table. East also has to find a discard on the fourth diamond, and he may think it safe to follow dummy and part with a spade. Do you see what will happen if he does?

After winning the fourth diamond South will cross to the queen

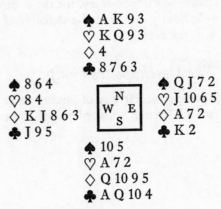

```
                 ♠ A K 9 3
                 ♡ K Q 9 3
                 ◇ 4
                 ♣ 8 7 6 3
 ♠ 8 6 4                      ♠ Q J 7 2
 ♡ 8 4          N             ♡ J 10 6 5
 ◇ K J 8 6 3  W   E           ◇ A 7 2
 ♣ J 9 5         S            ♣ K 2
                 ♠ 10 5
                 ♡ A 7 2
                 ◇ Q 10 9 5
                 ♣ A Q 10 4
```

of hearts and lead a club, finessing the queen when East plays low. A spade to the king will be followed by another club, and when the king appears East will be allowed to hold the trick. That will be the end of the defence. By playing the clubs in such a manner as to keep West off lead, South assures himself of three club tricks and his contract.

What can the defenders do? Well, if East had realized that the contract was bound to make unless his partner had the jack of clubs, he might have seen the need to get out of the way. If East discards the king of clubs on the fourth diamond, the declarer is held to eight tricks.

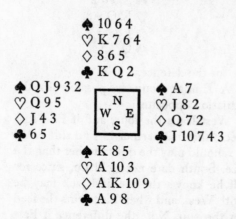

♠ 10 6 4
♡ K 7 6 4
♢ 8 6 5
♣ K Q 2

♠ Q J 9 3 2
♡ Q 9 5
♢ J 4 3
♣ 6 5

♠ A 7
♡ J 8 2
♢ Q 7 2
♣ J 10 7 4 3

♠ K 8 5
♡ A 10 3
♢ A K 10 9
♣ A 9 8

The example opposite is similar. West led the queen of spades against three no trumps and East won the trick with the ace. The spade return was allowed to run to the jack, and a third round of spades cleared the suit as East discarded a club.

The declarer proceeded with care, entering dummy twice in clubs in order to lead diamonds towards his own hand. If East had played the queen of diamonds he would have been allowed to hold the trick. In fact East played low both times, and South developed his ninth trick by conceding the third round of diamonds to the queen.

East missed an opportunity at trick three. If he throws the queen of diamonds on the third spade, South is held to eight tricks, for he cannot develop an extra trick without allowing West to gain the lead.

But South need not have offered this hostage to fortune. The hold-up in spades was unnecessary, for the contract is in no danger if the spades break 4–3. South can never be defeated if he wins the second round of spades with the king.

The Deschapelles Coup

This spectacular way of forcing an entry to partner's hand is named after a famous French whist player of the early nineteenth century.

North opens one diamond and
raises his partner's response of
one no trump to three no trumps.

West leads the five of hearts to
the queen and ace. East continues with the jack of hearts, and
then has to ask himself how he
can put partner on lead to run the
rest of the suit. If he reflects that
the only useful card that West
may hold is the queen of clubs,
he may find the right answer and
switch to the king of clubs. This
is the Deschapelles Coup – the

```
                     ♠ A J 5
                     ♡ Q 9
                     ◇ A K J 9 4 3
                     ♣ A 7
  ♠ 8 7 3                      ♠ 9 6 4 2
  ♡ K 8 7 5 4 2    N           ♡ A J
  ◇ 6            W   E         ◇ Q 8 5
  ♣ Q 8 5          S           ♣ K 9 6 2
                     ♠ K Q 10
                     ♡ 10 6 3
                     ◇ 10 7 2
                     ♣ J 10 4 3
```

sacrifice of a high card in exchange for the chance of promoting an entry for
partner.

Note that a switch to a small club would not be good enough. South
would play the ten, and West would be unable to drive out the ace without
destroying his potential entry card.

After the return of the king of clubs and the failure of the diamond queen
to drop, South can do nothing except go three down with as much grace as
he can muster.

D   [97]

7

The Attack on Entries

*Blocking – holding up in a trump contract – avoiding a ruff –
second hand high – defence – holding up in defence – shutting out
a long suit – the Merrimac Coup*

It is not enough to know how to look after your own entries; you must also
learn how to prevent the opponents from making the best use of theirs. On
hands where the defenders threaten to establish too many tricks, you may
have to launch an all-out assault on their lines of communication, knocking
out their entries prematurely, blocking their suits, and generally making it
hard for them to cross from hand to hand.

One of the most effective ways of putting the defenders out of touch with
each other is the hold-up play. We have already seen some examples of the
technique in an earlier chapter.

Sometimes the correct play is by no means obvious. On this instructive
hand a slip by the declarer was counterbalanced by a defensive error, so that
the par result was achieved in spite of the worst efforts of both sides.

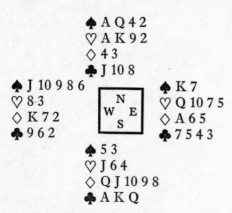

♠ A Q 4 2
♡ A K 9 2
◇ 4 3
♣ J 10 8

♠ J 10 9 8 6   ♠ K 7
♡ 8 3   ♡ Q 10 7 5
◇ K 7 2   ◇ A 6 5
♣ 9 6 2   ♣ 7 5 4 3

♠ 5 3
♡ J 6 4
◇ Q J 10 9 8
♣ A K Q

South played in three no
trumps on the lead of the jack of
spades. He counted six top tricks
and saw that three more could be
developed in diamonds. The
spade finesse was clearly an unnecessary risk, and South therefore played the ace at trick one.
A diamond was won by West
with the king, another spade was
led, and a low card was played
from dummy. East won with the
king but could find no profitable
continuation, and the declarer

made ten tricks in comfort.

East missed a chance to defeat the contract at the first trick. If he had unblocked by throwing his king of spades under the ace, he could have won the first diamond and cleared the spades while his partner still held the king of diamonds as an entry card.

But South had no need to give East this opportunity. He should have held up on the first round of spades and put up dummy's ace on the second round. The defenders would then have been powerless to defeat the contract.

Blocking

A good time to reject a hold-up is when you can see that the enemy suit must be blocked.

You play in three no trumps on the lead of the six of hearts. Clearly if you hold up the ace until the second round you will succeed whenever East has the ace of clubs and also when the hearts are 4–3.

♠ K 8 5
♡ A 4
◇ A 9 5
♣ Q J 9 3 2

However, you can virtually make certain of your contract by playing the ace of hearts at trick one.

```
      N
   W     E
      S
```

The reasoning is as follows: the Rule of Eleven tells you that East has two cards higher than the six and they must both be honour cards, for with three honours West would have led one rather than his fourth-highest card.

♠ A 3
♡ 9 7 5 2
◇ K Q 8 4
♣ K 10 5

Hence in the dangerous case where the suit is divided 5–2, West must have something like K J 8 6 3 and East Q 10. Not so dangerous after all, since the suit is blocked. You should therefore play the ace of hearts at once and knock out the ace of clubs before the hearts can be unblocked.

Similar opportunities to block the run of a suit occur in the following situations:

(a)   A 10 4   (b)   7 6

Q J 9 8 5   ```N / W E / S```   K 3   Q 9 3   ```N / W E / S```   A 10 8 5 4

               7 6 2   K J 2

In diagram (a) if West leads the queen of spades, you can block the suit by rising with the ace. East cannot unblock his king without establishing dummy's ten as a second stopper.

In (b) West leads the three of his partner's suit. East takes his ace and returns the five. Now, if you can read the position, you may succeed by going up with the king and attacking East's entry before the suit can be unblocked.

Holding Up in a Trump Contract

It is not only at no trump play that the hold-up can be a winning move. In a trump contract it is occasionally right to hold up in a suit that contains no loser.

You play in four hearts on the lead of the king of clubs. There are nine top tricks, and you should be able to establish a tenth in diamonds. The only danger is that both the king of diamonds and the ace of spades may be badly placed, in which case the defenders may score four tricks before you can make ten.

Ideally, you need to establish an extra trick in diamonds without allowing East to gain the lead. Does that suggest a solution?

Try the effect of holding up the ace of clubs at trick one. You can win a diamond switch with the ace, discard your jack of diamonds on the

♠ 7 6 4
♡ Q 9 5
◇ A Q 10 2
♣ A 10 5

```
      N
   W     E
      S
```

♠ K 8 3
♡ A K J 8 6 3 2
◇ J 4
♣ 7

ace of clubs, and then run the queen of diamonds, discarding a spade if East does not cover. With West on lead your king of spades is safe from attack, and eventually you will be able to discard another spade on the established ten of diamonds.

In effect, the hold-up in clubs is an assault on East's hypothetical diamond entry, enabling you to take a ruffing finesse into the safe hand.

When the defenders attack a suit in which you hold A x opposite two or three small cards, it is often right to hold up on general principles. By conceding your loser at once, you stop the defenders using this suit to cross from one hand to the other at a later stage.

♠ A 7
♡ K 8 6 3
◇ 8 7 2
♣ K 10 8 3

♠ K 5 4
♡ J 10 9 7 2
◇ A 4
♣ A Q 5

Your contract is four hearts, and West leads the queen of diamonds on which East plays the nine. A diamond trick must always be lost, and as a matter of sound technique you should let the defenders have it immediately, playing the four of diamonds at trick one.

The advantages of the hold-up may not be apparent at this point, but a look at the full hand will show the difference that it may make.

If you win the ace of diamonds at trick one, East will win the first trump

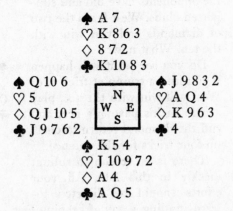

♠ A 7
♡ K 8 6 3
◇ 8 7 2
♣ K 10 8 3

♠ Q 10 6   ♠ J 9 8 3 2
♡ 5   ♡ A Q 4
◇ Q J 10 5   ◇ K 9 6 3
♣ J 9 7 6 2   ♣ 4

♠ K 5 4
♡ J 10 9 7 2
◇ A 4
♣ A Q 5

and return his club. On regaining the lead in trumps he will play a low diamond to his partner's ten, and the club ruff will put you one down. After your hold-up in diamonds, however, the defence expires for lack of entries.

Often a hold-up is needed for reasons of control, to stop the defenders from running away with more tricks than you can afford to lose.

You open three spades, partner raises to four, and West leads the

♠ 3
♡ A 4
◇ A K 9 6 3
♣ K Q 9 6 5

♠ K Q J 10 8 7 4
♡ 7 6 2
◇ Q 8
♣ 4

king of hearts.

It is an awkward lead, for the defenders are threatening to take a spade, two hearts and a club. Clearly you cannot afford to win the first trick and play a trump.

An alternative play is to try for an immediate discard on the third round of diamonds, but that will succeed only when the diamonds break 3–3.

The right move is to allow the king of hearts to win the first trick. This retains control of the situation and puts West in a quandary. If he continues with a second heart, you will be able to cross to hand with the queen of diamonds and ruff your third heart with dummy's lone trump.

West may switch to trumps in order to prevent the heart ruff, but that need not bother you. Once the ace of spades has gone you can stand a switch back to hearts, for you can come to hand with the queen of diamonds, draw the remaining trumps, and take a leisurely discard on the third round of diamonds.

Avoiding a Ruff

It is always aggravating when a perfectly good contract is defeated by an enemy ruff. At times the ruff will be unavoidable, but in a surprising number of cases there will be an opportunity to take counter-measures.

You play in four hearts after the opponents have bid and supported clubs. West leads the two of diamonds and you win with the ten. What now?

Do you see what will happen if you lead a trump at trick two? West will win with the ace, play a club to his partner's ace, and ruff the diamond return to chalk up four tricks for the defence.

There is no reason to submit meekly to this fate. All your efforts should be directed towards finding a way of keeping East off lead, and a little thought will convince you that this can be done only if West holds the jack of spades. You should cash the ace of spades at trick two. Then overtake your queen with dummy's king and continue with the ten of spades, discarding the losing club from your hand when East plays low.

This play has been called the Scissors Coup because it has the effect of snipping the enemy line of communication. You exchange your club loser for a spade loser, at the same time placing the lead firmly in the West hand. Unable to put his partner on lead, West is denied the opportunity of ruffing a diamond except with the ace of trumps.

Second Hand High

In the normal course of events it is correct for the second player to play low when a small card is led. He thus preserves his high cards for their proper task of capturing enemy honours. In a situation where an enemy honour card has to be forced out without delay, however, it may be right to play 'second hand high'.

♠ Q 7 4
♡ A 10 5
◇ A J 10 4
♣ 9 8 3

♠ K 6 2
♡ Q J 9 8 6 3
◇ Q 9 3
♣ A

You play in four hearts after West has overcalled in spades. West leads the king of clubs to your ace, the queen of hearts runs to the king, and East returns the nine of spades.

West is likely to have five or six spades for his overcall. With six he will take the ace and give his partner a ruff, and your contract will depend on the success of the diamond finesse. If West has five spades, however, you can succeed even when the diamond finesse is wrong, provided that you play the king of spades to force out the ace at trick three. You can win the spade continuation with the queen, draw the remaining trumps, and run the nine of diamonds. If East produces the king he will have no spade left to lead, and you will eventually discard your losing spade on the fourth round of diamonds.

Note the difference if you play low on the first round of spades. West will also play low, allowing dummy's queen to win, and when East gets in with the king of diamonds a further spade lead will give West two tricks in the suit.

DEFENCE

The occasion for the play of a high card second in hand is perhaps easier to recognize in defence. In the two examples below, dummy has a long suit with no outside entry.

(a)   A J 10 9 4   (b)   A J 9 6 3

K 6   [W N E S]   Q 7 3   Q 10 5   [W N E S]   K 7 4

         8 5 2   8 2

In (a) South leads the eight and runs it if West plays low. He is then sure to make four tricks in the suit, whether or not East takes his queen immediately. West can do better by playing his king on the first round. If South plays low in dummy, the queen must score a second trick for the defence. And if the king is captured by the ace, East can restrict the declarer to two tricks in the suit by holding up his queen until the third round.

In (b) West should go up with the queen on the first round. Then declarer can make no more than one trick in the suit. If West plays low, South will finesse dummy's nine, making two tricks even if East holds up.

A different reason for playing a high card second in hand is seen in the next two examples. Here the object is not to gain extra tricks for the defence but to deny the declarer an additional entry.

(c)   K 9 6 3   (d)   A 10 6

J 8 5 4   W E   7   Q 9 4   W E   8 7 5 2

         A Q 10 2   K J 3

In (c) South plays the ace and queen and continues with the two. If West follows with the eight, South gains an extra entry to dummy by finessing the nine. It may therefore pay West to make the blocking play of the jack, restricting dummy to one entry in the suit.

In (d) the position is not so clear-cut and the defence is more difficult. Needing two entries to dummy South leads the three, intending to finesse dummy's ten. West can frustrate this plan by going in with the queen.

Holding Up in Defence

The declarer normally has an easy time when he is permitted to go freely from hand to hand. His task is greatly complicated when the defenders refuse to release their high cards at an early stage.

Here is a hand from a multiple team contest on which a double hold-up made a difference of two tricks. After a Precision auction and a transfer bid, the heart game was played 'upside-down' at a number of tables.

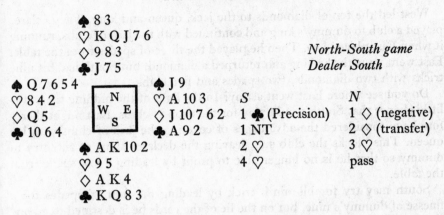

♠ 8 3
♥ K Q J 7 6
♦ 9 8 3
♣ J 7 5

North-South game
Dealer South

♠ Q 7 6 5 4   ♠ J 9
♥ 8 4 2   ♥ A 10 3
♦ Q 5   ♦ J 10 7 6 2
♣ 10 6 4   ♣ A 9 2

♠ A K 10 2
♥ 9 5
♦ A K 4
♣ K Q 8 3

S		N
1 ♣ (Precision)		1 ♦ (negative)
1 NT		2 ♦ (transfer)
2 ♥		3 ♥
4 ♥		pass

Play normally began with a spade to the jack and ace, then a heart to the king and ace. South won the diamond return, drew trumps, knocked out the club ace and claimed eleven tricks.

But at one table South was up against a 'difficult' defender who refused to take his ace of trumps at trick two. Although South did not know it, the contract was already dead. East won the second heart and returned a diamond to the ace. In an effort to create an entry to dummy, South played the king of clubs, but East was not tempted to part with his second ace. South then tried a low club to dummy's jack. This time East won with the ace and played a second diamond to the king.

Taking his last chance, South cashed the king of spades and ruffed a spade in dummy with the six of hearts. East over-ruffed with the ten and cashed a diamond to put the contract one down.

At times a devastating attack on the entry position can be launched by the simple expedient of blocking one of the declarer's suits. A defender missed his opportunity on the next hand.

♠ A 10 9 3
♥ 8 6 5
♦ J
♣ K J 10 4 3

Love all
Dealer North

♠ 8 7 2   ♠ K J 6 5
♥ K 10 4   ♥ A J 7
♦ 10 9 8 6 3 2 ♦ Q 7 5
♣ 8   ♣ Q 5 2

♠ Q 4
♥ Q 9 3 2
♦ A K 4
♣ A 9 7 6

W	N	E	S
	pass	1 NT	Dbl
2 ♦	3 ♦	pass	3 ♥
pass	3 ♠	pass	3 NT
all pass			

West led the ten of diamonds to the jack, queen and king. The declarer played a club to dummy's king and continued with the jack of clubs, running it when East played low. Then he played the three of spades from the table. East went up with the king and returned a diamond, but South had his nine tricks with two diamonds, two spades and five clubs.

Do you see where East went astray? In the light of the bidding there was little chance that South would play for the drop in clubs. East might therefore have considered the advantages of covering the jack of clubs with his queen. This blocks the club suit, leaving the declarer short of an entry to dummy so that he is no longer able to profit by leading a low spade from the table.

South may try for his ninth trick by leading the four of spades for a finesse of dummy's nine, but on the lie of the cards he is destined to go one down.

One of the most effective defensive moves is to force the declarer to use an entry before he is ready to do so. The next hand is of a type that comes up over and over again.

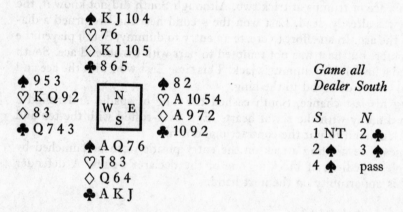

♠ K J 10 4
♡ 7 6
♢ K J 10 5
♣ 8 6 5

♠ 9 5 3   ♠ 8 2
♡ K Q 9 2   ♡ A 10 5 4
♢ 8 3   ♢ A 9 7 2
♣ Q 7 4 3   ♣ 10 9 2

♠ A Q 7 6
♡ J 8 3
♢ Q 6 4
♣ A K J

Game all
Dealer South

S	N
1 NT	2 ♣
2 ♠	3 ♠
4 ♠	pass

The opening lead is the king of hearts, on which East drops the ten. West continues with the two of hearts and East wins the second trick with the ace. How should he continue?

East may think of trying for the fourth defensive trick in clubs, but if he counts points he will realize that West cannot have much in clubs. In any case there is a stronger line of defence. Top priority should be assigned to an attack on dummy's entries in an effort to shut out the diamond suit. East's correct move at trick three is to play another heart, forcing dummy to ruff (from West's lead of the two of hearts at the second trick South is known to have a third heart).

Consider the effect of this defence on the declarer's chances. If South draws trumps, East is in a position to restrict him to two diamond tricks by holding up his ace until the third round, and the defence must eventually score a club trick. More likely, South will draw only two rounds of trumps before tackling the diamonds. However, West will echo in trumps to show a third trump and will also echo in diamonds to indicate a doubleton. East will then take his ace of diamonds on the second round and lead a third diamond to give his partner a ruff.

Shutting Out a Long Suit

On some hands the way to shut out a long suit is just to keep playing the suit until the declarer loses touch with dummy.

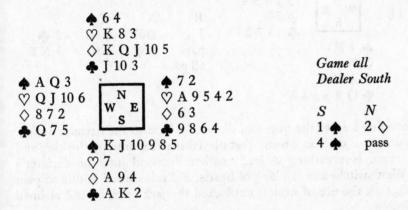

```
              ♠ 6 4
              ♡ K 8 3
              ◇ K Q J 10 5
              ♣ J 10 3                    Game all
 ♠ A Q 3          ♠ 7 2                    Dealer South
 ♡ Q J 10 6       ♡ A 9 5 4 2
 ◇ 8 7 2    W  E  ◇ 6 3                    S        N
 ♣ Q 7 5    S     ♣ 9 8 6 4                1 ♠      2 ◇
              ♠ K J 10 9 8 5              4 ♣      pass
              ♡ 7
              ◇ A 9 4
              ♣ A K 2
```

West leads the queen of hearts, on which dummy plays the three, East the two and South the seven. It seems natural for West to continue with another heart, but this defence will give the declarer no problems. He will ruff and lead trumps from his hand, knocking out the ace and the queen, and he will eventually discard his losing club on one of the long diamonds.

If West regards his partner's two of hearts at the first trick as a distributional signal, showing an odd number of cards in the suit, he will realize that there is not likely to be a second heart trick for the defence. The only other candidate for the role of setting trick is the queen of clubs, and before she can come into her own the diamond suit must be immobilized. This is achieved by switching to a diamond at trick two, and by leading diamonds again each time West is in with his high trumps.

The third diamond lead cuts the link between the two hands. Since West still has a small trump, the declarer can make no further use of the diamond suit and has to fall back on the club finesse. Unlucky – one down!

The Merrimac Coup

When the declarer has blockage trouble in his long suit, the defenders should not hesitate to attack his outside entries even at the cost of a possible trick. On the following hand a defender failed to appreciate the declarer's problem.

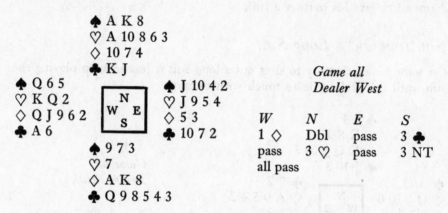

	♠ A K 8	
	♡ A 10 8 6 3	
	◇ 10 7 4	
	♣ K J	

♠ Q 6 5		♠ J 10 4 2
♡ K Q 2		♡ J 9 5 4
◇ Q J 9 6 2		◇ 5 3
♣ A 6		♣ 10 7 2

	♠ 9 7 3	
	♡ 7	
	◇ A K 8	
	♣ Q 9 8 5 4 3	

Game all
Dealer West

W	N	E	S
1 ◇	Dbl	pass	3 ♣
pass	3 ♡	pass	3 NT
all pass			

The opening lead of the queen of diamonds went to the declarer's king. South led a small club on which West played the ace, dummy the king and East the two. Not wishing to lead another diamond into the declarer's tenace, West switched to the king of hearts, but this caused South no pain at all. He took the ace of hearts, unblocked the jack of clubs and claimed ten tricks.

On the bidding South was marked with the queen of clubs but not necessarily with the ten, and West should have seen the need to attack the entry in the South hand before the clubs could be unblocked. He can do this by leading the jack of diamonds at trick three. This gives the declarer an extra diamond trick, but it shuts out the club suit and makes the contract impossible.

The sacrifice of a high card for the sake of killing the entry to a long suit is known as the Merrimac Coup. Note the similarity to the Deschapelles Coup discussed in the last chapter. In both cases an honour card is led to drive out a higher honour, but while the object of the Deschapelles Coup is to create an entry for partner the purpose of the Merrimac Coup is purely destructive.

Here is a further example of this type of play:

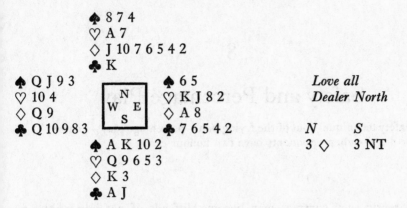

```
                ♠ 8 7 4
                ♡ A 7
                ◇ J 10 7 6 5 4 2
                ♣ K
♠ Q J 9 3                        ♠ 6 5              Love all
♡ 10 4          N                ♡ K J 8 2          Dealer North
◇ Q 9       W       E            ◇ A 8
♣ Q 10 9 8 3    S                ♣ 7 6 5 4 2        N        S
                ♠ A K 10 2                          3 ◇      3 NT
                ♡ Q 9 6 5 3
                ◇ K 3
                ♣ A J
```

South thought that three no trumps would be an easier game than five diamonds, but he rather regretted his choice when West led the ten of clubs and dummy went down.

A small diamond was led from the table at trick two, and East did the right thing by going up with the ace to block the suit. A club return would have enabled the declarer to claim eleven tricks, but East made no mistake. He switched to the king of hearts, taking out dummy's remaining entry and killing the diamond suit stone dead. On this defence there was no way for the declarer to make more than eight tricks.

8

Safety and Percentage Play

Safety technique – out of the frying pan – percentage play – finesse
or drop – when opponents have two honour cards

An apparently easy contract may become difficult, if not impossible, to
fulfil when a key suit breaks badly. Since there is no way of avoiding bad
breaks altogether, it is worth while learning how to minimize their effect
by the exercise of forethought and the use of safety technique.

The general theme of safety has a wide application over the whole field
of dummy play. All the techniques at the declarer's disposal are concerned
with safeguarding the contract in one way or another. The term 'safety
play', however, is usually reserved for the methods of handling combinations
of cards in a single suit to ensure maximum safety.

Some safety plays cost nothing, being simply a matter of playing the
cards in the correct order to protect against a bad break. Others are true
insurance plays where a trick is given up, perhaps unnecessarily, in order
to avoid all risk of losing two tricks in the suit. The trick lost represents the
premium on the insurance policy that guarantees the contract. Obviously,
you must be sure that you can afford to pay the premium. The correct play
on many combinations of cards depends on the number of tricks you can
afford to lose in the suit.

Safety play will not guarantee your contract in every case. It may do no
more than improve your chances slightly by protecting against a particular
distribution. But if you learn the correct way of handling the various card
combinations you will have a big edge over the lazy players who cannot be
bothered to study.

First let us have a look at a situation where nothing can go wrong if the
cards are handled sensibly.

Safety Technique

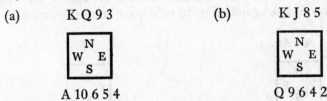

(a) K Q 9 3

```
N
W   E
S
```

A 10 6 5 4

(b) K J 8 5

```
N
W   E
S
```

Q 9 6 4 2

The safe play in diagram (a) is well known. Start with the king or queen from dummy. Then, if either defender proves to be void, you have a marked second-round finesse against the jack.

Diagram (b) shows a related position. You can guard against A 10 x x in either hand by playing an honour from dummy first.

It is different if another intermediate card is missing.

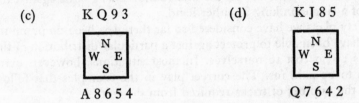

(c) K Q 9 3

```
N
W   E
S
```

A 8 6 5 4

(d) K J 8 5

```
N
W   E
S
```

Q 7 6 4 2

In (c) there is no way of avoiding a loser if West is void in the suit. But if East is void you can make five tricks by starting with the ace, subsequently finessing twice against the jack and ten. Similarly, in (d) you should start with the queen to cater for a possible void in the East hand. When West is void you must always lose two tricks.

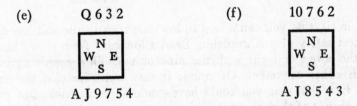

(e) Q 6 3 2

```
N
W   E
S
```

A J 9 7 5 4

(f) 10 7 6 2

```
N
W   E
S
```

A J 8 5 4 3

In (e) the correct play is to finesse against the king. But you should lead the queen, not a small card, from dummy. This ensures against loss when West is void.

In (f), if the lead is in dummy you will naturally protect yourself against a void in the West hand by taking a first-round finesse. The ten from dummy is better than a small card, for it has been known for an unwary defender to cover from Q x. If the lead is in your own hand and dummy has only one entry, the safe play is a low card towards the ten. If West shows out you can later finesse against East to hold your loss to one trick.

(g)   A 6 5   (h)   J 5

```
    N              N
 W     E        W     E
    S              S
```

K 10 7 4 3   A Q 7 6 4 2

Start with the ace in (g) and continue with a low card from dummy. If East plays low, the safety play is to insert the ten. This protects against the loss of two tricks when West began with a singleton. In (h) there is no way of making all six tricks in the suit. To give yourself the best chance of making five tricks, play the ace on the first round. This guards against the possibility of a singleton king in either hand.

In the safety plays we have considered so far there has been no premium to pay. We have been able to protect against a particular distribution of the enemy cards at no cost to ourselves. In most situations, however, extra security has to be paid for. The correct play in the examples that follow depends on the number of tricks required from the suit.

(i)   A 10 6 3   (j)   A K 4

```
    N              N
 W     E        W     E
    S              S
```

K 9 5 4 2   9 8 7 6 5 2

Suppose, in (i), that you can afford to lose one trick in the suit but not two. A perfect safety play is available. Lead a low card from either hand and cover the seven or eight with the nine or ten. This guards against Q J 8 7 with either opponent. Of course it may transpire that the suit breaks 2–2, in which case you could have made an extra trick. But you gave up the chance of this overtrick with your eyes open, deliberately conceding one trick in the suit to make sure of not losing two.

Needing six tricks in (j), you have to play out the ace and king and hope for a 2–2 break. However, if five tricks are all you need, lead the two from hand and cover West's three with the four. You thus avoid two losers when West has Q J 10 3.

If you cannot afford a loser in (k) you must take a first-round finesse of

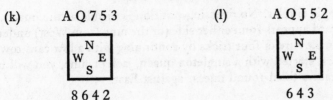

(k) A Q 7 5 3   (l) A Q J 5 2

8 6 4 2   6 4 3

the queen, hoping to find West with K x. If four tricks in the suit are your
target, however, it is better to play the ace on the first round. If nothing
interesting happens, return to hand in another suit and lead towards the
queen. This line avoids two losers when East has the singleton king.

Similarly, in (1) you have to take two finesses against the king if you need
to score five tricks in the suit. If you can afford a loser and have a plentiful
supply of entries to your own hand, the ace on the first round is again the
best play. If the king fails to drop, return to hand and lead twice towards
dummy's remaining honours.

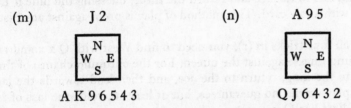

(m) J 2   (n) A 9 5

A K 9 6 5 4 3   Q J 6 4 3 2

Seven tricks will roll in on (m) if the suit breaks 2–2 or if the queen is
singleton. The way to make sure of six tricks, however, is to lead a low card
from hand towards the jack. This caters for Q 10 8 7 in either hand.

Needing six tricks in (n), lead the queen for a finesse. If your aim is to
make sure of five tricks, the correct play is to lead the five from dummy,
guarding against a void in either hand.

(o) J 5 3   (p) 10 5 3

A K 6 4 2   A K 8 4 2

In (o), if four tricks in the suit are all you need, you should cash the ace
and continue with a low card towards the jack. This avoids the loss of two
tricks when East has a singleton, and you gladly give up the chance of an
overtrick when either defender has the queen doubleton.

Diagram (p) is similar. No finessing position is visible at the outset, but if an honour card appears from either side (or the nine from West) under the ace, you can make sure of four tricks by continuing with a low card towards the ten. If West started with a singleton queen, jack or nine, you will be in a position to take a third-round finesse against East.

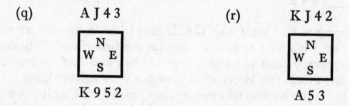

(q) A J 4 3

(r) K J 4 2

K 9 5 2

A 5 3

Needing all the tricks in (q), lead low from hand with the intention of finessing the jack. You will make four tricks when West has Q x x, Q x or singleton queen. To make sure of three tricks from this combination of cards, however, lead low to the ace and return the three, finessing the nine if East follows suit with a low card. This method of play is proof against any distribution.

To make all four tricks in (r), you need to find West with Q x x and take a second-round finesse against the queen. For the optimum chance of three tricks, lead to the king, return to the ace, and then lead towards the jack. This safety play carries no guarantees, but at least it avoids the loss of two tricks when East has Q x.

Some safety plays are designed to avoid the loss of more than two tricks in a suit.

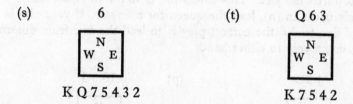

(s) 6

(t) Q 6 3

K Q 7 5 4 3 2

K 7 5 4 2

To avoid two losers in (s) you would need to find East with A x, leading from dummy to the king or queen and playing a low card on the second round. For the best chance of avoiding three losers, play low from both hands on the first round. This guards against a singleton ace with either defender. If there is a singleton other than the ace you must always lose three tricks.

Diagram (t) is similar. Needing four tricks, you must lead low to an honour and duck on the way back, hoping to find the right defender with

A x. But if you can afford two losers you can guard against a singleton ace by playing low from both hands on the first round.

(u) A J 5 3   (v) A 5

(N W E S)

10 6 4 2   J 10 6 4 3

If you need three tricks in (u), the normal play is to lead low from hand for a finesse of the jack. You will succeed when West has K Q x or a doubleton honour. However, this method will result in the loss of three tricks when East has a singleton king or queen. If two tricks are all you need from the suit, you can make sure of them by cashing the ace on the first round and then leading a low card towards your ten (or a low card from hand towards the jack).

Needing three tricks in (v), play the ace and continue with the five, playing a low card from hand no matter what East plays. If the suit breaks 3–3 it makes no difference what you do. And if it breaks 4–2, West is more likely to have K x or Q x than a small doubleton.

Now that we have almost exhausted the alphabet let us move on to consider the proper application of safety technique within the context of a complete hand. Unfamiliar card combinations may pose new problems, but with experience comes the knack of improvizing a safety play to meet the situation.

West leads the eight of diamonds against your contract of four spades. You win with the ace and draw trumps, which break kindly, West discarding a diamond on the third round. When you lead a small club from hand West plays the six. Which card should you play from dummy?

♠ 9 8 6 4
♡ J 8 7 2
♢ A J
♣ K 7 3

(N W E S)

♠ A K Q 3
♡ A 4
♢ 9
♣ Q 10 8 5 4 2

If the clubs lie favourably you may be able to make twelve tricks, discarding three hearts from dummy on your long clubs. But you have contracted for only ten tricks and you should be concerning yourself with the possibility of bad breaks, not good ones. You will get an unpleasant shock, for instance, if you play the king of clubs and East shows out. You will then be short of an entry to establish the club suit and the contract will go two down.

No doubt you are ahead of me on this one. Yes, of course, you should

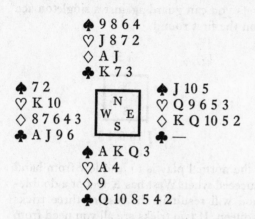

♠ 9 8 6 4
♡ J 8 7 2
◇ A J
♣ K 7 3

♠ 7 2
♡ K 10
◇ 8 7 6 4 3
♣ A J 9 6

♠ J 10 5
♡ Q 9 6 5 3
◇ K Q 10 5 2
♣ —

♠ A K Q 3
♡ A 4
◇ 9
♣ Q 10 8 5 4 2

protect yourself against the possibility of a bad break in clubs by covering the six with dummy's seven. This gives up the chance of making twelve tricks but guarantees the success of the contract.

The distribution you are guarding against is shown opposite.

At an early stage in the play of a hand you may not be sure whether you can afford a safety play or not. In that case you must try to find out before tackling the critical suit.

You play in four hearts and receive the lead of the jack of diamonds. How should you plan the play?

You can count one loser in each of the minor suits, a potential loser in spades, and one or two possible losers in trumps. A safety play is available in trumps, of course. By playing the six of hearts to your king and returning a low heart for a finesse of the nine, you can hold your trump losers to one trick when the suit breaks no worse than 4–1. Should you make this safety play?

At present you cannot answer that question, since everything depends on the spade position. First you must find out whether you have a spade loser or not. Then you will know if you can afford to lose a trump trick.

♠ A Q 7 4
♡ A 9 6
◇ K 8 4
♣ 7 6 3

♠ 6 5
♡ K J 5 4 2
◇ A 7 2
♣ A K 2

Win the first trick with the ace of diamonds and lead a spade for a finesse of the queen. If the finesse loses, you will need to bring in the trump suit without loss. When you regain the lead you must take your best chance by playing the ace of hearts and finessing against the queen on the second round.

If the spade finesse wins, you can afford to lose a trump trick. You will therefore play the trumps for safety, leading the six to your king and returning a small trump to dummy's nine.

Out of the Frying Pan . . .

Safety is, it must be remembered, a relative matter. A safety play designed
to avoid the loss of more than one trick in a particular suit may turn out
to be far from safe in relation to the hand as a whole. Here is an example of
the sort of thing that can happen when a player concentrates exclusively on
the problems of one suit:

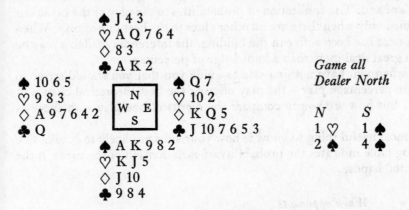

```
              ♠ J 4 3
              ♡ A Q 7 6 4
              ◇ 8 3
              ♣ A K 2                    Game all
 ♠ 10 6 5           ♠ Q 7               Dealer North
 ♡ 9 8 3           ♡ 10 2
 ◇ A 9 7 6 4 2     ◇ K Q 5
 ♣ Q               ♣ J 10 7 6 5 3        N      S
              ♠ A K 9 8 2               1 ♡    1 ♠
              ♡ K J 5                   2 ♠    4 ♠
              ◇ J 10
              ♣ 9 8 4
```

The opening lead of the queen of clubs was won by the ace. At trick two
the declarer led a low spade to his king, East playing the seven and West
the six. Realizing that a perfect safety play to guard against Q 10 x x in
either hand was available, South continued with a low spade to dummy's
jack.

Of course, you can see what happened. East won the queen of spades,
cashed the king of diamonds, and led a club for his partner to ruff. The ace
of diamonds then took the setting trick.

In a way South was unlucky, for a 4–1 trump break was more probable
than a 6–1 club break. However, when the five of trumps failed to appear
on the first round South might have judged that someone was echoing to
show three trumps, in which case it could do no harm to cash the other top
spade. On the lie of the cards this play would have made a difference of
three tricks.

Percentage Play

When safety is not the main consideration, there may still be certain advantages in playing a suit, or a complete hand, in one way rather than another.
It is customary to express the chance of success of any line of play in per-

centage terms. Thus we can say that a simple finesse is a 50 per cent chance. In other words it is as likely to lose as to win.

In a narrower sense the term 'percentage play' has come to mean the play that offers the best chance of success in any given situation. A player who takes his best chance is said to be 'playing the percentages' or 'playing with the odds'. A player who adopts an inferior line of play is said to be 'going against the odds'.

Mind you, there may be sound reasons for going against the odds on any particular hand. The application of probabilities to the play of the cards can be justified only when there are no other clues to the best line of play. When an opponent has been active in the bidding, the inferences available may be worth a great deal more than a knowledge of percentages.

It is when you have nothing else to guide you that you should strive to make the percentage play – the play offering the best theoretical chance of success. But how are you to compare the merits of one play with those of another?

The most useful thing to know is how your suits are likely to break. The following table indicates the probability of each division of the cards in the opponents' hands.

When opponents hold	Division	Probability
2 cards	1–1	52%
	2–0	48%
3 cards	2–1	78%
	3–0	22%
4 cards	2–2	40%
	3–1	50%
	4–0	10%
5 cards	3–2	68%
	4–1	28%
	5–0	4%
6 cards	3–3	36%
	4–2	48%
	5–1	15%
	6–0	1%

When opponents hold	*Division*	*Probability*
7 cards	4–3	62%
	5–2	30·5%
	6–1	7%
	7–0	0·5%

A point worth remembering is that when the opponents have an odd number of cards in a suit the most probable division is the most even one. When opponents have an even number of cards, however, an uneven break is the most probable.

There is no need to commit this table to memory, but a knowledge of the main points can be useful in helping to determine the best line of play. It is immediately seen, for instance, that a simple finesse (50 per cent) is a better shot than relying on a 3–3 break (36 per cent), but a worse bet than playing for a 3–2 break (68 per cent).

Finesse or Drop

From the preceding table we can extract information about the likelihood of an enemy honour card dropping.

| *When opponents have* | *Probability of an honour card being* | | |
	Singleton	*Doubleton*	*Trebleton*
2 cards	52%	48%	—
3 cards	26%	52%	22%
4 cards	12%	40%	38%
5 cards	6%	27%	41%
6 cards	2·5%	16%	36%
7 cards	1%	9%	27%

This in turn enables us to formulate a general rule for finessing.

When opponents have	
2 cards	Play for the drop.
3 or 4 cards	Finesse against the king but not against the queen or jack.
5 or 6 cards	Finesse against the king or queen but not against the jack.
7 cards	Finesse against the king, queen or jack.

When Opponents Have Two Honour Cards

If two honour cards in a suit are missing, the king and the queen for example, they will be divided between the opponents 52 per cent of the time. They will both be in the same hand 48 per cent of the time, 24 per cent of the time on your left and 24 per cent of the time on your right.

Taking a double finesse therefore gives you an excellent chance of success. With A J 10 opposite small cards, you will fail to make two tricks only when the king and queen are both behind the ace. The probability of making two tricks is 76 per cent.

The declarer paid the penalty for going against the odds in a typical 'finesse or drop' situation on the hand below. The setting was a pairs tournament, where overtricks are of vital importance.

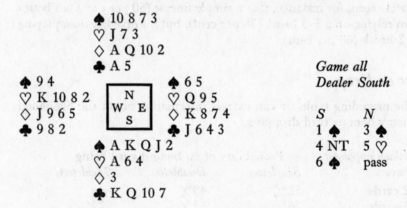

♠ 10 8 7 3
♡ J 7 3
◇ A Q 10 2
♣ A 5

♠ 9 4
♡ K 10 8 2
◇ J 9 6 5
♣ 9 8 2

♠ 6 5
♡ Q 9 5
◇ K 8 7 4
♣ J 6 4 3

♠ A K Q J 2
♡ A 6 4
◇ 3
♣ K Q 10 7

Game all
Dealer South

S	N
1 ♠	3 ♠
4 NT	5 ♡
6 ♠	pass

West led the five of diamonds against the spade slam. South put up the ace, drew trumps in two rounds, and played off the top clubs, discarding a heart from dummy. The jack of clubs failed to drop, but South lost only one heart trick and was confident of scoring well for making his vulnerable slam.

He did not score well. A number of players bid and made the grand slam, while most of those who stopped in six made thirteen tricks by finessing against the jack of clubs on the second round of the suit. This is clearly the correct percentage play, the finesse giving a 50 per cent chance of the extra trick against a 36 per cent chance of dropping the jack doubleton or trebleton (see table on previous page).

See if you can apply your knowledge of percentages in the play of the next hand.

You arrive in six diamonds and receive the lead of the jack of spades. How do you plan the play?

♠ 8 6 5
♡ A Q 6 4
◇ K J 9
♣ Q 7 2

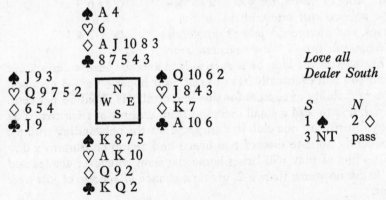

There are eleven immediate winners in sight, and the obvious line of play is to win the ace of spades, draw trumps, and then try the heart finesse for the twelfth trick. This gives you a fifty-fifty chance of success

Is there anything better? Well, it may occur to you that there is a possibility of making a sixth trump trick on this hand by the use of reverse dummy technique. Win the spade lead, play a heart to the ace and ruff a heart high. Cross to dummy with the queen of clubs, ruff another heart high and play a low trump to dummy's nine. After ruffing the fourth heart high, you can lead your last trump to dummy's jack and continue with the king of trumps, discarding a losing spade from hand. If all has gone well, you will be able to score three more clubs to bring your total up to twelve tricks.

The dummy reversal will succeed whenever the trumps break 3–2. A glance at the table on page 118 tells you that this is a 68 per cent chance, a significant improvement on the 50 per cent chance of the heart finesse. The dummy reversal is therefore the percentage play on this hand.

When a declarer goes against the odds in the play of the hand it is not normally a matter of perversity. The most likely explanation is that he simply failed to see the superior line of play. Here is a deal on which the declarer did not give himself the best chance:

♠ A 4
♡ 6
◇ A J 10 8 3
♣ 8 7 5 4 3

♠ J 9 3   ♠ Q 10 6 2
♡ Q 9 7 5 2   ♡ J 8 4 3
◇ 6 5 4   ◇ K 7
♣ J 9   ♣ A 10 6

♠ K 8 7 5
♡ A K 10
◇ Q 9 2
♣ K Q 2

Love all
Dealer South

S	N
1 ♠	2 ◇
3 NT	pass

West led the five of hearts to the jack and ace. Seeing nothing else to try, South immediately ran the nine of diamonds to East's king. A heart came back and South was unable to make more than eight tricks.

The diamond finesse offered a straight fifty-fifty chance, but better odds were available in the club suit. The correct play, after winning the ace of hearts, is to lead a diamond to the ace and return a club from the table. If East takes his ace, the club suit provides enough tricks for the contract. If East plays low and allows South to score a club trick, a switch back to diamonds sets up enough tricks in that suit.

This line of play succeeds whenever the king of clubs loses to the ace, for West can make no damaging return from his side of the table. It also works when East has the ace of clubs provided that the suit breaks 3–2. Add in the slight possibility of dropping a singleton king of diamonds and the total chance of success comes to a healthy 85 per cent, a big improvement on the 50 per cent chance of the diamond finesse.

At the table, opponents tend to get restive if you delay for too long in choosing between alternative plays. Under pressure of time it is not always easy to select the line that offers the best chance, but the declarer who has some idea of how his suits are likely to break has a decided advantage.

You land in six spades and West leads the ten of clubs to dummy's king. There is a bit of a shortage in the trump department, but for all that it is not a bad slam. How do you plan the play?

♠ K Q 9
♡ A 5 4
◇ A K Q 5 2
♣ K 6

```
    N
  W   E
    S
```

♠ A J 10 4
♡ Q 6 3
◇ 8 6
♣ A 7 4 3

Lacking the entries to ruff both of your losing clubs in dummy, you have to look to the red suits to supply an extra trick. One line of play worth considering is to lead a small heart from the table at trick two. That is likely to work if East has the king of hearts, for you will subsequently be able to ruff one club in dummy, draw trumps, and discard the other losing club on a top diamond. But if West captures your queen of hearts with the king he is sure to lead another heart to knock out the ace, and you will eventually have to rest your hopes on a 3–3 diamond break. The probability of success for this line of play is about 58 per cent.

A better shot is to lead a small diamond from dummy at trick two. You can win any return, ruff one club in dummy, draw the outstanding trumps, and subsequently hope to discard two hearts and a club on dummy's diamonds. This line of play will bring home the slam whenever spades and diamonds break no worse than 4–2, giving a chance of success of just over 70 per cent.

♠ 10 8 4 2
♡ J 10 6 2
◇ 9 7 4
♣ K 5

```
      N
   W     E
      S
```

♠ A Q J 7 6 3
♡ A Q
◇ A K 5
♣ 9 2

West leads the queen of clubs against your contract of four spades. East captures dummy's king with the ace and returns a diamond to your ace. How should you continue?

Your prospects are diminished considerably by the lack of an entry in dummy. Most players would shrug their shoulders and lay down the ace of spades. If the king dropped, they would be able to draw the remaining trump and play on hearts, losing at most two clubs and one heart trick.

What are the chances of this line of play? You know from the table on page 118 that the spades will break 2–1 78 per cent of the time, and it is not hard to work out that there is one chance in three of the singleton being the king. That gives you a 26 per cent chance of dropping the king with your ace.

You can obtain better odds, however. The contract can always be made if the trumps are 2–1 with the king of hearts in the East hand, which is a 39 per cent shot.

Three entries are needed in dummy, so you will have to do some careful unblocking. Lead the queen or jack of spades from hand at trick three. Presumably an opponent will win with the king, cash a second club, and lead another diamond to your king. Now lead the seven of spades to dummy's ten and return a heart for a finesse of the queen. If this succeeds, cash the ace of hearts, play the six of spades to dummy's eight, and continue with the jack of hearts. When East covers, ruff high, lead the three of spades to dummy's four, and cash the ten of hearts for a discard of your losing diamond.

Finally, here is a deal to illustrate how percentages may be affected by enemy bidding:

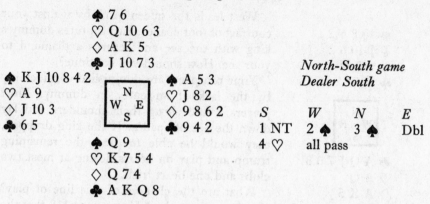

♠ 7 6
♡ Q 10 6 3
◇ A K 5
♣ J 10 7 3

North-South game
Dealer South

♠ K J 10 8 4 2   ♠ A 5 3
♡ A 9   ♡ J 8 2
◇ J 10 3   ◇ 9 8 6 2
♣ 6 5   ♣ 9 4 2

♠ Q 9
♡ K 7 5 4
◇ Q 7 4
♣ A K Q 8

S	W	N	E
1 NT	2 ♠	3 ♠	Dbl
4 ♡	all pass		

West led the jack of spades to his partner's ace, won the spade return with his king and switched to the jack of diamonds. South won in dummy and led a heart to the king and ace. He was subsequently unable to avoid the loss of a second trump trick for one down.

South made the normal percentage play in trumps, failing to see that it did not apply in the context of this hand. In the absence of bidding by the opponents, South would have been correct to play as he did, for he would succeed whenever West had two or three trumps including the jack.

The position changes, however, when the ace of hearts is marked in the West hand by the bidding. Now the odds are heavily in favour of winning the first diamond in hand, leading a small trump to the queen, and ducking on the way back when the jack does not appear.

Assuming the 3–2 trump break needed for the success of the contract, this line of play gains over South's chosen line when West has A x or A x x and loses to it only when West has A J x.

9

Further Tactical Moves

A safety finesse – loser-on-loser – transferring a ruff – ducking for
safety – keep your options open

The subjects discussed in the last few chapters, communication and safety
plays, are prominent in the field of tactics. We go on to examine some
assorted tactical strokes – all plays that are important enough to merit a place
in the tool-bag of the serious player. Some of the hands in this chapter
might have been classified as safety plays or communication plays, but in
each case there is an additional theme that sets them apart.

A Safety Finesse

The finesse is generally regarded as a hazardous type of play that offers no
better than a fifty-fifty chance of success. Yet there are times when a simple
finesse can guarantee your contract. Consider the example below.

You play in four spades on the lead of the
king of hearts. The first task is to get rid of
your heart loser, so you win with the ace, cash
the ace and queen of clubs, and lead a low spade
to dummy's king, both defenders following with
small cards. Both follow to the king of clubs as
you discard the losing heart.

♠ K 6 4
♡ 9 7 6 2
♢ 8 4
♣ K 8 7 2

```
      N
   W     E
      S
```

Your next move is to lead a diamond from
the table. East goes up with the king and returns the ten of spades. Should you play the
ace or the jack?

♠ A J 9 7 5 2
♡ A 5
♢ Q 6 3
♣ A Q

From the probability table in the last chapter
you can calculate that the chances are slightly
better than even that the queen will drop. But
there is little in it and you should certainly not be guided by probabilities
here. Forget about the best chance of avoiding a trump loser and concen-

trate on the safety of the contract. Then you may see that the finesse of the jack of spades gives you a perfect safety play. West is welcome to score the queen if he has it, for that will leave an unassailable small trump in dummy to take care of the third round of diamonds.

Loser-on-Loser

Cards that lose tricks may be divided into two categories. The first comprises plain losers – cards that lose a trick but do nothing for you in return. We can call these unproductive losers.

The other category consists of constructive losers. These are cards which, in the process of losing the trick, serve the purpose of promoting eventual winners for you.

Often both types of losers will be present in the same hand, and when you have any choice in the matter you should aim to lose constructively rather than unproductively.

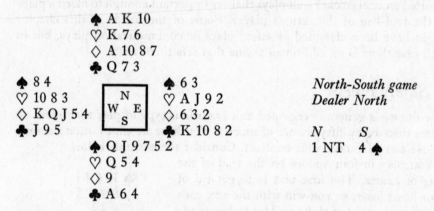

```
                   ♠ A K 10
                   ♡ K 7 6
                   ◇ A 10 8 7
                   ♣ Q 7 3
 ♠ 8 4                         ♠ 6 3          North-South game
 ♡ 10 8 3          N           ♡ A J 9 2      Dealer North
 ◇ K Q J 5 4    W     E        ◇ 6 3 2
 ♣ J 9 5           S           ♣ K 10 8 2     N     S
                   ♠ Q J 9 7 5 2                1 NT  4 ♠
                   ♡ Q 5 4
                   ◇ 9
                   ♣ A 6 4
```

West leads the king of diamonds to dummy's ace, and you note ruefully that three no trumps by North would have been unbeatable. Still, you must have good chances in four spades. Eight top tricks are visible, a ninth can be developed in hearts, and the tenth might come from the queen of clubs.

In clubs you have either one or two losers, depending on the position of the king. When the king is with East, however, your two losers in the suit are of the unproductive type. In hearts there are also two losers, one constructive (in losing to the ace the king promotes the queen) and one unproductive. In diamonds there are no losers in your hand, but the picture changes if you glance across the table. Dummy has two losers in diamonds and both are of the constructive variety. The queen and the jack are the only high diamonds left, and once these are out of the way the ten of diamonds will provide your tenth trick, irrespective of the position of the king of clubs. On this deal you should plan to exchange the three unproductive losers in your hand for two constructive losers and one winner in diamonds.

The first move is to test the trump position by cashing the ace. If trumps are 4–0 you will have to abandon the plan to use dummy's diamonds, drawing trumps instead and hoping to find the king of clubs well placed. When both defenders follow to a round of trumps, you can go ahead with the loser-on-loser play. Lead the seven of diamonds and discard a club (not a heart) from your hand. On winning the trick, West will no doubt switch to a heart or a club. In either case you will win in hand, play a second trump to dummy's ten, and continue with the eight of diamonds. This time you must discard a loser from the suit that West attacked. Now the defenders are free to cash the ace of hearts in addition to the two diamond tricks they have already made, but your remaining unproductive loser is discarded on dummy's ten of diamonds.

Note that it is essential that your first discard should be a club. That is the suit that contains the two unproductive losers and it is vital to give yourself time to discard them both. If your first discard is a heart, the defenders can attack clubs and score a club trick in addition to two diamonds and a heart.

Transferring a Ruff

Another form of loser-on-loser play is useful when you are ruffing out a side suit and have reason to fear an over-ruff. By discarding an unproductive loser instead of ruffing, you may be able to transfer your ruff to another suit.

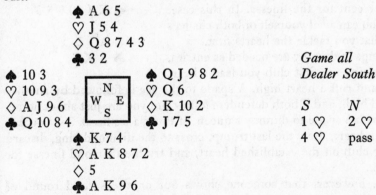

```
              ♠ A 6 5
              ♡ J 5 4
              ◇ Q 8 7 4 3
              ♣ 3 2                        Game all
♠ 10 3                 ♠ Q J 9 8 2         Dealer South
♡ 10 9 3     N         ♡ Q 6
◇ A J 9 6  W   E       ◇ K 10 2            S      N
♣ Q 10 8 4     S       ♣ J 7 5             1 ♡    2 ♡
              ♠ K 7 4                      4 ♡    pass
              ♡ A K 8 7 2
              ◇ 5
              ♣ A K 9 6
```

West leads the ten of spades against your contract of four hearts. There are four top tricks in the black suits and you can probably count on four trump tricks in your hand. Clearly you will need two ruffs in dummy to bring the tally up to ten tricks.

So you win the ace of spades and start on the clubs, playing the ace and king and ruffing the third round in dummy. Returning to hand with the king of spades, you play the fourth club on which West plays the queen. You might ruff with the jack of hearts, but if that is over-ruffed you will subsequently have to lose a spade, a diamond and a further trump trick for one down.

Rather than risk everything on the position of the queen of hearts, you should have recourse to loser-on-loser technique, discarding the losing spade from dummy on your losing club. The effect is to transfer dummy's ruffing potential from clubs to spades.

West is likely to switch to a trump at this point, but it makes no difference what he does. You play low from dummy and win the trump in hand, then lead your third spade, ruffing with the jack of hearts. You still have a diamond and a trump to lose, but that is all.

Loser-on-loser play may also help to establish a long suit in dummy. The time to employ it is when you are not rich enough in trumps to ruff the suit out.

Suppose you have to play a contract of six spades on the lead of the jack of clubs. There are eleven top tricks, and the twelfth may come either from the long heart suit or from the diamond finesse.

♠ A Q
♥ A 7 6 4 3
♦ K 8 3
♣ 8 6 5

```
      N
   W     E
      S
```

♠ K J 10 9 5 3
♥ 5
♦ A J 2
♣ A K 7

If you had to choose between the two chances you would pick the heart play, for the probability of the 4–3 break is 62 per cent compared with 50 per cent for the finesse. In this case, however, you can avail yourself of both chances provided that you tackle the hearts first.

The trumps in dummy are needed as entries, so after winning the first club you lead a heart to the ace and ruff a heart high. A spade to the ace is followed by another heart ruffed high, and if both defenders follow suit you are just about home. Continue with a spade to dummy's queen. If the spades break 3–2 you can ruff a fourth heart, draw the last trump, cross to the diamond king, discard your losing club on the established heart, and try the diamond finesse for an overtrick.

Suppose, however, that someone shows out on the second round of spades. Now you cannot afford to ruff another heart, for that would establish a trump trick for the defence. Instead, you must fall back on loser-on-loser play, discarding a club or a diamond from your hand on the fourth heart. When you regain the lead you can draw the remaining trumps, and the fifth heart in dummy will provide a parking place for your remaining loser.

Ducking for Safety

The problem of establishing a long suit that you suspect will break badly can sometimes be overcome by the adoption of an unusual type of safety play.

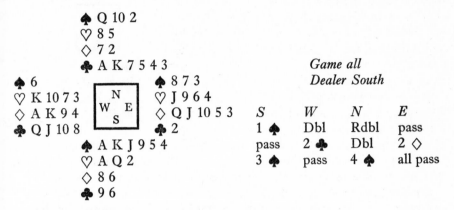

```
              ♠ Q 10 2
              ♡ 8 5
              ◇ 7 2
              ♣ A K 7 5 4 3            Game all
  ♠ 6                   ♠ 8 7 3        Dealer South
  ♡ K 10 7 3    ┌─────┐ ♡ J 9 6 4
  ◇ A K 9 4     │  N  │ ◇ Q J 10 5 3   S      W      N      E
  ♣ Q J 10 8    │W   E│ ♣ 2            1 ♠    Dbl    Rdbl   pass
                │  S  │
                └─────┘
              ♠ A K J 9 5 4            pass   2 ♣    Dbl    2 ◇
              ♡ A Q 2                  3 ♠    pass   4 ♠    all pass
              ◇ 8 6
              ♣ 9 6
```

West starts with the king of diamonds, on which his partner plays the queen. Instead of continuing the suit, West makes the ominous switch to the queen of clubs. To your great relief, East follows suit when you play dummy's ace. How should you continue?

The lie of the enemy cards is clearly marked by the bidding. It is no good relying on the queen of hearts for your tenth trick since West is bound to have the king. Nor can you hope to ruff a club in dummy. East is likely to have three trumps, and if you concede a heart trick before drawing trumps you will surely suffer a club ruff.

There is only one other place to look for the tenth trick and that is in the club suit itself. But the suit cannot be developed after drawing trumps, and if you touch clubs before East's trumps have been extracted how can you avoid a damaging ruff?

The solution – simple once you think of it – is to duck a club on the second round. First lead the two of spades to your ace, just to check that the trumps are not 4–0, then lead the nine of clubs, playing low in dummy when West covers. The defenders have no answer to this manoeuvre. West may lead a diamond to his partner's ten and East may switch to a heart, but you play the ace, cross to the ten of spades, ruff a low club and return to

E   [129]

dummy with the queen of spades, drawing East's last trump in the process. Now the king of clubs extracts West's last card in the suit and your losing hearts go away.

The same sort of safety duck may be employed when you need to establish a second suit in your hand.

You arrive in six hearts and West leads the four of trumps. East plays the ten on dummy's five and you win with the jack.

Your first thought is that you have probably underbid the hand, for there is an excellent chance of making all thirteen tricks. Having contracted for only twelve tricks, you should look for the safest possible way of making the small slam.

♠ Q 7 6 2
♡ A Q 5
◇ 7 2
♣ A 8 7 5

```
      N
   W     E
      S
```

♠ A
♡ K J 9 8 6 3
◇ A K Q 6 5
♣ 9

What could go wrong? The only thing that might bother you is a bad diamond break. If you draw trumps and subsequently find the diamonds 5–1 or 6–0, you will have no more than eleven tricks. A 6–0 diamond break may be too hard to handle, but you can always make sure of the small slam when the suit breaks 5–1 provided that you are willing to give up the chance of making thirteen tricks.

With a two-suited hand like this, it is almost always right to test the side suit before drawing trumps. But it may not be good enough to play the ace and king of diamonds at tricks two and three. If a defender ruffs the second diamond and returns a trump, you will be left with only one trump in dummy and two losing diamonds to dispose of.

The solution, as you have probably seen, is to play a low diamond on the second round, conceding the trick to the defenders. Now a 5–1 diamond break has no terrors for you. Even if a trump is returned, you still have a trump left in dummy with which to ruff your remaining diamond loser.

Keep Your Options Open

Inexperienced declarers often come to grief through allowing a defender to force them to make a critical guess at a premature stage in the play. Ideally, you should try to manage the play so as to take advantage of all the chances that are available. Often this is just a matter of tackling your suits in the right order.

♠ 5 2
♡ J 7 5
◇ A Q 10 4
♣ A 8 7 4

```
    N
 W     E
    S
```

♠ A 10 4
♡ A Q 6
◇ J 9 5 2
♣ K Q 3

West leads the six of spades against your contract of three no trumps, and you allow East's queen to hold the first trick. East returns the eight of spades to the ten and jack, and West continues with the nine of spades to knock out your ace. How do you plan the play?

There will be no problem if the diamond finesse is right, and it may seem natural to run the nine of diamonds at trick four.

Have you considered, though, what will happen if the finesse loses? East will return a heart, and you will have to make an immediate choice between finessing in hearts and going up with the ace of hearts and relying on a 3–3 club break for the ninth trick. Probabilities favour the finesse (50 per cent as against 36 per cent), but whatever you do may be wrong and you should never have allowed yourself to be placed in this position.

The way to give yourself both chances is to test the clubs before touching the diamonds. Lead a club to the ace at trick four and return a club to your king. If both defenders follow suit, continue with the queen of clubs. Then you can switch to diamonds, running the nine. The difference is that when the finesse loses and East returns a heart, you know what you have to do. If the clubs break 3–3 you go up with the ace of hearts and take your nine tricks. If the clubs break badly, you try for a second heart trick by taking the finesse.

Sometimes the play to preserve an option takes on the character of avoidance play. On the next hand you must avoid giving the dangerous defender an opportunity to capture an honour card until you discover how your suit is breaking.

Your contract is six hearts and West leads the ten of spades. Either defender could have the queen of spades, but it is clearly unnecessary to risk everything on a finesse at this point. You win with the ace and East follows with the three. Trumps are drawn with the ace, king and queen, East discarding a small club on the third round. How should you continue?

For top tricks you have two spades, four hearts, one diamond and two clubs. A club ruff will provide a tenth trick, an eleventh can be developed in diamonds, and the twelfth may come from either a favourable diamond break

♠ A K J
♡ Q J 7 3
◇ J 7 6 2
♣ 9 4

```
    N
 W     E
    S
```

♠ 7 5 4
♡ A K 10 5
◇ A Q 5
♣ A K 6

or a successful spade finesse. You will naturally tackle diamonds first, for a 3–3 diamond break will render the spade finesse unnecessary.

The normal play in the diamond suit is to lead a low card for a finesse of the queen, but that will not be good enough here. If West produces the king of diamonds he will certainly return another spade, and you will be on the familiar guess between the spade finesse and the diamond break. Whatever you do, you will have lost one of your options. To give yourself all the chances you must take the diamond finesse the other way round, leading a low card to the ace and returning the five towards dummy's jack. If West beats air with the king, the spade finesse will not be needed, and if East has the king of diamonds he will be unable to attack spades from his side of the table. Either way, you will not be compelled to take a position in spades until you have discovered how many diamond tricks are available.

Note that you slightly increase your chances of making three diamond tricks by playing the ace on the first round. You will make three tricks when either defender has a singleton king, when West has the king doubleton and whenever the suit breaks 3–3. But the big gain comes from the fact that you retain the option of the spade finesse as well.

A defensive hold-up can sometimes be overcome by exercising your option to switch to another suit.

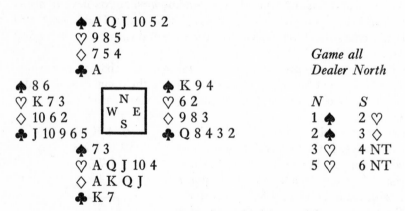

```
        ♠ A Q J 10 5 2
        ♡ 9 8 5
        ♢ 7 5 4
        ♣ A                          Game all
♠ 8 6              ♠ K 9 4          Dealer North
♡ K 7 3     N     ♡ 6 2
♢ 10 6 2  W   E   ♢ 9 8 3           N       S
♣ J 10 9 6 5  S   ♣ Q 8 4 3 2       1 ♠     2 ♡
        ♠ 7 3                       2 ♠     3 ♢
        ♡ A Q J 10 4                3 ♡     4 NT
        ♢ A K Q J                   5 ♡     6 NT
        ♣ K 7
```

West leads the jack of clubs, inconveniently taking out the entry card for dummy's spades. Chances of establishing the spade suit are not too bright, and it may appear that the contract depends on the success of one of two finesses.

Nevertheless, it is still correct to play on spades first, for if the king appears on the first round you will have enough tricks without the heart finesse. At trick two you play a diamond to your hand and return a spade for a finesse of the ten. This finesse is likely to win. Even if East knew that your hearts were nearly solid, it would still be correct for him to hold up his king of spades in the hope that you are unwise or greedy enough to repeat the finesse.

You are having none of that, of course. With a second spade trick in the bag, you switch promptly to hearts, establishing the extra tricks needed for your contract in that suit.

Note the painful dilemma in which East finds himself. If he wins the king of spades it is the only trick for the defence. If he holds up he kills the spade suit, but now the defenders score only one heart trick. It is a case of 'heads you win, tails they lose'.

When there is a winner in dummy opposite a void in your hand, the defenders can sometimes be faced with a similar dilemma.

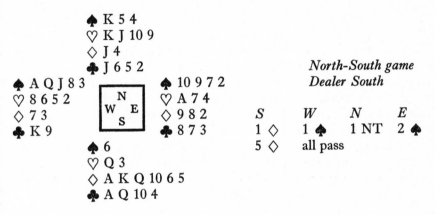

♠ K 5 4
♡ K J 10 9
◇ J 4
♣ J 6 5 2

♠ A Q J 8 3   ♠ 10 9 7 2
♡ 8 6 5 2   ♡ A 7 4
◇ 7 3   ◇ 9 8 2
♣ K 9   ♣ 8 7 3

♠ 6
♡ Q 3
◇ A K Q 10 6 5
♣ A Q 10 4

North-South game
Dealer South

S	W	N	E
1 ◇	1 ♠	1 NT	2 ♠
5 ◇	all pass		

Suppose that West attacks in spades, leading the ace and continuing with the queen. It would not be a good idea to play dummy's king, for any discard from your hand at this stage would be premature. You do not know whether you want to discard a heart or a club. You should therefore keep your options open by playing low from dummy and ruffing the queen of spades.

Draw trumps, discarding a club from the table, and then impale East on the horns of the dilemma by leading the queen of hearts to dummy's king. If East wins and returns a club, you can go up with the ace and discard all your losing clubs on dummy's winners. If East holds up the ace of hearts, you promptly discard your remaining heart on the king of spades and switch to clubs. It is a sadistic sort of play.

The only way for the defenders to defeat your contract is to cash the aces of both major suits and then lead a second heart. This cuts the link with dummy, and East's third trump spoils your enjoyment of the hearts.

In the final example a similar manoeuvre is combined with loser-on-loser play.

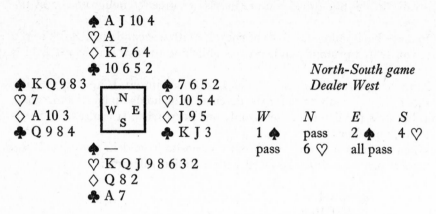

♠ A J 10 4
♡ A
◇ K 7 6 4
♣ 10 6 5 2

♠ K Q 9 8 3
♡ 7
◇ A 10 3
♣ Q 9 8 4

♠ 7 6 5 2
♡ 10 5 4
◇ J 9 5
♣ K J 3

♠ —
♡ K Q J 9 8 6 3 2
◇ Q 8 2
♣ A 7

North-South game
Dealer West

W	N	E	S
1 ♠	pass	2 ♠	4 ♡
pass	6 ♡	all pass	

You play in six hearts after an interesting, if unscientific, auction. West leads the king of spades and you are in with a chance.

Any discard would be premature, so you play the four of spades from dummy, ruff in hand, and lead the two of diamonds to put West on the spot. If West takes his ace it will be the only trick for the defence. More likely, West will play low, allowing dummy's king to win. Now is the time for your loser-on-loser coup. Play the ace and jack of spades, discarding both remaining diamonds from your hand. West is welcome to score the pueen of spades, for when you regain the lead you will cross to the ace of hearts and discard your club loser on the ten of spades.

Trump Control

Avoiding a premature ruff – when not to leave a trump out – handling a two-suiter – loser-on-loser again – leaving a trump in dummy
– countering trump promotion – defence – save that trump –
timing the promotion

We have already noted the function of trumps as controlling cards which
confer the power of veto over the defenders' long suits. The declarer can
continue to exercise this veto as long as his trumps last out, but the supply
of trumps is never inexhaustible. Indeed, there are times when the declarer
starts with only a slender numerical superiority, and there may then be a
serious danger of losing control of the hand.

The loss of control can often be ascribed to lack of foresight, faulty
timing, or general carelessness. It may be a mistake, for example, to release
your high cards in the trump suit at an early stage in the play. If the trumps
break badly, you may then find that instead of you drawing the enemy
trumps the defenders end up by drawing yours, and that is humiliating, to
say the least.

The contract is four spades and West leads
the king of hearts to your ace. How should you
plan the play?

It would be asking for trouble to play off the
ace and king of spades, for the trumps might
prove to be 4–1. You would then have to turn
to the clubs, but if the defender with the long
trumps also has the ace of clubs he will glee-
fully draw your trumps and have a fiesta with
the heart suit.

Nor would it be a good idea to ruff a heart at
trick two. That would weaken your control of
the heart situation, quite apart from increasing
the risk of an eventual over-ruff.

♠ 8 7 5 2
♡ 6
◇ A 9 5
♣ K J 9 6 3

```
    N
 W     E
    S
```

♠ A K 9 4
♡ A 9 5 3
◇ K 7 2
♣ Q 10

On this hand you can afford two trump losers, and the correct play is to draw just one round of trumps before tackling the clubs. If an opponent wins the first club and forces dummy to ruff a heart, play a second club before cashing your second top trump. Now a 4–1 trump break has no terrors for you, since you can ruff another heart in dummy and discard your fourth heart on a winning club. Your diamond loser is also discarded on a club, and you lose at most two trumps and the ace of clubs.

Here is a further exercise in control.

♠ 9 6 4 3
♡ 8 2
◇ A K 5 2
♣ K Q 7

```
    N
W       E
    S
```

♠ A 8 7 2
♡ A K 7 4
◇ Q 8 3
♣ 8 5

Against your contract of four spades West leads the jack of clubs to the queen and ace. East returns a club to the nine and king. How should you play?

This time you need to find the spades 3–2 since you can afford only two trump losers. But it would be a mistake to play the ace and another spade. That might enable the defenders to draw a third round of trumps and then, if the diamonds fail to break evenly, you will be a trick short.

You need four tricks from trumps to go with your six winners in the side suits, and you should plan to retain control by winning the ace of trumps on the second round of the suit. Play a low trump from both hands at trick three. Win any return, cash the ace of trumps and then play on the side suits, leaving the master trump outstanding. You just go about your business of cashing winners and cross-ruffing. A defender may ruff or over-ruff with the master trump at any time, but that will be the third and final trick for his side.

When your trumps have work to do, it is generally right to leave an enemy master trump at large. Forcing it out uses up two precious trumps of your own and at best loses a tempo.

The next example continues the same theme.

You are in four hearts for a change, and West leads the jack of clubs. How should you play?

The only certain loser outside the trump suit is the ace of diamonds. You can therefore afford two trump losers provided that you do not also lose a spade trick.

The percentage play to give you the best chance of three trump tricks is to cash the ace of hearts on the first round, guarding against the possibility of a singleton king with West. However, you should be willing to give up this

♠ K 9 5
♡ A 8 6
◇ Q 7 6 3
♣ A 4 3

```
    N
W       E
    S
```

♠ A Q 7 2
♡ Q 7 5 4 3
◇ K 4
♣ K 6

small advantage for reasons of control. If you play the ace of hearts and continue with a heart to your queen, the contract will be in danger when West is able to win with the king and continue with a third heart, drawing the last trump from dummy. You will then be dependent on a 3–3 spade break.

The proper play is to win the first trick with the ace of clubs and lead a low heart from dummy towards your queen. Now you will succeed when East has four hearts headed by the king, and also whenever the hearts break 3–2 irrespective of the position of the king. If the queen of hearts loses to the king, you will win the second round of trumps with the ace and switch to spades, leaving the master trump outstanding. A defender may ruff when he pleases, but you will always be able to ruff your fourth spade in dummy, thus losing only two trumps and a diamond.

Avoiding a Premature Ruff

Over-eagerness to ruff a loser in dummy can often result in a loss of control. The following hand illustrates this in a striking way.

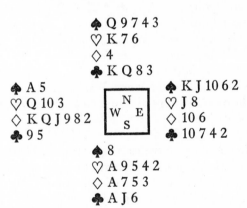

♠ Q 9 7 4 3
♡ K 7 6
◇ 4
♣ K Q 8 3

♠ A 5
♡ Q 10 3
◇ K Q J 9 8 2
♣ 9 5

♠ K J 10 6 2
♡ J 8
◇ 10 6
♣ 10 7 4 2

♠ 8
♡ A 9 5 4 2
◇ A 7 5 3
♣ A J 6

You play in four hearts after West has made an overcall in diamonds. The opening lead is the diamond king.

The way to ensure defeat is to win the first trick and ruff a diamond at trick two. You may then play off the top trumps and turn your attention to the clubs, but West will ruff the third club and cash two diamonds plus the ace of spades.

The early ruff damages your prospects in two ways, by losing control of the diamond situation and by removing from dummy an entry that is needed at a later stage.

There are several methods of retaining control on this hand. One is to allow the king of diamonds to win the first trick. You can subsequently ruff a small diamond in dummy and continue with the king, ace and another trump (in this case you do not leave the master trump at large because you have already done your ruffing in dummy, because you still have the ace to control the diamonds, and because you cannot afford to have the run of the clubs interrupted by a ruff).

An alternative line is to win the first diamond and duck a heart at trick two. You will later be able to ruff a diamond, draw trumps and claim your ten tricks.

The simplest and best way to play the hand is to win the first trick, cash the top trumps and play on clubs, leaving the master trump at large. If West declines to ruff, you discard the spade on the fourth round of clubs. You can then ruff a spade in hand, ruff a diamond in dummy, and claim one of the two remaining trumps in your hand as the tenth trick.

There are times when it is advisable to leave two enemy trumps out, conceding an extra trump trick, perhaps unnecessarily, for the sake of control.

Suppose in the first instance that your contract is four spades. West leads a heart to his partner's ace and East plays another heart, forcing you to ruff.

♠ 3
♡ 8 7 3
♢ K J 9 6 5
♣ K Q 6 2

```
    N
  W   E
    S
```

♠ A K J 10 7 2
♡ 5
♢ Q 7 3
♣ A 9 5

In spite of your strong spade suit, the contract is not guaranteed. You can be sure that the defenders will force you in hearts each time they gain the lead. However, with a loser in each of the red suits, you must give yourself the best chance of losing only one trump by crossing to dummy in clubs and leading the trump for a finesse. You will succeed when the trumps are 4–2 and the queen with East, and also whenever the trumps are 3–3. You will fail when West has Q x or Q x x x, for after ruffing the third heart you will need to use all your trumps to draw the outstanding trumps, and the defenders will have at least one more heart to cash when they come in with the ace of diamonds.

Now suppose that you are in three spades on the same opening lead and continuation. You can afford to lose two trumps in addition to a heart and a diamond, and after ruffing the second heart you should take the precaution of playing off the ace and king of trumps. If the queen falls on the second round, you will be able to draw the remaining trumps and make eleven tricks and your only worry will be how to explain to partner why you are not in game. If the queen does not drop, you are still home when both defenders follow suit. You simply switch to diamonds, leaving two trumps outstanding. You can ruff the next heart and continue to cash side winners, allowing the defenders to score their trump tricks when they please. You thus avoid defeat when West has something like: ♠ Q x x x, ♡ K J x x x, ♢ A x, ♣ x x.

♠ J 9 3
♡ 8 6 5
◇ A Q 8 4
♣ K Q 2

♠ —
♡ A 9 7 4 2
◇ K 7 5
♣ A J 10 7 4

West leads the king of spades against your contract of four hearts and you ruff the first trick. How should you continue?

Is it one of those hands where you have to duck a trump and take your ace on the second round? That would certainly be the right play if the contract were five hearts, in which case you would need a 3–2 trump split.

The difficulty is that the hearts may break 4–1. If you duck a heart, ruff the spade return and cash the ace of hearts, you will be in real trouble if someone shows out. You may switch to clubs, but sooner or later (and probably sooner) will come a club ruff, two rounds of trumps and an avalanche of spades.

Playing in four hearts you can afford to lose three trump tricks. The way to cope with all 4–1 breaks is to cash the ace of hearts at trick two and then play on the side suits, leaving three trumps at large for the defenders to take when they like.

When Not to Leave a Trump Out

It is time to have a look at the sort of hand on which it is wrong to leave a master trump at large.

The defenders start with three rounds of clubs against your contract of four spades. You ruff and cash the ace and king of spades. Do you see what will happen if you leave the master trump out and play on diamonds? East will ruff the third diamond, and although you will be able to discard a losing heart on this trick you will be left with a further heart loser in your hand.

On this hand you must play a third round of spades to force out

♠ 8 4
♡ 9 6 2
◇ A Q J 5 4
♣ 9 8 3

♠ J 9
♡ K 10 5 4
◇ 10 9 7 2
♣ K Q 10

♠ Q 10 2
♡ J 8 3
◇ 8 6
♣ A J 7 6 4

♠ A K 7 6 5 3
♡ A Q 7
◇ K 3
♣ 5 2

the master trump. Then you can win any return and run the diamonds without fear of interruption, discarding both losing hearts. A running suit in dummy with no outside entry is usually a point of recognition for this type of play. You must, of course, be sure that you can afford the loss of tempo involved in conceding a trick to the defenders, which normally means you can have no quick losers in the outside suits.

Note that East missed his chance at trick two. If he overtakes the second club and returns a heart, the contract can never be made.

Handling a Two-Suiter

Two-suited hands can pose difficult problems in control, especially when the defenders launch a forcing attack. When the side suit is less than solid, it is almost always right to tackle the side suit before touching trumps.

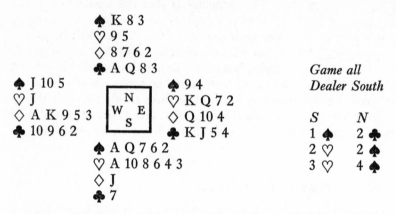

```
                ♠ K 8 3
                ♡ 9 5
                ◇ 8 7 6 2
                ♣ A Q 8 3                   Game all
  ♠ J 10 5               ♠ 9 4              Dealer South
  ♡ J              ┌─────┐  ♡ K Q 7 2
  ◇ A K 9 5 3      │  N  │  ◇ Q 10 4        S        N
  ♣ 10 9 6 2       │W   E│  ♣ K J 5 4       1 ♠      2 ♣
                   │  S  │                  2 ♡      2 ♠
                   └─────┘                  3 ♡      4 ♠
                ♠ A Q 7 6 2
                ♡ A 10 8 6 4 3
                ◇ J
                ♣ 7
```

West starts with top diamonds against your optimistic game and you have to ruff the second round. Now your plan must be to try to establish the heart suit or, failing that, to make all your trumps separately. You play the ace of hearts and continue with a heart to the nine and queen.

It is bad news when West discards a club, but good news that the heart shortage is on the right side of dummy. You ruff the diamond return and persevere with a third heart. If West ruffs, you can over-ruff, draw trumps in two rounds and concede a heart to establish the suit. West will no doubt discard a second club instead of ruffing, and you will ruff in dummy with the three of spades. The ace of clubs and a club ruff come next, and a fourth heart catches West in the same dilemma. If he ruffs, you over-ruff, draw trumps and claim eleven tricks. West will therefore discard once more, whereupon you ruff with the eight of spades and score three more tricks on a high cross-ruff to land your contract.

Note that even one round of trumps before tackling the hearts would have been fatal.

On certain hands you can retain control only by establishing a trump winner for the enemy.

Suppose that by good bidding you arrive in a contract of six diamonds. West leads the queen of hearts and you ruff.

Since the clubs are solid you can afford to test diamonds first, taking care to unblock the ace from dummy. It looks like thirteen tricks until East discards on the second diamond. Now you have to exercise a little care. You cannot afford to return to hand by ruffing a heart, for that would leave West with a trump more than you. The safe

```
                    ♠ A K Q 7
                    ♡ 10 7 6 3
                    ◇ A Q J
                    ♣ A K
        ♠ J 4                    ♠ 10 8 6 5
        ♡ Q J 9 2      N         ♡ A K 8 5 4
        ◇ 10 8 4 3   W   E       ◇ 6
        ♣ 9 6 5        S         ♣ 8 7 3
                    ♠ 9 3 2
                    ♡ —
                    ◇ K 9 7 5 2
                    ♣ Q J 10 4 2
```

play is to unblock the ace and king of clubs and then overtake dummy's remaining diamond with your king. That establishes West's ten of diamonds as a winner, but it is the only trick for the defence. You now abandon trumps and play clubs and then spades until West ruffs.

Now suppose, on the same hand, that your partner insists on playing in the inferior contract of six spades. East leads a top heart and North has to ruff in dummy. How should he continue?

As the cards lie he can scramble home by way of a club to the king, a heart ruff, a club to the ace, a heart ruff, and the queen of clubs for a discard of the fourth heart. After a diamond to the ace and three top trumps, North can revert to diamonds and make twelve tricks.

However, that is a poor line of play that succeeds only because of the 3–3 club break. Correct play protects against 4–2 breaks in both black suits. At trick two North should play a small spade from both hands. By conceding a trump at a time when dummy can take care of a further heart lead, North retains control. On regaining the lead he draws trumps, and eventually discards all his heart losers on the clubs.

Loser-on-Loser Again

The 4–3 trump fit is particularly vulnerable to a forcing attack. Often the declarer has to resort to loser-on-loser play, waiting until the short trump hand can cope with the enemy suit.

♠ 9 7 5
♡ K 10 3
◇ 9 8 5 2
♣ A Q J

```
      N
  W       E
      S
```

♠ 6
♡ A Q J 5
◇ A K 7 3
♣ K 8 7 2

You play in four hearts and the defenders start with two rounds of spades. There appear to be ten tricks, but you will lose control of the hand if you ruff the second spade and subsequently discover the trumps to be 4–2.

The remedy lies in a repeated loser-on-loser play. Discard a losing diamond on the second spade, and a further losing diamond when the defenders continue with a third spade. All is then under control, for dummy can deal with a fourth spade lead by ruffing high. You can continue with four rounds of trumps, and you will make your contract whenever the trumps break no worse than 4–2.

Leaving a Trump in Dummy

A solid 5–3 trump fit gives you a sense of security that is sometimes illusory. The contract may be in danger on a forcing attack even when the opposing trumps break 3–2.

You play in four spades after East has opened with a bid of one heart. (Yes, three no trumps is easier if you can get there.) West leads the ten of hearts to dummy's ace. How do you plan the play?

♠ K 9 5
♡ A 7 2
◇ J 8 7 4
♣ Q 8 2

```
      N
  W       E
      S
```

♠ A Q J 10 3
♡ 8
◇ 9 6 5 2
♣ A K 4

There are nine top tricks and the tenth will have to come from diamonds. Establishing a diamond trick will involve giving up the lead three times, and the danger is that repeated forces in hearts will run you out of trumps. That will certainly be your fate if you draw three rounds of trumps immediately.

However, you can always get home if both spades and diamonds break 3–2. It is safe enough to draw two rounds of trumps, but then you must switch to diamonds. You can ruff the heart return and lead another diamond, ruff the third heart and lead a third diamond. Now, if the defenders lead a fourth heart, you can ruff in dummy while discarding the fourth diamond (or a club) from your hand. Return to the ace of clubs, draw the last trump and you have ten tricks.

The ace of trumps is a powerful controlling card which enables you to win a trump trick at a time convenient to yourself. So far in these examples you have always held the trump ace, and there have been several instances where the success of the contract depended on whether you took your ace on the first or the second round.

When the defenders have the ace of trumps, however, you lose the right to determine which round of trumps you will win. The choice passes to the defenders, who will naturally elect to take the ace at the moment when they can do the most damage.

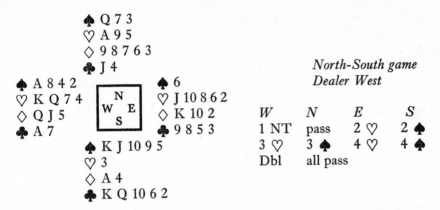

	♠ Q 7 3		
	♡ A 9 5		
	◇ 9 8 7 6 3		

North-South game
Dealer West

W	N	E	S
1 NT	pass	2 ♡	2 ♠
3 ♡	3 ♠	4 ♡	4 ♠
Dbl	all pass		

West leads the king of hearts to dummy's ace. How should you plan the play?

In a sense you can count your ten tricks, with four spades, four clubs and the two red aces, but the double sounds ominous. If West has four trumps headed by the ace, repeated heart leads will put the contract at risk. Your best chance is that West can be persuaded to take his ace on the first or second round, so at trick two you lead a small trump to your jack. If West wins this trick you can ruff the heart return, knock out the ace of clubs, and discard your losing diamond on the third heart. Dummy will then be able to take care of a further heart lead and you will make your contract.

But let us suppose that West knows his way around and holds up his ace of trumps, holding up again when you continue with the ten of trumps. Now a third round of trumps will prove fatal. Having waited patiently for the moment when dummy is exhausted of trumps, West will take his ace and force you with a heart. If you draw his last trump, he will be able to give his partner three more heart tricks when he gains the lead with the ace of clubs. Whatever you do, you will have to go at least one down.

But there is no need to throw in the sponge. After two rounds of trumps you should switch to clubs, leading low to the jack and back to the king and ace. After ruffing the heart return you will still be unable to afford a trump lead, but you can pick off West's trumps by leading clubs through him. If he ruffs with the eight of spades at any time, you can over-ruff with the queen, return to the ace of diamonds and continue with the clubs. If West starts discarding diamonds, of course, you must cash the ace of diamonds before the last club to make sure that it is not ruffed.

Note the point of leaving the queen of spades in dummy. You need a trump higher than the eight for over-ruffing purposes.

What if it is the king of trumps rather than the ace that is missing?

You open with a forcing bid, and partner has no chance to wriggle off the hook until you are in four hearts. The defenders attack in spades and you have to ruff the third round. How should you continue?

♠ J 8 4
♡ 8 6 5
♢ J 7 6
♣ J 7 4 3

```
      N
   W     E
      S
```

♠ 9 3
♡ A Q J 10 9
♢ A K
♣ A K Q 6

You can afford to lose a heart trick, and there would appear to be little point in crossing to the jack of clubs for a heart finesse, thereby exposing yourself unnecessarily to the risk of a club ruff. You may therefore be tempted to play the ace of hearts and continue with the queen. That will serve all right if the hearts are 3–2, but suppose they are 4–1. By releasing the ace of hearts on the first round you promote the king to first rank, giving the defender with the king the right to choose when he will take his trick. A defender with four trumps will naturally elect to keep his king for the third round when dummy's last trump is played. A further spade lead will then promote a second trump trick for the defence.

On this hand you must try to persuade the defenders to take their king of trumps on the first or second round, while dummy still has the eight of hearts as protection against a fourth round of spades. Retain the ace of hearts in your hand, leading the queen at trick four. If this is allowed to win, continue with the jack of hearts. If the king is again held up, just cash the ace of hearts and play on the side suits, allowing the defender to score his king of trumps when he likes.

Let us try the same hand opposite a slightly weaker dummy.

♠ J 8 4
♡ 8 6
◇ J 7 6 5
♣ J 7 4 3

```
      N
   W     E
      S
```

♠ 9 3
♡ A Q J 10 9
◇ A K
♣ A K Q 6

Again you are in four hearts and again you are forced to ruff the third spade. Should you play the same way?

This time there is less going for the lead of the queen of hearts at trick four because, having only two trumps in dummy, you cannot profitably repeat the manoeuvre if the king of hearts is held up. Does this mean that you should just play out the ace and queen of hearts and hope for a 3–3 split?

Not at all. Although you cannot cope with K x x x in the West hand, you can still succeed against K x x x with East. Lead the queen of hearts from hand as before. If the king wins the trick, the eight of hearts in dummy will protect against a further spade lead. If the queen of hearts is allowed to win, cross to the jack of clubs in dummy and return the eight of hearts for a finesse of the ten. If the finesse succeeds, continue with the ace of hearts and then go about your business of cashing winners in the side suits.

Countering Trump Promotion

As declarer you will frequently find yourself in the familiar situation where the defenders are threatening to promote extra tricks for themselves in the trump suit. Usually what happens is that the defender on your right leads a suit in which both you and the player on your left are void. If you ruff low you will surely suffer an over-ruff, while if you ruff high you are likely to promote a trump trick for the defenders.

On some hands there will be no answer to this defence, but at times it may be possible to take evasive action.

                                ♠ J 10 5
                                ♡ K Q 4
                                ◇ K 7 6 3
                                ♣ A 6 2

Love all
Dealer North   ♠ A 6   ♠ K Q 9 8 7 3
                        ♡ 10 9 7 5 2   ┌─────┐   ♡ A 8 6
                        ◇ J 9 4   │ N │   ◇ 5
| W | N | E | S | ♣ Q 8 5   │ W E │   ♣ J 7 4
|---|---|---|---| │ S │
| | 1 NT | 2 ♠ | 3 ◇ | └─────┘
all pass   ♠ 4 2
                                ♡ J 3
                                ◇ A Q 10 8 2
                                ♣ K 10 9 3

The defenders begin with three rounds of spades, putting you under immediate pressure. If you ruff the third spade, either low or high, you will have to lose a trump trick as well as two spades, a heart and a club.

Loser-on-loser technique will come to your rescue here. Instead of ruffing the third spade, discard one of your losing clubs. Now dummy can take care of a further spade lead, and your remaining club loser will eventually be discarded on the third round of hearts.

The same considerations apply when your right-hand opponent attempts an uppercut, as in the next hand.

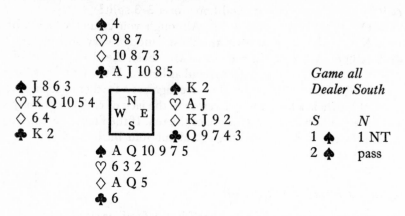

```
              ♠ 4
              ♡ 9 8 7
              ◇ 10 8 7 3
              ♣ A J 10 8 5                Game all
  ♠ J 8 6 3              ♠ K 2            Dealer South
  ♡ K Q 10 5 4   N       ♡ A J
  ◇ 6 4       W    E     ◇ K J 9 2
  ♣ K 2          S       ♣ Q 9 7 4 3       S      N
              ♠ A Q 10 9 7 5               1 ♠    1 NT
              ♡ 6 3 2                       2 ♠    pass
              ◇ A Q 5
              ♣ 6
```

West leads the king of hearts and East plays the ace. When the jack of hearts is returned, West overtakes with the queen and cashes the ten. Then comes a fourth heart, and East makes a nuisance of himself by ruffing with the king of spades. What do you do?

With all four hands on view, it is easy to see that if you over-ruff you will subsequently have to lose two trumps and a diamond in addition to the three heart tricks already lost. The right move is to dodge the uppercut by discarding your losing diamond on the fourth trick. Your only other loser will be a trump, for you can take the diamond finesse when in dummy with the ace of clubs.

DEFENCE

Let us now examine the subject of trump control from the point of view of the defenders. We have already seen something of the power of the ace of trumps in defence. A holding of A x x x in trumps is an enormous asset when you are playing a forcing game, particularly if you can hold up the ace until dummy is out of trumps.

A forcing defence is less likely to succeed when you have A x x in trumps, but there may still be a big advantage in holding up the ace. There are certain hands on which the declarer needs to draw exactly two rounds of trumps and then, perhaps, cross-ruff. If you take your ace on the first round you make it easy for him to attain his objective. By holding up for one round you can upset his timing. If he plays a second round of trumps you can counter with a third round, while if he starts his cross-ruff after one round of trumps he may run into an over-ruff. Here is an example:

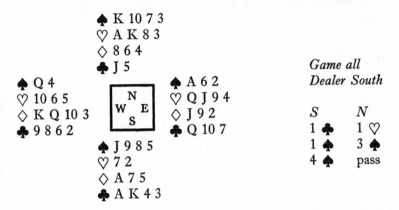

♠ K 10 7 3
♡ A K 8 3
◇ 8 6 4
♣ J 5

♠ Q 4
♡ 10 6 5
◇ K Q 10 3
♣ 9 8 6 2

♠ A 6 2
♡ Q J 9 4
◇ J 9 2
♣ Q 10 7

♠ J 9 8 5
♡ 7 2
◇ A 7 5
♣ A K 4 3

Game all
Dealer South

S	N
1 ♣	1 ♡
1 ♠	3 ♠
4 ♠	pass

West attacks in diamonds and South wins the second round. He then leads the eight of spades, on which West plays the four and dummy the three. If East wins with the ace he can give his partner a further diamond trick, but that is the end of the road for the defence. When South regains the lead he will play a second trump, heaving a sigh of relief when the queen appears. After winning with the king he will cash the top cards in his side suits and cross-ruff the remainder for ten tricks.

To defeat the contract East must hold up the ace of spades, denying South the chance of winning the second round. Now the declarer has no good move to make. If he plays a second trump, East wins and continues with a third trump, leaving South a trick short. And if South tries for the cross-ruff without playing any more trumps, he is eventually over-ruffed by West with the queen of spades.

Perhaps, instead of planning a cross-ruff, the declarer may have ideas of establishing a side suit. In the next example South would again be glad of the chance to win the second round of trumps.

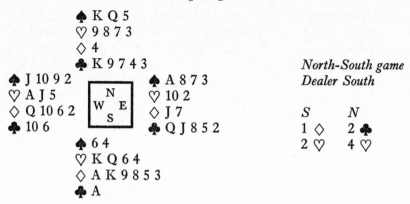

♠ K Q 5
♡ 9 8 7 3
◇ 4
♣ K 9 7 4 3

♠ J 10 9 2   ♠ A 8 7 3
♡ A J 5   ♡ 10 2
◇ Q 10 6 2   ◇ J 7
♣ 10 6   ♣ Q J 8 5 2

♠ 6 4
♡ K Q 6 4
◇ A K 9 8 5 3
♣ A

North-South game
Dealer South

S	N
1 ◇	2 ♣
2 ♡	4 ♡

The lead of the jack of spades draws the king and ace, and the spade return goes to the queen. The declarer leads a heart to his king and the ball is in West's court. If West parts with the ace of hearts the declarer's worries are over. He ruffs the spade return, cashes the ace of diamonds, ruffs a small diamond in dummy and returns to hand with the queen of hearts. He can then ruff a second diamond with impunity, return a club to his ace, and play diamonds from the top until West takes the final trick for the defence with the jack of hearts.

Once again, the hold-up in trumps is the killing move. If the declarer plays a second trump West will cash a third, and South will find himself unable to make more than eight tricks. And if South tries to establish the diamonds without playing a second trump he will run into an over-ruff.

Save That Trump

When the declarer has shown a two-suited hand in the bidding, a forcing defence is indicated and the defenders must take care to preserve their trump length. In this context it is important to realize that three cards may constitute adequate 'length' when the declarer's trumps are being shortened.

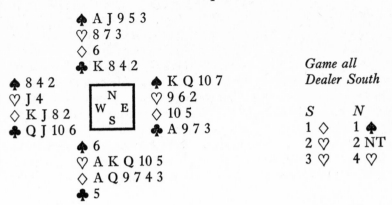

♠ A J 9 5 3
♡ 8 7 3
◇ 6
♣ K 8 4 2

♠ 8 4 2
♡ J 4
◇ K J 8 2
♣ Q J 10 6

♠ K Q 10 7
♡ 9 6 2
◇ 10 5
♣ A 9 7 3

♠ 6
♡ A K Q 10 5
◇ A Q 9 7 4 3
♣ 5

Game all
Dealer South

S	N
1 ◇	1 ♠
2 ♡	2 NT
3 ♡	4 ♡

West attacks with the queen of clubs and South has to ruff on the second round. He cashes the ace of diamonds, ruffs a diamond in dummy, returns to hand with the ace of hearts and ruffs another diamond with dummy's last trump.

The critical point of the hand has been reached. It seems natural for East to seize the opportunity of making a cheap trick in trumps by over-ruffing with the nine, but if he does so the contract cannot be defeated. South will win the spade return in dummy, ruff a spade, draw trumps in one more round and concede a diamond.

If East discards a spade on the third diamond instead of over-ruffing, the contract cannot be made. After returning to hand with a ruff in one of the black suits, South can draw trumps and concede a diamond as before, but the difference is that it takes two more rounds to draw the trumps and South has no way back to the established diamonds in his hand.

It is perhaps easier to see the advantages of refusing to over-ruff when you are sitting behind the declarer.

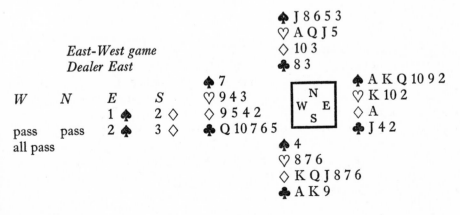

♠ J 8 6 5 3
♡ A Q J 5
◇ 10 3
♣ 8 3

East-West game
Dealer East

♠ 7
♡ 9 4 3
◇ 9 5 4 2
♣ Q 10 7 6 5

♠ A K Q 10 9 2
♡ K 10 2
◇ A
♣ J 4 2

W	N	E	S
		1 ♠	2 ◇
pass	pass	2 ♠	3 ◇
all pass			

♠ 4
♡ 8 7 6
◇ K Q J 8 7 6
♣ A K 9

East wins the opening spade lead with the nine and continues with the ace of spades, which South ruffs with the six of diamonds. If West makes the mistake of over-ruffing, the declarer will be in control. He will win the heart return with the ace, play the ace and king of clubs and ruff the third club in dummy, and then play a trump to East's ace. He can afford to ruff the next spade high, draw trumps, and concede a trick to the king of hearts.

Now try discarding a heart from the West hand instead of over-ruffing at trick two. Whether South goes for the trumps straight away or after ruffing his third club in dummy, he will be unable to make more than eight tricks. When in with the ace of diamonds East plays another spade, reducing South to the same number of trumps as West and causing him to lose control.

Timing the Promotion

We have seen that, when given the chance, the declarer will discard a loser rather than ruff in a position where an extra trump trick may be promoted for the defence. When aiming for a trump promotion, therefore, it is important for defenders to take all the tricks they can in the side suits first. Here is an example:

```
                    ♠ K 6 4
                    ♡ Q 8 3
                    ◇ 10 8 6 5
                    ♣ A Q 7                    Game all
 ♠ A 10 8                      ♠ 3            Dealer East
 ♡ 9 2          ┌─────────┐    ♡ A K J 10 6 4
 ◇ Q 7 4 3      │ W   N  E│    ◇ K 9 2        W    N    E    S
 ♣ J 9 6 2      │     S   │    ♣ 10 8 5                 1♡   1♠
                └─────────┘
                    ♠ Q J 9 7 5 2           1 NT  3♠   all pass
                    ♡ 7 5
                    ◇ A J
                    ♣ K 4 3
```

West leads the nine of hearts and East wins with the ten. Recognizing the possibility of promoting an extra trump trick for his partner, East may continue with the ace and king of hearts. But this defence is not good enough. Instead of ruffing, South simply discards the losing jack of diamonds, and the only other trick for the defenders is the ace of spades.

East should realize that the defenders need to score either two diamonds and a trump or one diamond and two trumps if the contract is to be defeated, and at trick two he should switch to the two of diamonds. Now the declarer is doomed to lose five tricks, whether he plays the ace of diamonds or the jack.

Part Three

BREAKING THROUGH THE BARRIER

Card Reading

Counting the hand – think of the bidding – anti-percentage – the
chain of assumption – count it out – defence

Anyone who can count up to thirteen has the makings of a master player.
The first tentative steps into expert country are taken when a player
attempts to reconstruct in his mind the distribution of all four suits in the
unseen hands. And this involves nothing more difficult than adding up to
thirteen – the number of cards in each suit of the pack and also the number
of cards dealt to each player.

Although the arithmetic is simple, a genuine effort of concentration is
required when you first start counting. It is all too easy to go astray if an
early discard is missed. Suppose, for example, that you and dummy have
seven hearts between you and that East shows out on the second round. As
well as taking careful note of the discard, you must register mentally that
West is marked with five hearts. If West subsequently follows suit twice in
both spades and clubs before showing out, you will know beyond any doubt
that he started with four diamonds. And this knowledge may enable you to
make a certainty of your contract.

To begin with, counting may seem like hard work, but if you persevere
you will discover that it soon becomes second nature. When you find yourself making a contract by taking a deep finesse that you *know* must be right,
you will realize that all the effort has been worth while.

A complete count of the hand will seldom be achieved until a late stage
in the play, and you may have to commit yourself to a line of play before
this. Then you will have to fall back upon an inferential count, relying on
clues from the bidding, the opening lead and the early play to build up your
picture of the enemy hands.

It is not only the distribution that concerns you but also the location of
the high cards. By relating the number of high-card points a player has
already shown up with to his bidding, or his failure to bid, you will often
be able to infer that he must have, or cannot have, a particular card.

Counting the Hand

Here is a simple counting situation:

You play in five diamonds after West has made an overcall in hearts. West attacks with his top hearts and East discards a spade on the third round.

After ruffing and drawing trumps you will have ten top tricks, and the contract will depend on a successful finesse in spades which you can take either way. Already at trick three you have some

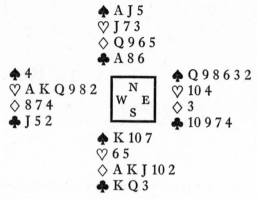

♠ A J 5
♡ J 7 3
◇ Q 9 6 5
♣ A 8 6

♠ 4
♡ A K Q 9 8 2
◇ 8 7 4
♣ J 5 2

♠ Q 9 8 6 3 2
♡ 10 4
◇ 3
♣ 10 9 7 4

♠ K 10 7
♡ 6 5
◇ A K J 10 2
♣ K Q 3

vital information about the distribution. You know that West began with six hearts and East with two. When you draw trumps you note with interest that West follows three times while East discards a spade and a club. The picture is becoming clearer. Now you know that West began with nine red cards and therefore only four black ones.

If you had to make a decision about the spades at this point you would be inclined to finesse against East, who is marked with ten cards in the black suits. But there is no need for haste. You can discover more about the distribution by playing three rounds of clubs. When both defenders follow suit, probability gives way to certainty. West is known to have started with six hearts, three diamonds and three clubs, and therefore precisely one spade. If you prefer to count the East hand you can do so just as easily. East has shown up with two hearts, one diamond, four clubs, and therefore six spades.

Problems tend to vanish when you know where the cards lie. You play the ace of spades, and when the queen does not drop you take the marked finesse against East.

Counting enables you to play as though you had seen your opponents' hands. In fact you have seen them – in your mind's eye.

In the next example we shall work with only two hands on view.

East, the dealer, opens with a non-vulnerable bid of three spades. You come in with three no trumps, and North raises to six no trumps.

♠ Q J
♡ A K 5
◇ K 10 7 2
♣ K 9 6 4

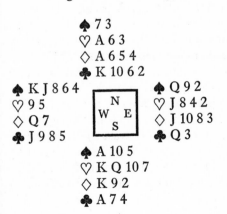

♠ K 5
♡ Q J 6
◇ A Q 6 3
♣ A Q J 7

West leads the seven of spades to his partner's ace and East returns the ten of spades, on which West plays the two. How should you play?

There are eleven top tricks and the twelfth will have to come from diamonds. Chances are good, for you would normally expect East to be short in diamonds in view of his advertised length in spades. You can cope with that easily enough by finessing against the jack of diamonds if East shows out on the first or second round.

However, it would be a mistake to tackle the diamonds immediately. First you should play on the other suits in order to gain some indication of how the diamonds may lie. Suppose that, after winning the second spade, you cash the ace of clubs and East discards a spade. Then you investigate the lie of the hearts, and on the third round East discards another spade.

Now you realize that, against all expectations, it is East who has the diamond length. His hand can be counted as seven spades, two hearts, four diamonds and a void in clubs. Your remaining chance is that West's singleton diamond is one of the higher cards – the jack, the nine or the eight. So you play the king of diamonds and await West's card with bated breath. If it is the eight or the nine, continue with the two of diamonds from dummy, finessing the six if East plays low. That will make him hold his cards closer to his chest for the next few hands. It makes no difference if East plays high on the second round of diamonds, for after winning the trick you can return to the king of clubs and repeat the finesse to pick up four diamond tricks.

At times you may have to concede a number of tricks to the defenders before you can obtain an accurate count.

The contract is three no trumps and West leads the six of spades. You allow the queen to win the first trick, cover the return of the nine of spades with the ten, and win the ace on the third round, discarding a diamond from the table.

There are eight top tricks and

♠ 7 3
♡ A 6 3
◇ A 6 5 4
♣ K 10 6 2

♠ K J 8 6 4
♡ 9 5
◇ Q 7
♣ J 9 8 5

♠ Q 9 2
♡ J 8 4 2
◇ J 10 8 3
♣ Q 3

♠ A 10 5
♡ K Q 10 7
◇ K 9 2
♣ A 7 4

chances for a ninth in either clubs or hearts. Naturally you plan to concede a trick to the 'safe' defender, East, who has no more spades. At trick four you play a low club and put in the ten from dummy. East wins with the queen and returns a diamond, on which you play the nine and West the queen. Since you cannot afford to concede a trick to West, you win with the ace and play off the ace and king of clubs. East discards a diamond on the third round, dashing your hopes of scoring an extra club trick.

However, the evidence that West started with five spades and four clubs makes it easy for you to count out the hand. West has already produced the queen of diamonds, and you know that he has three more red cards. To gather the final piece of the jigsaw, lead a diamond to your king. When West follows suit he can have no more than two hearts, and you make sure of your contract by playing the king of hearts, then a heart to the ace and a finesse of the ten on the way back.

If West had shown out on the second diamond, of course, you would have played for the drop in hearts with equal certainty.

Think of the Bidding

Valuable clues to the distribution of the cards are available when a defender has been active in the bidding.

♠ A 5
♡ 10 7 6 3
◇ A 7 4 3
♣ 10 6 4

```
  N
W   E
  S
```

♠ K Q 8 7 6 3
♡ 5
◇ 6 2
♣ A K J 3

Game all
Dealer West

W	N	E	S
1 ♡	pass	pass	2 ♠
3 ◇	3 ♠	pass	4 ♠
all pass			

West begins with top hearts and you ruff on the second round. When you test the trumps with the king and ace, West follows once and then discards a diamond. How do you continue?

Having a loser in trumps, one in hearts and one in diamonds, you cannot afford to lose a club trick. The obvious method of trying to avoid a club loser is to take a finesse, but if you think back to the bidding you will realize that the finesse cannot be the right play here. For his vulnerable bid of three diamonds West must surely have five cards in the suit, and he will not have fewer hearts. Add in the trump that he has played and there is room in his hand for no more than two clubs. Hence the club finesse, even if it succeeds, will not enable you to avoid a loser in the suit.

The only chance is to assume that West has the queen of clubs. Play a club to your ace, cash the queen of trumps and continue with the king of clubs, hoping for the queen to drop.

Enemy bidding provides a useful indication not only of the distribution of the suits but also of the high-card content of the defenders' hands. Valuable negative inferences arise when a defender fails to make a bid. Here is an example of the sort of situation that crops up quite regularly.

Love all
Dealer West

♠ K J 8 7 4
♡ 7 2
◇ 6 4
♣ K Q 7 5

W	N	E	S
pass	pass	pass	1 ♠
Dbl	4 ♠	all pass	

```
      N
   W     E
      S
```

♠ A Q 10 6 3
♡ K J 5 4
◇ A 8 5
♣ 4

West leads the king of diamonds, East plays the nine and you win with the ace. You draw trumps, East discarding the three of diamonds on the second round, and then lead the club from your hand, hoping to slip past the ace. But West goes up with the ace of clubs, cashes the queen of diamonds and leads a third diamond for dummy to ruff. What now?

With only two discards available on the clubs, you need to guess the heart position correctly. If you reflect on the bidding, however, you will realize that there is no need for guesswork because the position is clearly charted. West has already produced the king and queen of diamonds and the ace of clubs, and yet he passed originally. He may well have the queen of hearts to account for his second-round double, but he can hardly have the ace, for with thirteen high-card points he would not have failed to open the bidding.

When East plays low on the lead of a heart from dummy, therefore, you can put up the king with complete confidence.

Anti-Percentage

An inference from the bidding may be strong enough to persuade you to abandon the normal percentage play in a suit. The probabilities can be useful when there is nothing else to guide you, but an ounce of inference will always be worth a pound of percentage.

♠ 8 7 5 3
♡ J 9 5 3
♢ K Q 6
♣ K 2

Game all
Dealer West

	W	N	E	S
	1 ♠	pass	pass	2 ♡
	pass	3 ♡	pass	4 ♡
	all pass			

♠ 6 2
♡ A Q 10 8 4 2
♢ 7 4
♣ A J 5

When West leads the king of spades, East overtakes with the ace and returns the nine of spades to his partner's ten. West continues with the queen of spades and East discards a small club. After ruffing, how should you play?

You cannot avoid losing a trick to the ace of diamonds, and you must therefore pick up the trumps without loss. The percentage play is to take the finesse, which will succeed roughly twice as often as playing for the drop. But the percentage tables take no account of the enemy bidding. They do not allow for the fact that East passed his partner's opening bid and subsequently produced the ace of spades. It is surely hardly possible for East to have the king of hearts as well, for with seven high-card points he would not have passed his partner out in one spade.

You should therefore reject the trump finesse on this hand. Just play the ace of hearts at trick four and enjoy the expression on West's face if his king tumbles down.

The Chain of Assumption

Players soon learn the value of making simple assumptions about the location of enemy cards. If a particular card must be in a certain position to give you a chance for your contract, you must assume that it is so placed and plan your play accordingly. Similarly, if the contract will be in danger only when a particular card lies badly, assume that it does lie badly and consider what follows from that. The chain of logic that extends from an arbitrary assumption of this sort will often lead to helpful conclusions about the position of other key cards.

Game all   ♠ A Q J 5
Dealer East   ♡ K Q 6 5
                                            ◇ K J 3
                                            ♣ 8 4

W	N	E	S
		1 ♡	pass
pass	Dbl	2 ♡	3 ♠
pass	4 ♠	all pass	

♠ A Q J 5
♡ K Q 6 5
◇ K J 3
♣ 8 4

```
      N
  W       E
      S
```

♠ 10 8 7 6 3 2
♡ —
◇ Q 7 6 4
♣ K 7 2

West leads the nine of hearts, the king draws the ace, and you ruff the first trick. How should you continue?

At first glance the contract looks fairly secure, for the ace of clubs is likely to be right on the bidding. But suppose that it is wrong. Then you would have four potential losers – a spade, a diamond and two clubs.

One thing is certain. If West has the ace of clubs he cannot have the king of spades as well, for with seven high-card points he would not have passed his partner's opening bid. That being the case, you may as well give yourself the chance of dropping a singleton king by leading a trump to the ace at trick two.

To look at it from another angle, if the spade finesse is working there is no need for you to take it, for in that case the ace of clubs will certainly be in the East hand. The distribution you have to guard against is the following:

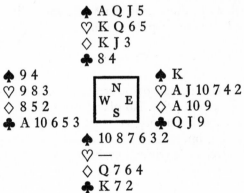

♠ A Q J 5
♡ K Q 6 5
◇ K J 3
♣ 8 4

♠ 9 4   ♠ K
♡ 9 8 3   ♡ A J 10 7 4 2
◇ 8 5 2   ◇ A 10 9
♣ A 10 6 5 3   ♣ Q J 9

♠ 10 8 7 6 3 2
♡ —
◇ Q 7 6 4
♣ K 7 2

Count it Out

On certain hands you may discover how to play the trumps by first investigating the side suits.

You play in four spades after East, playing five-card majors, has opened with a bid of one heart.

West leads the seven of clubs to his partner's king. East continues with the ace and a third club, and West ruffs with the four of spades. The nine of hearts is then led to your king, and when you cash the ace of spades West plays the five and East the six. How should you continue?

The problem is whether to finesse in spades or play for the drop. What do you know about the hand? Firstly, that East started with four clubs and West with two. Secondly, East is likely to have exactly five hearts and West three,

♠ 10 9 3
♡ 6 4
◇ A 10 7 6 2
♣ Q 6 3

```
      N
  W       E
      S
```

♠ A K J 8 2
♡ A K 7
◇ 4
♣ J 10 9 5

for with a doubleton in both hearts and clubs, West would probably have elected to lead his partner's bid suit. For your contract to have a chance you must assume that East began with two or three trumps, which would leave him with one or two diamonds.

Doest that suggest anything? Yes, of course, you can find out how to play the trumps by testing the diamonds. Lead a diamond to the ace and return a diamond for a ruff. If East shows out on the second diamond, you will know that he began with the guarded queen of spades. After ruffing the third heart in dummy, therefore, you will finesse in trumps to land your game.

And if East follows to the second diamond, you will simply play out the king of spades and hope to drop the queen.

DEFENCE

For the declarer, counting can be of great value, as we have seen, but for the defenders it is beyond price. No player can hope to rise above the ruck in defence without making a serious effort to count the hand and to keep track of what is going on.

A count of the declarer's tricks may be all that is needed.

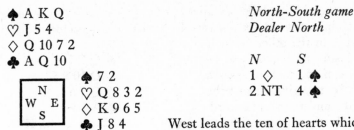

♠ A K Q
♡ J 5 4
◇ Q 10 7 2
♣ A Q 10

♠ 7 2
♡ Q 8 3 2
◇ K 9 6 5
♣ J 8 4

North-South game
Dealer North

N	S
1 ◇	1 ♠
2 NT	4 ♠

West leads the ten of hearts which is allowed to win the first trick. South wins the continuation of the king of hearts with the ace, draws two rounds of trumps. West following low-high, and leads the two of diamonds from the table. Over to you.

South is marked with six trumps by both the bidding and the play. He has already scored the ace of hearts, and you can see that he can make two further tricks in clubs by finessing. It follows that if South has any other high card – either the ace of diamonds or the king of clubs – he cannot be prevented from making ten tricks. You must assume partner to have these cards, and you should step up with the king of diamonds on the first round in order to protect yourself against a possible ruffing finesse in the suit. The full hand may be as shown here.

Do you see what happens if you play low on the diamond lead? Partner wins with the ace and gives you your heart trick, but South later ruffs out your king of diamonds to establish a discard for his losing club.

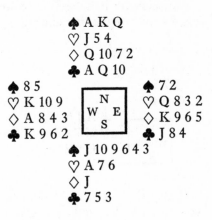

♠ A K Q
♡ J 5 4
◇ Q 10 7 2
♣ A Q 10

♠ 8 5
♡ K 10 9
◇ A 8 4 3
♣ K 9 6 2

♠ 7 2
♡ Q 8 3 2
◇ K 9 6 5
♣ J 8 4

♠ J 10 9 6 4 3
♡ A 7 6
◇ J
♣ 7 5 3

More often it is a count of distribution that will tell you what to do.

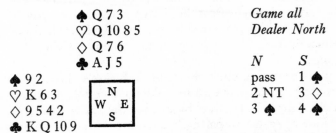

♠ Q 7 3
♡ Q 10 8 5
◇ Q 7 6
♣ A J 5

♠ 9 2
♡ K 6 3
◇ 9 5 4 2
♣ K Q 10 9

Game all
Dealer North

N	S
pass	1 ♠
2 NT	3 ◇
3 ♠	4 ♠

Your lead of the king of clubs is allowed to win the first trick, partner playing the four and declarer the six. What now?

F

In this case the bidding tells you all you need to know. South is marked with at least nine cards in spades and diamonds, and therefore no more than four cards in the other suits. If he has two losing hearts, he will be able to dispose of one of them as soon as he gets in by finessing against the queen of clubs and taking a discard.

Consequently there is no time to be lost. You must switch at once to the three of hearts in order to make sure of any heart tricks that are going. The heart switch cannot cost anything, even if South has the ace and the jack, and it may be essential if the contract is to be defeated. One possible hand is shown here.

♠ Q 7 3
♡ Q 10 8 5
◇ Q 7 6
♣ A J 5

♠ 9 2   ♠ K 10 4
♡ K 6 3   N   ♡ A J 9 2
◇ 9 5 4 2   W   E   ◇ 8 3
♣ K Q 10 9   S   ♣ 8 7 4 3

♠ A J 8 6 5
♡ 7 4
◇ A K J 10
♣ 6 2

Occasionally it is feasible to work out the distribution of the complete hand from the bidding and the opening lead.

♠ 10 8 7 3 2   *Love all*
♡ A J 5   *Dealer South*
◇ 7 5
♣ A 8 3

          ♠ A J 9 4
  N   ♡ K 7 4 3
W   E   ◇ Q 9 2
  S   ♣ J 5

S	N
1 ♡	1 ♠
2 NT	3 ♡
3 NT	pass

West leads the three of diamonds on which you play the queen and South the king. The ten of hearts is then run to your king. How should you continue?

South can have no more than four hearts since he preferred to play in no trumps. He is also marked with four diamonds by your partner's lead of the three. And a further inference can be drawn from the opening lead. With a five-card club suit partner would presumably have led a club rather than a diamond. And if partner has no more than four clubs South must also have four.

Now the picture is becoming clear. South has a 1-4-4-4 shape, and his singleton spade must be an honour card to make up his quota of points. It follows that you can defeat the contract by cashing the ace of spades, continuing with the four of spades to partner's honour card, and scoring two further spade tricks on the return. The full hand:

Players are sometimes tempted to cash their tricks too quickly in situations where a little counting would keep them straight.

Your opening spade lead is won in dummy and the king of hearts is played to your ace, East following with the two. South ruffs the next spade and draws trumps with the queen and jack, East discarding a spade and a low club. Then comes the four of diamonds to the eight, queen and ace. How should you continue?

Looking at the string of diamond winners in dummy and thinking of all

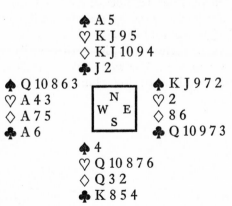

the discards South will be able to make, you may feel an urge to play the ace and another club in an attempt to take any tricks that are available in the suit. That would be short-sighted, however. South is known to have started with one spade and five hearts, and therefore seven cards in the minor suits. It follows that after taking his discards on the diamonds South will still have two clubs left in his hand.

A passive diamond return is all that is required. South will eventually have to open up the clubs himself.

Returning a diamond brings in a worthwhile penalty of 300, while cashing the ace of clubs would have produced a paltry 100.

Counting can also prove to be an effective safeguard against trickery. The declarer pulled off a neat swindle on this hand.

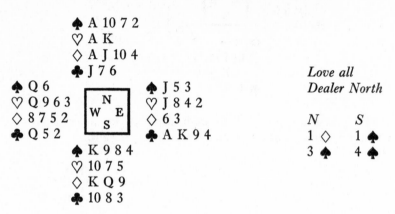

♠ A 10 7 2
♡ A K
◇ A J 10 4
♣ J 7 6

♠ Q 6
♡ Q 9 6 3
◇ 8 7 5 2
♣ Q 5 2

♠ J 5 3
♡ J 8 4 2
◇ 6 3
♣ A K 9 4

♠ K 9 8 4
♡ 10 7 5
◇ K Q 9
♣ 10 8 3

Love all
Dealer North

N	S
1 ◇	1 ♠
3 ♠	4 ♠

The opening lead of the three of hearts went to dummy's king. After drawing two rounds of trumps with the ace and king, South continued with the king of diamonds, the nine of diamonds to the ace, and the jack of diamonds from the table. Not wishing to waste his master trump on air, East discarded the nine of clubs. South unsportingly produced the queen of diamonds, and the rest was a matter of routine. A heart to the ace was followed by the ten of diamonds, and South was in a position to make ten tricks whether East ruffed or not.

All credit to the declarer, but if East had been counting he would not have fallen into the trap. East can tell that the defenders need three club tricks to defeat the contract. From the bidding, the opening lead and the early play it is apparent that South began with four spades and three hearts. It follows that if he has two diamonds, as seems likely, he must have four clubs and a discard will be of no use to him. The safety play for East, therefore, is to ruff the third diamond and lead a low club, catering for Q x x or Q x with West.

12

Deception

Creating an illusion – finessing technique – deception with small
cards – faking a finesse – inducing a continuation – slipping past
the queen – the disappearing trick – defence – obligatory false
cards – playing the known card – deceptive leads – the false echo

The first-class card player is not content with winning the tricks that are
rightfully his but is always on the watch for a chance of stealing a trick from
under the noses of his opponents. Stolen fruit has a special flavour, and
many players derive more satisfaction from a good swindle than from the
most brilliant technical coup.

A deceptive play is not an easy thing to improvise on the spur of the
moment, nor is a deceptive style something that comes naturally. It is a
product of hard work and experience. First you have to know exactly what
you are trying to achieve. Basically, deception is just a matter of concealing
your strengths and weaknesses from the opponents until it is too late for
them to damage you. There are a hundred small ways of laying a false trail,
and it is as well to study the common positions in advance so that you will
have a chance of recognizing them when you meet them at the table.

Remember, above all else, that a deceptive play is of little use unless it is
made smoothly and naturally. Any hesitation is liable to give the show
away. Try to maintain the same tempo in your play whether you are
following suit with a normal card or attempting an outrageous bluff.

As declarer you do not have to worry about misleading your partner, and
you can therefore select your cards with a view to causing the maximum confusion within the ranks of the enemy. But this does not mean that you should
choose your cards at random. Whether you are contemplating winning the
trick with an honour or following suit with a low card, there will usually be a
right card and a wrong card to play from the point of view of deception. The
right card is the one that will leave the defenders in doubt about your holding
in the suit. It will often be possible to suggest a continuation when that is
what you want, and to induce a switch when that will suit you best.

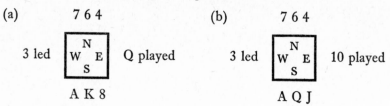

(a)   7 6 4   (b)   7 6 4

3 led   Q played   3 led   10 played

A K 8   A Q J

Suppose that in diagram (a) you intend to win the first trick. Should you play the ace or the king?

The answer depends on whether you are playing a suit or a no trump contract. At no trumps you should win with the king, leaving open for East the possibility that his partner may be able to take the rest of the tricks in the suit. If you win with the ace the defenders are likely to place you with the king as well, for with only one stopper in the suit you would probably hold up for a round or two.

In a suit contract, however, you should win the first trick with the ace. Each defender may then form the impression that his partner holds the king.

In diagram (b) you should win with the queen, leaving West guessing about the location of the jack. If he decides that his partner has it, he may lead into your tenace again.

(c)   7 6 4   (d)   J 10 4

3 led   J played   3 led   5 played

K Q 5   A Q 9

In diagram (c) the king is the card to create ambiguity for West. Placing his partner with the queen, West may again lead away from his ace when he regains the lead.

In diagram (d) the most plausible ruse is to put up the jack from dummy as though trying to induce a cover and to overtake smoothly with the queen when East plays low. When next on lead, West may continue the attack, expecting your ace to fall.

Creating an Illusion

It is often possible to give a defender a headache by dropping a high card from your hand.

You are playing in a trump contract and West leads the king of this side suit. If there is a possibility of discarding one of your losers on another suit, try the effect of dropping the queen on the first round. West may then fear to continue in case his ace is ruffed.

```
            J 6 5
          ┌─────────┐
          │   N     │
A K 9 8 4 │ W     E │  10 7 3
          │   S     │
          └─────────┘
            Q 2
```

In certain circumstances, this type of play may be effective when you hold the king.

(a)
```
            J 8 4
          ┌─────────┐
          │   N     │
A led     │ W     E │  3 played
          │   S     │
          └─────────┘
            K 2
```

(b)
```
            10 8 4
          ┌─────────┐
          │   N     │
J led     │ W     E │  A played
          │   S     │
          └─────────┘
            K 2
```

In (a) suppose that West, who has pre-empted in this suit, leads the ace against your trump contract. You can be sure that East's three is a singleton, and your only chance of avoiding a second-round ruff is to drop your king under the ace. Not wishing to establish dummy's jack, West is likely to switch and you may later be able to dispose of your other loser in the suit.

In (b) it is East who has pre-empted and West leads the jack to his partner's ace. Again you should ditch the king in an effort to persuade East that it is you who have the singleton.

Mind you, it is not always the highest card that is the most deceptive when your aim is to avert an enemy ruff.

(c)
```
            K 7 6 2
          ┌─────────┐
          │   N     │
3 led     │ W     E │  A played
          │   S     │
          └─────────┘
            Q J 10
```

(d)
```
            K 7 6 2
          ┌─────────┐
          │   N     │
3 led     │ W     E │  Q played
          │   S     │
          └─────────┘
            J 10 9
```

You are playing in a trump contract in (c) and the defenders attack this side suit. West's three is an obvious singleton and your only chance of avoiding a ruff is to drop your jack under the ace. The jack is the one card which, from East's point of view, could be single in your hand. West would not lead the three from Q J 3 or J 10 3, but he might from Q 10 3.

In (d) you play low from dummy and East wins with the queen. Again, the middle card is the only one to create ambiguity for East. Drop the ten under the queen.

Finessing Technique

On the face of it a finesse represents a fifty-fifty chance, but the declarer who has cultivated a deceptive style will always be able to get rather better odds. One way of putting a defender under pressure is by forcing him to make an early decision.

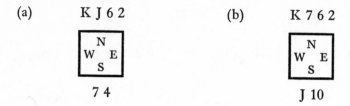

(a)	K J 6 2	(b)	K 7 6 2

7 4   J 10

Suppose, in diagram (a), that you are in a slam contract that depends on a correct guess in this suit. The way to give yourself the best chance is to lead a small card from hand at the earliest opportunity, before West knows much about your holdings in the other suits. If West has the ace he will be under considerable pressure to play it, because for all he knows you may have a singleton in this suit and a certain loser elsewhere. If West plays low without hesitation, therefore, a good case can be made for finessing the jack.

In (b) many players would lead the jack and watch for a reaction, but a competent defender in the West seat will play low with a wooden face and leave you with the guess. It is actually better to lead the ten from hand, especially if you are marked with shortage in the suit. West may then think you have no alternative to the play of the king from dummy, and he is more likely to play the ace if he has it.

When leading a high card from a sequence for a finesse, consider whether you would like to have it covered or not. The highest of the sequence is the card most likely to induce a cover, and the lowest will be best when you wish to slip past the enemy honour card.

(c)   A 7 6   (d)   A K J 3   (e)   A 7 6 3

Q J 9   10 9   Q J 10 5

In diagram (c) you would like West to cover if he has the king and you should therefore lead the queen. West should not cover, of course, unless he has the ten as well, but players often go wrong in this situation.

If dummy has no outside entries in (d), the play of the queen by West will block the suit. West is more likely to cover the ten than the nine, so lead the nine for the first finesse.

In (e), having no reason to induce a cover from West, you should lead the ten from hand. If West now plays the king, there is some presumption that this may be a singleton and you may consider running the seven on the way back.

Good technique will enable you to win not only the finesses that are right but also some of those that are wrong.

(f)　　A Q 7 6 3　　　　　(g)　　A 9 6 3

```
   N              N
 W   E          W   E
   S              S
```

J 10　　　　　　　　　　Q 10

Suppose, in (f), that the king is marked in the East hand. There is no need to despair if you cannot afford a loser in the suit. Lead your jack to the ace and return a small card, and there is a good chance that East will play low, expecting you to ruff.

If West leads the jack in diagram (g), the same ruse can be tried. Go up with the ace, dropping the queen from hand, and return the three. Only a very suspicious East will consider playing his king on the second round.

It is often possible to put your right-hand opponent under this kind of pressure by making the first lead of a suit away from the honour cards in dummy.

(h)　　A Q 8 4　　　　　(i)　　K 8 7 6 3

```
              N                          N
 J 10 6 5   W   E   K 9 2    Q 10 5 2   W   E   A 9 4
              S                          S
```

7 3　　　　　　　　　　J

Suppose that you can afford to lose one trick in (h) and need to develop two tricks in the suit. The way to play on East's nerves is to start by leading a low card from dummy. You can always try the finesse on the next round, but meanwhile East may save you the trouble by going up with the king.

In diagram (i), if the bidding marks the ace in the East hand, try the effect of leading the three from dummy. Again East may go up, fearful of allowing you to score a singleton queen.

Deception With Small Cards

While the deployment of high cards is important, the good player achieves just as many deceptive effects from the way he handles his small cards. In certain routine situations there are well-known methods of crossing the enemy signals.

	(a)	Q 7 5			(b)	Q 7 5	
A K J 8 6		N W E S	10 9 3	A K J 8 6		N W E S	4 3
		4 2				10 9 2	

In diagram (a) West leads the king of a side suit that he has mentioned in the bidding and his partner plays the three. To give West a problem you must play the four. Like the silver foil deployed from a warplane for the purpose of confusing the enemy radar, this false card may persuade the defenders to waste their ammunition on the wrong target. If West believes that his partner has started an echo to show a doubleton, he will continue the suit to your advantage.

Diagram (b) shows the opposite situation. West leads the king and his partner starts an echo with the four. This time you would like West to switch and give you a chance to pull trumps, and you should therefore play the two. This leaves open for West the possibility that his partner started with 10 9 4.

Obviously you cannot afford to take time to think in these situations. Fortunately there is a simple rule to follow. As declarer, behave exactly as though you were a defender, starting an echo when you wish to induce a continuation and playing your lowest card when you hope for a switch.

At no trumps as well there may be big rewards if you can persuade a defender that his partner has played an encouraging card.

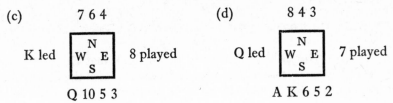

(c)   7 6 4   (d)   8 4 3

K led   8 played   Q led   7 played

      Q 10 5 3   A K 6 5 2

In diagram (c) your play of the five on the first round may cause West to think he has hit the jackpot.

In (d) you are lucky enough to attract a lead in a suit you have concealed in the bidding. However, if you win and return the suit the defenders will have a chance to switch their attack. It is better to play the five on the first round. West is then likely to continue, putting you a tempo ahead.

When there is a long suit in dummy the defenders will normally try to signal their length to each other. There is no reason why you should not join in the fun.

(e)   K Q J 8 2   (f)   K Q J 8 2

9 5 4   A 10 7   5 4   A 10 7

       6 3   9 6 3

Assuming there is no outside entry to dummy, your only chance of making two tricks in (e) is to persuade East to hold up his ace for two rounds. You may succeed, but only if you lead the six on the first round. East may then read his partner for 4 3 and allow you to steal a second trick when you lead an honour from dummy on the next round.

In (f) you would like East to take his ace on the second round. In this case the only chance is to lead the three on the first round. East will then have to guess whether his partner's five is the start of an echo or the lowest from 9 6 5.

In some cases your play will depend on your estimate of who holds the missing ace.

Again there is no side entry in dummy and you would naturally like the defenders to take their ace on the second round.

K Q 10 9

If you believe West to have the ace, the best shot is to lead the jack and continue with the five. If West is persuaded that his partner has started an echo to show four cards in the suit, he will see no point in

J 5 2

holding up his ace a second time. Note that West must be made to play ahead of his partner on the second round, since East's next card will expose the position.

The suit must be tackled differently if you think that East has the ace. Lead the five for a 'finesse' of the nine and continue with the king from the table. If East, holding A x x, believes that his partner has J x x x, he may take his ace on the second round.

Against defenders who habitually echo to show distribution, concealing a low card may pay dividends in a suit contract as well.

K Q 10 8

J 9 6  A 7 4 2

5 3

When you lead the five to dummy's queen, East may fear to hold up lest his partner has started an echo with four cards in the suit. The subsequent play is always easier if the defenders can be persuaded to take their aces on the first round.

It is often a good move to conceal a small card when leading towards dummy or when following suit. Even when you have no specific purpose in mind it can do no harm to create a spot of confusion in the enemy ranks

When entering dummy in this suit, lead the five rather than the two if you fear a switch. Each defender may believe the other to be echoing and may return the the suit when he gains the lead.

A K 4

Q 5 2

Faking a Finesse

Look out for opportunities of creating the impression that you are taking a finesse.

(a) A Q J 6

K 4 2

(b) 7 6

A K Q J

Needing to enter dummy in diagram (a) in order to lead another suit, avoid giving the show away by using the ace. Lead the four to dummy's jack. West may believe that his partner is holding up the king and echoing, while East may receive the impression that his partner has the king, in which case he will credit you with high cards that you do not possess in the other suits.

In (b), suppose you are playing in a trump contract and need a discard in dummy before touching trumps. The best chance is to lead from dummy for a 'finesse' of the queen and continue with the ace and jack. If West has a doubleton he may refrain from ruffing, expecting his partner to have the king.

Inducing a Continuation

Many deceptive manoeuvres are designed to steer the defenders away from a potentially damaging switch. One good way of suggesting a continuation is by pretending to have a loser in the suit led.

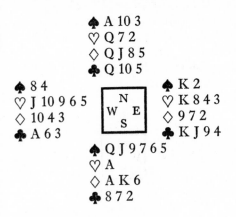

♠ A 10 3
♡ Q 7 2
◇ Q J 8 5
♣ Q 10 5

♠ 8 4
♡ J 10 9 6 5
◇ 10 4 3
♣ A 6 3

♠ K 2
♡ K 8 4 3
◇ 9 7 2
♣ K J 9 4

♠ Q J 9 7 6 5
♡ A
◇ A K 6
♣ 8 7 2

West leads the jack of hearts against your contract of four spades. The king of hearts is almost certainly with East, and to give yourself the best chance you must play the queen from dummy in an attempt to persuade the defenders that you have a second heart in your hand. The queen is covered by the king and ace, and the spade finesse loses to East. Now East is likely to try to put his partner in with a heart, and one of your losing clubs will eventually be discarded on dummy's fourth diamond.

If you play low from dummy to the first trick, East will certainly switch when he comes in with the king of spades, and he may well decide that his best chance is to find his partner with the ace of clubs.

Another telling move is to win the first trick with a higher card than is necessary. The situation illustrated in the next hand is well known, but it is always hard for the defenders to smell out this ruse.

You play in three no trumps, and West leads the four of spades to his partner's jack. Consider first what will happen if you make the normal play of winning with the queen. You can enter dummy in hearts and take the diamond finesse, but on winning with the king West will realize that there is no point in a spade continuation and his club switch will put you two down.

To improve your chances when the diamond finesse is wrong, win

```
                    ♠ 7 6
                    ♡ A K Q 3
                    ◇ Q 10 5 4
                    ♣ 10 4 3
    ♠ K 10 8 4 3            ♠ J 9 5
    ♡ 9 5 2         N       ♡ 8 6 4
    ◇ K 6       W     E     ◇ 7 2
    ♣ K 9 6         S       ♣ A J 8 5 2
                    ♠ A Q 2
                    ♡ J 10 7
                    ◇ A J 9 8 3
                    ♣ Q 7
```

the first trick with the ace of spades! In theory this gives the defenders the chance to put your contract six down, but in practice it will never happen. When West comes in with the king of diamonds he will continue with a low spade, confident that his partner has the queen.

Similar plays may be made with the following holdings when West is expected to win the first trick for the defence.

(a)   7 5   (b)   6

```
                 N                                      N
    Q 9 6 4 3  W     E  10 8 2        A Q 8 4 2  W     E  10 7 5
                 S                                      S
              A K J                                  K J 9 3
```

In both cases, when West leads the four and East plays the ten, you may persuade West to lead the suit again by winning with the king rather than the jack.

You may be able to convince the defenders that they are on the right track by sacrificing one of your sure tricks.

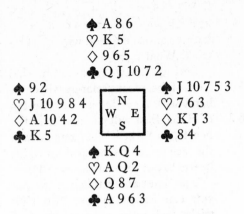

♠ A 8 6
♡ K 5
◇ 9 6 5
♣ Q J 10 7 2

♠ 9 2
♡ J 10 9 8 4
◇ A 10 4 2
♣ K 5

♠ J 10 7 5 3
♡ 7 6 3
◇ K J 3
♣ 8 4

♠ K Q 4
♡ A Q 2
◇ Q 8 7
♣ A 9 6 3

West leads the jack of hearts against your three no trumps, and you can count eleven easy tricks if the club finesse is right. Since you do not need eleven tricks, or even ten, you should take out a little insurance against an unfavourable club position by playing the king of hearts from dummy and dropping the queen from your own hand.

Now, when in with the king of clubs, West is likely to lead another heart, intent on establishing the suit while he still has the diamond ace as an entry. And you will gratefully take your nine tricks.

On the next hand it takes the play of an unexpected card to give a defender the green light.

West leads the king of clubs against your contract of three no trumps. How should you play?

It will not do to win the ace, for if West has a five-card club suit a losing diamond finesse will then defeat the contract. The normal procedure with this holding is to play low, preparing a Bath Coup against the defender on your left. But if you do this West is sure to switch, and a spade switch might enable the defenders to score three spades, a club and a diamond.

♠ 8 6 5
♡ K Q 3
◇ A Q 10 5
♣ 8 7 2

♠ K 4 2
♡ 10 6 4
◇ 8 6
♣ K Q 10 9 5

♠ Q J 9 7
♡ 9 5 2
◇ K 7 4 3
♣ 4 3

♠ A 10 3
♡ A J 8 7
◇ J 9 2
♣ A J 6

The card that gives you the best chance at trick one is the jack of clubs! West would then need to have a very suspicious nature to do anything but continue clubs. You can take the ace of clubs on the second round and finesse in diamonds with complete safety.

Slipping Past the Queen

The secret of bringing home impossible contracts lies in making it as hard as possible for the defenders to do the right thing.

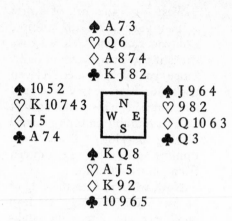

♠ A 7 3
♡ Q 6
◇ A 8 7 4
♣ K J 8 2

♠ 10 5 2
♡ K 10 7 4 3
◇ J 5
♣ A 7 4

♠ J 9 6 4
♡ 9 8 2
◇ Q 10 6 3
♣ Q 3

♠ K Q 8
♡ A J 5
◇ K 9 2
♣ 10 9 6 5

West leads the four of hearts against your contract of three no trumps and the queen wins the first trick. What now?

Seeing that two tricks are needed from clubs, most declarers will enter hand with a spade and run the ten of clubs. East will win and clear the hearts, and when West gets in with the ace of clubs he will cash his hearts to put the contract one down.

The point about this hand is that you can afford to lose two club tricks as long as you lose the first one to West, who cannot profitably lead another heart. Do you suppose that East will play the queen of clubs if you lead a low club from the table at trick two? Not if he is a creature of flesh and blood. Placing you with the ace of clubs, East will play low without a tremor, hoping to score his queen on the second round. And that will enable you to make your contract with an overtrick.

The Disappearing Trick

When conditions are right you may be able to persuade the defenders to telescope their tricks in the trump suit. The next hand shows one way in which this may be achieved.

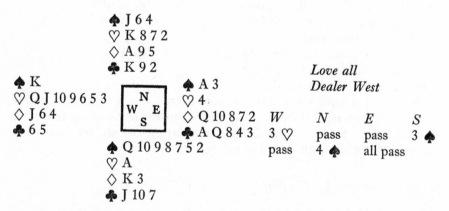

♠ J 6 4
♡ K 8 7 2
◇ A 9 5
♣ K 9 2

♠ K
♡ Q J 10 9 6 5 3
◇ J 6 4
♣ 6 5

♠ A 3
♡ 4
◇ Q 10 8 7 2
♣ A Q 8 4 3

♠ Q 10 9 8 7 5 2
♡ A
◇ K 3
♣ J 10 7

Love all
Dealer West

W	N	E	S
3 ♡	pass	pass	3 ♠
pass	4 ♠	all pass	

West leads the queen of hearts to your ace. How should you proceed? You are fortunate to have escaped a club lead, but you can see that there is still a danger of losing two tricks in each black suit. The king of hearts in dummy may appear to be of no use to you. However, East does not know the position and you can play on his ignorance by crossing at once to the ace of diamonds and playing the king of hearts. If East is persuaded to ruff with the three of spades, the hand is over. You over-ruff and lead a trump, and have the satisfaction of seeing the ace and king of trumps knock heads on the same trick.

DEFENCE

Although the defenders are handicapped to some extent by the need to exchange honest information with each other, they have a compensating advantage. Opportunities for deception are more plentiful in defence owing to the fact that both enemy hands are hidden from the declarer. The aim of the defenders should be to offer declarer, whenever possible, a plausible alternative to the winning line of play.

One of the commonest ways of creating a losing option for the declarer is seen in routine hold-up technique.

(a)	K Q 10 2		(b)	K Q 10 2

J 8 4 [N W E S] A 9 5	A 8 4 [N W E S] J 9 5
7 6 3	7 6 3

When South leads a low card to dummy's king in diagram (a), it will seldom be right for East to win with the ace. If he does, South is more or less forced to find the winning play of finessing the ten on the next round. If East placidly plays the five under dummy's king, there is a good chance that South will go wrong on the next round.

Did someone suggest that he should finesse the ten anyway? If he does that he may run into the position of diagram (b) where it is West rather than East who is playing a deep game.

Obligatory False Cards

There are many routine situations where the declarer is marked with length in a suit (often the trump suit), in which a defender *must* play a false card to create an alternative to the winning line of play. Otherwise there is no chance of the declarer going wrong. Here are some of the basic positions, most of which have a number of variations:

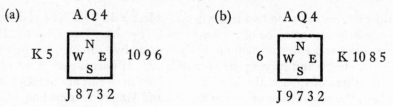

(a)   A Q 4   (b)   A Q 4

K 5   [N W E S]   10 9 6   6   [N W E S]   K 10 8 5

J 8 7 3 2   J 9 7 3 2

In diagram (a) when the declarer leads a low card from hand and finesses dummy's queen, East must drop the nine or the ten. Otherwise South will have no alternative to the winning play of the ace on the second round. The fall of the nine or ten gives him the option of returning to hand in another suit and leading the jack, hoping to pin the other intermediate card in the East hand.

In (b) South again leads a low card for a finesse of the queen. If East takes his king, that will be the only trick he makes in the suit for South will have a marked finesse against the ten on the third round. To give himself a chance of two tricks East must play the eight under the queen. South may then return to hand and run the jack, hoping for East's holding to be 10 8.

(c)   A 8 6 3   (d)   Q J 9 5

2   [N W E S]   J 9 5 4   10 8 6 2   [N W E S]   A

K Q 10 7   K 7 4 3

When South plays the king from hand in diagram (c), East must drop the nine in order to create a losing option. If he fails to do this, South is bound to continue by playing the seven to dummy's ace and taking the marked finesse on the third round. When the nine falls, however, South has a choice of finessing either way against the jack. He may well go wrong by playing the queen on the second round.

In passing it is worth noting that, if entries permit, South does better to start this combination by leading a low card from dummy. Now East cannot afford to play the nine, since for all he knows his partner may have a singleton ten.

Diagram (d) shows a similar position. South leads a low card towards dummy's queen, and West has a chance of a second trick in the suit only if he plays the eight.

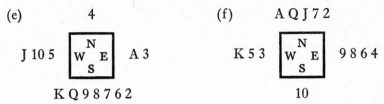

(e) 4

J 10 5 [N W E S] A 3

KQ98762

(f) AQJ72

K 5 3 [N W E S] 9 8 6 4

10

In (e) the declarer leads from dummy and puts on the king when East plays low. In order to create a losing option West must play the jack or the ten. If he plays the five, there will be nothing for South to try but the winning play of a low card on the second round.

Suppose, in (f), that the contract is no trumps. Needing tricks from this suit, South leads the ten, overtakes with dummy's jack and continues with the ace. Again he can hardly go wrong unless East plays the eight or the nine on the second round.

(g) K 4

J 10 [N W E S] A 7 5

Q98632

(h) J 9 5

7 6 4 [N W E S] Q 10

AK832

In diagram (g) South leads low to dummy's king. If East wins, South will have no option but to play the queen on the second round if he can afford only one loser in the suit. East should, of course, play the five under dummy's king and the seven on the next round. South is then virtually certain to finesse, playing for West to have A J or A 10 doubleton.

In (h) South starts by playing the ace and cannot go wrong if East follows tamely with the ten. But when East drops the queen a losing option appears. If South believes the queen to be a true card he will finesse dummy's nine on the next round.

(i) 10 5 4 2

K [N W E S] A J 9

Q 8 7 6 3

(j) Q 10 4

A J 9 [N W E S] 6 5 2

K 8 7 3

South leads a low card from dummy in diagram (i). If East plays the nine, the correct percentage play for declarer will be to play low from hand, since singleton ace or king in the West hand are twice as likely as singleton jack. If East plays the jack, however, South has to consider the possibility that West may have the singleton nine or A K 9, and he is likely to cover with the queen. Note that the play of the jack by East cannot cost a trick in this situation. East is never going to make more than one trick if South has both king and queen.

In diagram (j) South leads the three from hand. If West plays the nine, South will finesse the ten and continue with the queen to knock out the ace, and since he knows the location of the jack he will not do the wrong thing on the third round. But if West plays his jack on the first round there is a chance that declarer will go astray, particularly if he is short of entries to his hand. After winning with the queen, he may continue with the ten to knock out the ace, and then he is likely to finesse into West's hand on the third round.

Playing the Known Card

The last example raises an important issue. When a defender is known to have a certain card, he should plan to get rid of it at the first opportunity, for the declarer will not go wrong until he has seen it played.

(a)	K J 4		(b)	A Q 9 7 4	
Q 10 2	N W　E S	8 6 3	K J 10 3	N W　E S	8 6 2
	A 9 7 4			5	

In diagram (a) South leads the four for a finesse of the jack and continues with the king. West is known to have the queen, and he must play it on the second round to give himself a chance of making a trick in the suit.

Diagram (b) represents one of the side suits in a trump contract. Before tackling trumps, South plans to establish this suit. He starts by finessing dummy's queen and taking a discard on the ace. West should play the king, the card he is known to hold, on the second round, for until the king appears South knows that he can ruff low with impunity.

One excellent reason for playing a card you are known to hold is that it may be the only way to protect partner's honour cards. The situations that follow provide a good test of a defender's awareness at the table.

(c)   Q 10 7 5 2   (d)   7 6 4 3

J 9 3 [N W E S] A K   K Q [N W E S] 10 8 2

        8 6 4   A J 9 5

In diagram (c) the declarer leads a low card from hand and the finesse of the ten loses to the ace. On the second round West must not fail to give South a nudge in the wrong direction by playing the jack, the card he is known to hold. If West plays the nine, South will realize that he has nothing to lose by playing low from dummy, for if West started with K J 9 3 South must always lose three tricks in the suit.

In (d) South can afford to lose only one trick and starts by leading low to the nine and queen. When the next card is played from dummy East must protect his partner's chances by playing the ten, the card he is known to hold and the card he would now play from an original holding of K 10 2. If East plays a feeble eight on the second round, South will realize that his only chance is to go up with the ace in an attempt to drop the king.

It may take close defensive co-operation to build a plausible illusion.

A Q 10 9 6 4

J 7 2 [N W E S] K 3

    8 5

Suppose that the declarer needs to establish this suit at no trumps but has no outside entries in dummy. He starts by running the eight, and East, not one to give up without a struggle, calmly plays the three. That is good defence, but it will be to no avail unless West plays his part by putting in the jack on the next round. If West plays the seven, South will realize that he cannot hope to establish the suit against K J 7 2 in the West hand, and he may in desperation go up with the ace.

The principle of playing the card you are known to hold may with advantage be extended to include playing the card you will shortly be known to hold.

(f)   A Q 9 6 3   (g)   A 10 8 3

K 10 [N W E S] 7 4 2   K J 7 4 [N W E S] 6 5

      J 8 5   Q 9 2

When South leads a low card in (f), West's king is a dead duck. Its location will be known as soon as dummy's queen wins the trick, and it can cost nothing to play it on the first round. When the king appears, South may decide to finesse his eight on the second round.

In (g) the declarer leads the three from dummy for a finesse of his nine. West can see that if he wins with the jack his king will be picked up by a finesse and South will make three tricks in the suit. Since the location of the king will shortly be known, it must be a good move to play the king at once, thereby obscuring the position of the jack. Now South is sure to limit himself to two tricks in the suit.

Deceptive Leads

We are treading on dangerous ground here, for partners tend to rely heavily on the information received from opening leads. However, declarers can also benefit from honest information, and it does not pay for a defender to allow himself to be classified as a player who never departs from the conventional. The best time to try something different, naturally, is when it cannot matter if partner is deceived.

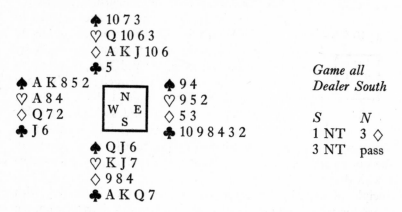

```
              ♠ 10 7 3
              ♡ Q 10 6 3
              ◇ A K J 10 6
              ♣ 5
♠ A K 8 5 2                ♠ 9 4
♡ A 8 4          N         ♡ 9 5 2
◇ Q 7 2       W   E        ◇ 5 3
♣ J 6            S         ♣ 10 9 8 4 3 2
              ♠ Q J 6
              ♡ K J 7
              ◇ 9 8 4
              ♣ A K Q 7
```

Game all
Dealer South

S	N
1 NT	3 ◇
3 NT	pass

If West makes the normal lead of the five of spades it is likely that the declarer will read the position correctly. In view of the danger of a 5–2 spade break, he will judge that he cannot afford to knock out the ace of hearts. Reluctantly, therefore, he will be forced to try the winning play of taking the diamond finesse.

West knows from the bidding about the threat of the diamond suit in dummy, and he should realize that this is a good occasion for an unorthodox lead of the two of spades. The fifth-best lead may deceive partner, it is true, but on this hand East's actions are not likely to affect the outcome. The important thing is that the lead of the two of spades stands a good chance of deceiving the declarer.

If South takes the lead at its face value – and he has no reason to do otherwise – he will see no point in exposing himself to the hazard of the diamond finesse. Instead he will play on hearts, expecting to lose no more than three spades and the ace of hearts. As it happens he will lose an extra spade, and with it some of his faith in human nature.

The False Echo

Another device that can be worth a lot of tricks to the defenders is the false echo, used in situations like the following:

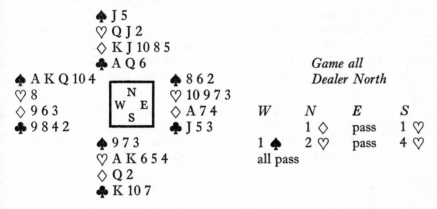

```
                ♠ J 5
                ♡ Q J 2
                ◇ K J 10 8 5
                ♣ A Q 6                Game all
♠ A K Q 10 4    ┌──────┐  ♠ 8 6 2      Dealer North
♡ 8             │  N   │  ♡ 10 9 7 3
◇ 9 6 3         │W   E │  ◇ A 7 4      W      N      E      S
♣ 9 8 4 2       │  S   │  ♣ J 5 3             1 ◇   pass   1 ♡
                └──────┘               1 ♠    2 ♡   pass   4 ♡
                ♠ 9 7 3                all pass
                ♡ A K 6 5 4
                ◇ Q 2
                ♣ K 10 7
```

West leads the king of spades, and at first glance it appears that the declarer can lose no more than two spades and the ace of diamonds. If East is alert, however, he may persuade South to lose a trump trick as well. Suppose that East plays the eight of spades on the first trick and follows with the two of spades when his partner continues with the ace. Both West and South are likely to be deceived. West will continue with the queen of spades, expecting his partner to have no more, and South will be reluctant to ruff low in dummy for fear of an over-ruff. South will probably decide to rely on a 3–2 trump break and ruff high in dummy, and the defenders will score the setting trick in trumps.

The declarer's fear of a ruff can often be used to deflect him from the winning line of play.

The contract is four spades and the opening lead the two of diamonds. When the king is played from dummy East wins with the ace and cashes the queen.

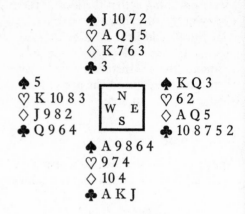

♠ J 10 7 2
♡ A Q J 5
◇ K 7 6 3
♣ 3

♠ 5   ♠ K Q 3
♡ K 10 8 3 ♡ 6 2
◇ J 9 8 2 ◇ A Q 5
♣ Q 9 6 4 ♣ 10 8 7 5 2

♠ A 9 8 6 4
♡ 9 7 4
◇ 10 4
♣ A K J

It is clear that on a normal defence – a diamond continuation or a club switch – the declarer will enter dummy by ruffing the jack of clubs and lead a trump, taking the double finesse and thus losing only two diamonds and one spade.

To give the defence a chance, East must lead a heart into the jaws of dummy's tenace at trick three. There is no certainty of success, but if South believes East's heart to be a singleton he may abandon the trump finesse in favour of playing the ace and another spade. And that will be one down.

We have seen that the declarer can produce startling effects by winning with a higher card than necessary, and the same ruse can work just as well for the defenders. On certain hands the declarer may be persuaded to repeat a losing finesse rather than take a winning one.

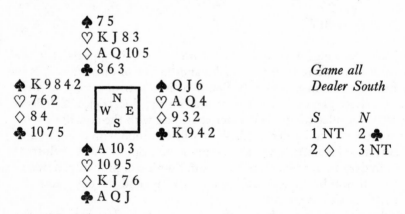

♠ 7 5
♡ K J 8 3
◇ A Q 10 5
♣ 8 6 3

♠ K 9 8 4 2   ♠ Q J 6
♡ 7 6 2   ♡ A Q 4
◇ 8 4   ◇ 9 3 2
♣ 10 7 5   ♣ K 9 4 2

♠ A 10 3
♡ 10 9 5
◇ K J 7 6
♣ A Q J

Game all
Dealer South

S	N
1 NT	2 ♣
2 ◇	3 NT

Try defending this hand from the East seat. Your partner leads the four of spades and the declarer holds up his ace until the third round, discarding a club from the table. He then runs the ten of hearts. Quick! What do you do?

Yes, of course, you should win with the ace and return a club, aiming to create the impression that it is the heart finesse and not the club finesse that is right. The declarer is likely to go up with the ace of clubs and repeat the heart finesse, and that will give you five tricks.

If you had won the first heart with the queen, South would have had no option but to take the club finesse. Without it he would not have enough tricks.

When the contract depends on a two-way finesse against a queen, it will sometimes be possible to point the declarer in the wrong direction.

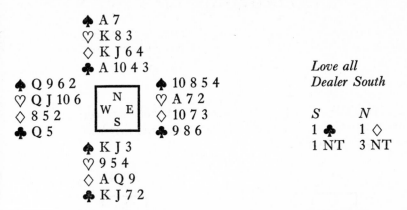

	♠ A 7	
	♡ K 8 3	
	◇ K J 6 4	
	♣ A 10 4 3	

Love all
Dealer South

♠ Q 9 6 2		♠ 10 8 5 4
♡ Q J 10 6	N	♡ A 7 2
◇ 8 5 2	W E	◇ 10 7 3
♣ Q 5	S	♣ 9 8 6

	♠ K J 3	
	♡ 9 5 4	
	◇ A Q 9	
	♣ K J 7 2	

S	N
1 ♣	1 ◇
1 NT	3 NT

West leads the queen of hearts on which dummy plays the three and East the seven. On the next round the jack of hearts is covered by the king and ace, and East continues with the two of hearts to West's ten.

At this point West can be confident that he has seen his partner's only high card, and he can tell that the contract will depend on the declarer's success in finding the queen of clubs. This is in theory a fifty-fifty chance, but West can load the odds heavily in his favour by refusing to cash the six of hearts, switching instead to a diamond at trick four.

If South believes the thirteenth heart to be with East, he will take the club finesse into the West hand, expecting to make his contract even if the finesse loses. It is not his day.

13

Throw-in Play

Elimination – the ruff and discard – defence to throw-in play –
protecting partner – unblocking – remember to count – make him
guess

Many combinations of cards will produce a better or more certain yield of
tricks if the defenders can be persuaded to make the first lead in the suit.
Here are some common examples:

K J 5   A 9 4

```
    N                                       N
 W     E                                 W     E
    S                                       S
```

A 10 3   K 10 5

In the first case you have two certain tricks and a two-way finesse against
the queen for a third, giving you a fifty-fifty chance of three tricks. However, all guesswork is eliminated if you can force one of the defenders to
lead the suit. You will then be certain of three tricks no matter who has the
queen.

In the second example there is little chance of a third trick if you have to
open up the suit yourself. If a defender leads it, however, a finessing position
appears and the prospects become rosier.

Q 10 7   A 10 6

```
    N                                       N
 W     E                                 W     E
    S                                       S
```

K 9 2   Q 4 3

Similar considerations apply in the above cases. If you have to tackle either of these combinations yourself, you cannot be sure of more than one trick. But if a defender can be persuaded to open them up, you are guaranteed two tricks irrespective of the position of the enemy honours.

With the above holdings you cannot count on a trick at all unless the defenders come to your aid by opening up the suit.

Tenaces gain in stature when there is a possibility of compelling a defender to lead up to them.

K 5

<table>
<tr><td>N</td></tr>
<tr><td>W   E</td></tr>
<tr><td>S</td></tr>
</table>

8 3

A Q

<table>
<tr><td>N</td></tr>
<tr><td>W   E</td></tr>
<tr><td>S</td></tr>
</table>

6 5

Normally the trick-taking potential of such holdings depends on whether the missing high card is with West or with East. But if East has to lead the suit you are assured of the maximum number of tricks no matter where the high card lies.

The play of the hand takes on a new dimension when you discover how to avoid the hazard of a finesse, and there is something very satisfying about throwing an opponent in to make a fatal lead. But there may be some careful planning to do before you reach the desired position. It is rare for a throw-in to come about accidentally.

Elimination

Naturally the defenders are not out to do you any favours and they will not lead into your tenaces if they have been left with any alternative. The essential preparation for throw-in play involves removing the alternatives. First you must eliminate the side suits, stripping the defender of safe cards of exit before putting him on lead in a situation where he has no option but to concede a trick on his return.

When a defender has been active in the bidding, it is often possible to place the high cards accurately. On the following hand, for example, it is the knowledge that a key finesse is sure to be wrong that turns the declarer's thoughts towards the possibility of a throw-in.

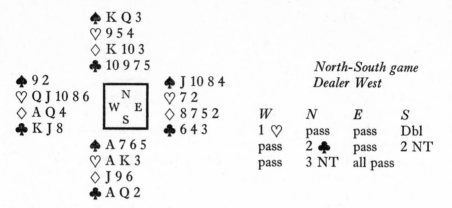

♠ K Q 3
♡ 9 5 4
◇ K 10 3
♣ 10 9 7 5

North-South game
Dealer West

♠ 9 2
♡ Q J 10 8 6
◇ A Q 4
♣ K J 8

♠ J 10 8 4
♡ 7 2
◇ 8 7 5 2
♣ 6 4 3

♠ A 7 6 5
♡ A K 3
◇ J 9 6
♣ A Q 2

W	N	E	S
1 ♡	pass	pass	Dbl
pass	2 ♣	pass	2 NT
pass	3 NT	all pass	

West leads the queen of hearts and the declarer can see only six immediate winners. The club finesse is sure to be wrong, but if two extra tricks can be developed in diamonds the ninth trick may come from spades.

South wins the first heart, therefore, and leads the nine of diamonds. West goes up with the ace in order to continue with the jack of hearts. South wins the second heart, finesses the ten of diamonds successfully, and then turns his attention to the spades. But when West discards the eight of clubs on the third spade, South has to look elsewhere for his ninth trick.

The position is now as shown here.

South has lost one trick and can afford to lose three more. He leads his diamond to dummy's king, removing West's last exit card, and then throws the lead to West with the nine of hearts. After cashing his three hearts, West has to concede the last two tricks by leading a club into South's major tenace.

When contemplating a throw-in, the declarer should try to retain a card of exit in the defender's suit. South would have been defeated in the last

♠ —
♡ 9
◇ K
♣ 10 9 7 5

♠ —
♡ 10 8 6
◇ Q
♣ K J

♠ J
♡ —
◇ 8 7
♣ 6 4 3

♠ 7
♡ 3
◇ J
♣ A Q 2

hand if he had held up on the first or second round of hearts, for he would then have had no means of throwing the lead to West at the critical moment.

Try the next one with only two hands on view.

♠ A 8 7 3
♡ 6 4
◇ A Q 8 6 3
♣ Q 9

♠ 5
♡ A K 7 5
◇ 5 2
♣ A K J 10 8 3

With no opposing bidding you reach a contract of six clubs, and West produces the awkward lead of a trump.

On any other lead you would expect to make twelve tricks by playing on cross-ruff lines. Now you will be able to ruff only one heart in dummy, and it looks as though the success of your slam will hinge on the diamond finesse.

However, if you are thinking along the right lines, you may realize that you can give yourself an extra chance by catering for the possibility of a throw-in. The elimination process must be started at once in order to remove as many of the defenders' exit cards as possible.

Play the ace of spades at trick two and continue with a spade ruff. Then play off the ace and king of hearts and ruff a heart, and we shall assume that both defenders follow to the third round of hearts. A further spade is ruffed, with both opponents again following suit.

When you draw trumps they prove to break 3–2, and you are left with the cards shown opposite.

Now, before trying the diamond finesse, you have nothing to lose by exiting with the heart. If West wins and leads a spade, you can ruff and take your last chance in diamonds. But if East has the outstanding heart he may have nothing but diamonds left in his hand, in which case all your problems will be solved.

The elimination was not complete in this particular case because you lacked an entry to ruff out dummy's last spade. But even a partial elimination can improve your chances considerably.

♠ 8
♡ —
◇ A Q 8
♣ —

♠ —
♡ 7
◇ 5 2
♣ J

The Ruff and Discard

It is not only when the opponents have to lead into your tenaces that you may stand to gain a trick in the end game. When you are playing in a trump contract it can be equally advantageous to have a defender lead a suit in which both you and dummy are void, for this will enable you to ruff in one hand while discarding a loser from the other.

Accordingly, when you have an adequate supply of trumps in both hands, you may be able to engineer a throw-in that offers the defenders the choice of two different methods of suicide – opening up a new suit to your advantage, or conceding a ruff and discard. Here is an example.

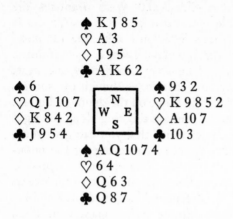

♠ K J 8 5
♡ A 3
◇ J 9 5
♣ A K 6 2

♠ 6
♡ Q J 10 7
◇ K 8 4 2
♣ J 9 5 4

♠ 9 3 2
♡ K 9 8 5 2
◇ A 10 7
♣ 10 3

♠ A Q 10 7 4
♡ 6 4
◇ Q 6 3
♣ Q 8 7

Your contract is four spades and West leads the queen of hearts to dummy's ace. There are nine top tricks and the tenth could come from a 3–3 club break. Failing that, there is always a chance of a trick from diamonds. But if you are thinking in terms of finessing the nine of diamonds, forget it. When the trumps break no worse than 3–1 you can make a certainty of the contract by elimination play.

Draw all the outstanding trumps and then test the club suit. When the 3–3 break fails to materialize, ruff the fourth club in your hand. The elimination is now complete and all that remains is for you to exit with your losing heart. It makes no difference which defender wins this trick. He will either have to open up the diamonds, thereby creating a trick for you in the suit, or return a heart, which will enable you to ruff in one hand while discarding a losing diamond from the other. Whatever they do, the defenders can make no more than one heart and two diamonds.

Loser-on-loser technique is often used in combination with throw-in play.

You play in five diamonds after West has bid strongly in spades. The opening lead is the king of spades, which you ruff. What do you think of your chances?

Since the ace of hearts is likely to be in the West hand, you have to think of some way of disposing of one of your heart losers in the event of the clubs failing to break evenly. A loser-on-loser elimination provides the answer.

Play a small trump to dummy at trick two, and if both defenders follow suit you are home. Ruff the small spade in hand, draw the remaining trump and play out the clubs, ruffing the

♠ Q 5 2
♡ 7 6 2
◇ A J 9 5
♣ 8 7 4

♠ —
♡ K 8 3
◇ K Q 10 7 6 2
♣ A K Q 5

fourth round in dummy if necessary. Then play the queen of spades from the table and discard a losing heart from your hand.

On winning with the ace of spades, West will be caught in the classical dilemma with no sound action to take. If he opens up the hearts, you will score a trick with your king. And if he plays another spade, you will ruff in dummy and discard a second heart from your hand. Either way you will make eleven tricks.

In all the examples that we have studied so far, the throw-in has been effected by leading a card in the opponent's suit. This need not always be the case, however. The throw-in card may in fact be in one of the critical suits. This usually comes about when the declarer has a deep finessing position so that the defenders cannot return the suit without conceding an extra trick in it.

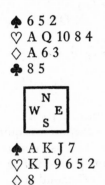

♠ 6 5 2
♡ A Q 10 8 4
◇ A 6 3
♣ 8 5

♠ A K J 7
♡ K J 9 6 5 2
◇ 8
♣ A Q

Your contract is six hearts, and West leads the queen of diamonds to dummy's ace. This is a good slam with eleven tricks in view (reversing the dummy and ruffing two diamonds in hand), and chances for the twelfth trick in the spade finesse, the 3–3 spade break and the club finesse.

It would certainly be unlucky if all these chances were to fail. Nevertheless, this is the sort of hand on which the success of the contract can be guaranteed by the use of elimination and throw-in technique.

Ruff a diamond high at trick two, lead a trump to to dummy and ruff another diamond high. Re-enter dummy in trumps, and then lead a spade with the intention of finessing the seven. A return of either black suit from West will give you the twelfth trick, as will a diamond return by conceding a ruff and discard.

If East plays the eight, nine or ten, on the first round of spades, win with the ace, return to dummy with a trump, and lead another spade. Again you will finesse the seven if permitted, and if East plays an intermediate card this time, you can afford to cover with the jack, for you will be left with a major tenace when West produces the queen.

Other card combinations suitable for the purpose of throw-in play in the critical suit include A J 10, A Q 9, K 10 x, or Q J x opposite small cards in dummy. In each case you lead from the table and cover East's card as cheaply as possible. If West wins, he will be unable to return the suit without allowing you to make one or two tricks as the case may be.

The next hand illustrates a similar but rather more complex throw-in, where a defender is given the choice of leading up to tenace positions in three suits.

West makes the safe lead of a trump against the contract of six hearts, and you draw a second round. There are eleven tricks and all kinds of chances for the twelfth, with finessing positions in both spades and clubs plus the option of finessing either way in diamonds.

In any case your first move should be to lead a low club to dummy's queen. If this loses to the ace and a club comes back, it will probably be best to go up with the king and cross-ruff diamonds and clubs, hoping for the king of diamonds or the jack of clubs to fall in three rounds and keeping the spade finesse to fall back on as a last resort.

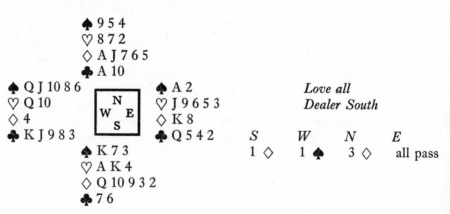

♠ A 7 3
♡ J 10 9 5
◇ A Q 10 3
♣ Q 4

♠ Q 9 5
♡ 8 4
◇ K 8 7 4
♣ A J 8 3

♠ 10 8 4 2
♡ 6 3
◇ 9 6 5 2
♣ 9 7 5

♠ K J 6
♡ A K Q 7 2
◇ J
♣ K 10 6 2

When the queen of clubs wins, however, you can make certain of your contract by throw-in play. Very little in the way of elimination is required. Just cash the ace of diamonds before returning the four of clubs for a finesse of the ten. West wins with the jack but is in the unhappy position of having to concede the twelfth trick whether he returns a spade, a diamond or a club.

Note the importance of cashing the ace of diamonds in order to take the guesswork out of the diamond position. Note also that in spite of the abundance of trumps in both hands, no ruff-and-discard element was present on this deal. The defender was faced with a choice of leading away from his high cards in three suits.

Sometimes it is the other way round. When the declarer has no tenace holding in either hand, it is only a ruff and discard that can help him. Here is an example of a pure ruff-and-discard elimination.

♠ 9 5 4
♡ 8 7 2
◇ A J 7 6 5
♣ A 10

♠ Q J 10 8 6
♡ Q 10
◇ 4
♣ K J 9 8 3

♠ A 2
♡ J 9 6 5 3
◇ K 8
♣ Q 5 4 2

♠ K 7 3
♡ A K 4
◇ Q 10 9 3 2
♣ 7 6

Love all
Dealer South

S	W	N	E
1 ◇	1 ♠	3 ◇	all pass

West leads the queen of spades to his partner's ace, and East returns a spade to your king. Looking at four losers in the side suits, you have to hope for the trump finesse to be right. But when you run the ten of diamonds, East produces the king and switches to a heart.

Now just one slim chance remains – that the hearts will divide 5–2. After drawing the remaining trump you must cash your second heart winner, then play a club to the ace and exit with the club ten. Now lack of communication prevents the defenders from scoring their winners in both major suits. Depending on where the club trick is won, the defenders can win either a heart or a spade but must then concede a ruff and discard, allowing you to get rid of your remaining major suit loser.

DEFENCE TO THROW-IN PLAY

To defend successfully in the end game it is essential to keep track of what is going on in the early play. Defenders often awake to the danger too late, when the throw-in is already upon them.

The warning signs are always there to be seen. When a defender has a vulnerable tenace holding, for instance, he should resolve that, come what may, he is not going to be thrown in to lead away from it. Early evasive action may avoid all further problems.

The most hurtful throw-ins are the self-inflicted ones. West has no one but himself to blame if he allows the declarer to throw him in on this hand.

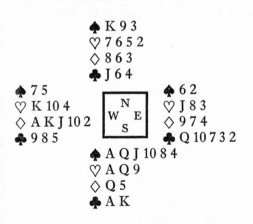

South opens with a forcing bid and eventually plays in four spades. West attacks with top diamonds, and when the queen drops on the second round he may consider it safe to continue with a third diamond. Do you see what will happen if he does?

South will ruff, play off the ace and king of clubs, enter dummy with the nine of spades and ruff the jack of clubs. A spade to the king will complete the process of elimination, and the declarer will be in a position to lead a heart from the table, covering East's card as cheaply as possible. On winning the trick, West will have to choose between returning a heart into the declarer's tenace and conceding a ruff and discard.

All this can be avoided if West refuses to help in the elimination of the side suits. A passive switch to a spade or a club at trick three defeats the contract, for South lacks the entries in dummy to eliminate both diamonds and clubs. He has to fall back on a straight heart finesse, and on the lie of the cards the contract is doomed.

Protecting Partner

It is not easy for the declarer to conceal his intentions when he is planning a throw-in. The process of elimination by ruffing out the side suits tends to focus attention on the critical suit, and the defenders ought to be able to work out what is going on. Nevertheless, a defender has to be wide awake to protect his partner from an imperfect throw-in in situations like the following.

(a) A Q 8

10 6 3 | N | K J 9
W   E
S

7 5 4 2

(b) 8 6 2

A Q 10 | N | J 9 5 4
W   E
S

K 7 3

Assume that the declarer has eliminated the side suits and has trumps left in both hands. In diagram (a) he leads a low card from hand and the ball is in West's court. If West contributes a low card, the play of the eight from dummy will restrict the defenders to one trick. In order to protect his partner from this potential throw-in West must play the ten. He has nothing to lose by this, for the defenders are never going to make more than one trick if the declarer has a card as high as the nine in his hand.

Similarly, when a card is led from dummy in diagram (b) East must rise with the jack to give the defenders three tricks.

Unblocking

The main line of defence against throw-in play depends on getting rid of unwanted high cards before they can become a liability. Obviously, if you unblock all your high cards you will be in no danger from a throw-in. You may not make any tricks, but that is another matter.

Beginners have to struggle against a natural reluctance to throw away what appears to be a sure trick. But with experience comes the knowledge that high cards are not always assets and that unblocking is both necessary and safe. In practice, unblocking seldom costs a trick, and when it does the trick usually comes back with interest.

Here are some examples.

A declarer who is planning a throw-in may cash the ace of this suit at an early stage in the play. West should not hesitate to drop his king under the ace. The play is completely safe since East is marked with both the queen and the ten. Holding either of these cards, South would have tackled the suit in a different manner.

```
            J 9 3
            ┌─────┐
            │  N  │
    K 4     │W   E│     Q 10 7 6 2
            │  S  │
            └─────┘
            A 8 5
```

(a)
```
            A 7 2
            ┌─────┐
            │  N  │
 10 9 5 3   │W   E│   Q J 6
            │  S  │
            └─────┘
            K 8 4
```

(b)
```
            A Q 9
            ┌─────┐
            │  N  │
    K J 7   │W   E│   10 6 5 2
            │  S  │
            └─────┘
            8 4 3
```

Suppose, in diagram (a), that East can see that he will have to make a lead that is favourable to the declarer if he wins the third round of this suit. He must start to unblock by playing his queen under dummy's ace on the first round. He can play the jack on the next round and thus avoid the throw-in. West might help by playing his ten on the first round, but even without this aid East should unblock.

The position in (b) is similar. When South leads a low card from hand, West must start to unblock by playing the jack if he judges that he cannot afford to be thrown in. When the declarer finesses the queen and continues with the ace, West can drop his king, relying on his partner for the ten.

It is always dangerous for a defender to leave himself with a singleton ace. Normal principles of defence may have to be abandoned in situations like the following.

```
            K J 7 4
            ┌─────┐
            │  N  │
    A 3     │W   E│   Q 10 9 6 5
            │  S  │
            └─────┘
            8 2
```

When South leads a low card from hand it is normal for West to play low in order to give South a guess. But if West has no safe exit in another suit, he may do better to play the ace at once rather than risk being thrown in on the second round.

Successful unblocking may call for a high degree of foresight on the part of a defender.

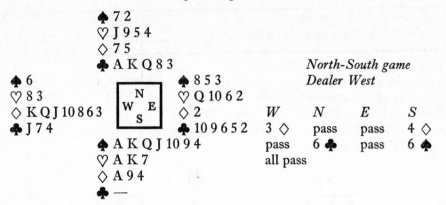

```
              ♠ 7 2
              ♡ J 9 5 4
              ◇ 7 5
              ♣ A K Q 8 3         North-South game
 ♠ 6                      ♠ 8 5 3    Dealer West
 ♡ 8 3          ┌─────┐   ♡ Q 10 6 2
 ◇ K Q J 10 8 6 3  │ N │   ◇ 2         W    N     E    S
 ♣ J 7 4        │W   E│   ♣ 10 9 6 5 2  3 ◇  pass  pass  4 ◇
               │  S  │
               └─────┘
              ♠ A K Q J 10 9 4       pass  6 ♣  pass  6 ♠
              ♡ A K 7               all pass
              ◇ A 9 4
              ♣ —
```

South wins the opening lead of the king of diamonds with the ace, gloomily notes the lack of entries to dummy, and plays the ace of spades on the off-chance that the eight will fall. Well, is he going to make this contract or not?

The answer depends on East's state of mental alertness and on the size of the trump he plays on the first round. If East is half asleep he will play the three, and the declarer will continue with the king of spades, the ace of hearts, and the four of spades to put East on lead. The return of either a club or a heart will enable the declarer to dispose of his three losers in the red suits.

If East is alive to the possibility that the declarer has no clubs, however, he will play the five of spades on the first round, preserving the three to make sure that he can never be thrown in. When the declarer continues with a second top trump, East will continue to unblock by playing the eight, and the declarer will have to settle for one down.

Remember to Count

A defender will sometimes be faced with a choice between two leads, either of which will be to the declarer's advantage. One of the alternatives may not be fatal, however, and a little counting will help to determine which is the lesser of the evils.

South plays in four hearts on the lead of the king of diamonds. He wins with the ace and runs the ten of hearts to East's king. A diamond is returned to the queen, and West exits safely with a trump. The declarer draws trumps with the ace and jack, West discarding a spade, then plays a spade to his king, a spade back to the ace, and a third spade to throw West on lead.

♠ A 9 5
♡ A J 9 3
◇ J 4
♣ K 9 6 5

♠ Q J 7 4   ♠ 10 6 3
♡ 5 2   N   ♡ K 8 4
◇ K Q 10 9 W E ◇ 8 7 6 3 2
♣ Q 7 2   S   ♣ J 8

♠ K 8 2
♡ Q 10 7 6
◇ A 5
♣ A 10 4 3

Now West is at the crossroads. He has nothing but clubs and diamonds left, and a lead of either suit looks highly dangerous. If he takes the trouble to count the declarer's hand, however, he will soon reach the right conclusion. South has shown up with four hearts and three spades. If he has only two diamonds, a diamond return will certainly permit him to ruff in one hand and discard from the other. But in that case South must have four clubs, and a discard in either hand will not help him.

The diamond return is therefore safe, despite appearances. It is only the club return that allows declarer to make his contract.

Make Him Guess

The last recourse of the defender who can see a throw-in looming ahead is deceptive discarding. Much can be achieved in this respect by enterprising defence. The unguarding of kings and queens is not as dangerous as one might think, for it is hard for the declarer to be sure of what is going on.

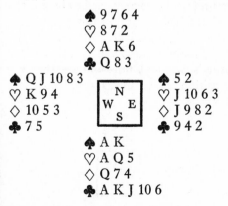

Certainly it is better to give the declarer a guess than to submit meekly to your fate.

South is in six clubs and West leads the queen of spades to the ace. After drawing trumps (West discarding a diamond), South cashes the king of spades, enters dummy with the king of diamonds and ruffs a spade (East discarding a heart). The play of the last trump extracts a heart from West, a heart from dummy and a diamond from East, and South then cashes the queen of diamonds.

[197]

Here is the position at this stage.

South plays his last diamond to dummy's ace, and if West tamely discards a spade he is bound to be thrown in at the next trick. South will continue with the nine of spades from dummy, putting West on lead and compelling him to yield the last two tricks in hearts.

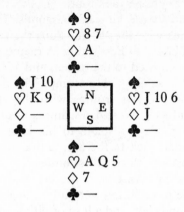

To give the declarer a guess West must discard the nine of hearts on the diamond. Now there will be no question of a throw-in, for the declarer knows that West has two spades and one heart left. South has to decide whether West has in fact bared the king of hearts or whether he never had the king in the first place. The choice lies between playing the ace of hearts or finessing the queen – a difficult decision to have to make with the fate of the slam in the balance.

Finally, when despite all his efforts a defender is thrown in and has to open up a new suit, he may still find a way of giving the declarer a guess.

(a)   A 10 5   (b)   A 10 5

Q 8 3 [N W E S] J 7 6 2   Q J 3 [N W E S] 8 7 6 2

K 9 4   K 9 4

If West has to open the suit in diagram (a), the correct card to lead is the queen. If a small card is led, the declarer has no option but to play for divided honours and he is bound to score three tricks. The lead of the queen gives the declarer a guess. He should probably play for divided honours anyway, winning with dummy's ace and finessing on the way back. But then he may run into the position shown in diagram (b), where again West leads the queen (or the jack).

(c)   K 7 4   (d)   K 7 4

A Q 9 2 [N W E S] J 5 3   Q 9 2 [N W E S] A J 5 3

10 8 6   10 8 6

Suppose that you have to lead from the West seat in diagram (c) and need three tricks from the suit. The situation is critical but not hopeless. Try the effect of leading the queen. If declarer plays low from dummy, continue with the two to give him a further headache.

Perhaps you think that declarer should go up with the king on the second round, but that will do him no good if the cards are distributed as in diagram (d). Should declarer cover the queen with the king on the first round? Then he may encounter diagram (e).

No declarer can hope to do the right thing every time. If you force him to guess, he will sometimes guess incorrectly.

(e)   K 7 4

Q J 9   [N / W   E / S]   A 5 3 2

          10 8 6

14

Trump Coups

The *coup en passant* – trump reduction – the grand coup – the
devil's coup – the smother play – defence against trump coups

We have seen in earlier chapters something of the strange, almost magical
properties of the trump suit. Now we are going to examine in greater depth
the ways in which an extra trump trick can be conjured out of thin air.
Consider this diagram.

Spades are trumps and South requires one of the three remaining
tricks. Clearly he will not get it if the
lead is in the South or the East hand.
And if West is on play, the lead of a
heart to the queen will give his partner
the rest of the tricks. But if the lead is
in dummy, South can always promote
a trump trick for himself by leading
the diamond. If East discards, South
scores a trump immediately, while if
East ruffs the diamond South discards
his losing heart and makes one of his
small trumps at the end.

```
              ♠ 9
              ♡ 5
              ◇ 7
              ♣ —
  ♠ —                    ♠ J 10
  ♡ J 9     ┌──────┐     ♡ Q
  ◇ Q       │  N   │     ◇ —
  ♣ —       │W   E │     ♣ —
            │  S   │
            └──────┘
              ♠ 7 6
              ♡ 8
              ◇ —
              ♣ —
```

Timing is the essence of all trump coups. The sequence of play has to be
so arranged that the lead is in the right place at the right time to transform
a losing trump into a winner.

The Coup en Passant

The play illustrated in that diagram, where the lead of a side suit from
dummy promotes a small trump in the declarer's hand, is known as the
coup en passant.

Here is the hand that gives rise to the ending:

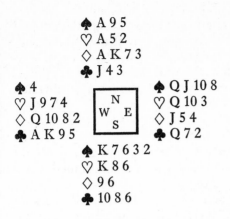

♠ A 9 5
♡ A 5 2
◇ A K 7 3
♣ J 4 3

♠ 4
♡ J 9 7 4
◇ Q 10 8 2
♣ A K 9 5

♠ Q J 10 8
♡ Q 10 3
◇ J 5 4
♣ Q 7 2

♠ K 7 6 3 2
♡ K 8 6
◇ 9 6
♣ 10 8 6

South plays in a contract of two spades and the defenders start with three rounds of clubs. East then plays the queen of spades to dummy's ace and South wins a second spade with his king, learning the bad news when West discards a club.

Now there appear to be three further losers, two spades and a heart, but proper technique causes one of them to disappear. South plays the ace and king of diamonds and ruffs a diamond in hand. After the king of hearts and a heart to the ace, the lead of the seven of diamonds achieves the *coup en passant*.

When the enemy trumps are held behind you there can be no *coup en passant*, of course, but you may still be able to make tricks with your small trumps if the defender on your left has exactly the right distribution.

Let us alter the East and West cards on the last hand.

Again the contract is two spades and again the defenders play three rounds of clubs and switch to trumps. East shows out on the second round of trumps and, as before, you appear to have three further losers.

This time you must hope for West to have four diamonds along with his four trumps. Play the ace and king of diamonds, ruff a diamond, cash the king of hearts, lead a heart to the ace and ruff the fourth diamond. The defenders are left in possession of the field, but only two tricks remain and East's queen of hearts falls uselessly under his partner's master trumps.

♠ A 9 5
♡ A 5 2
◇ A K 7 3
♣ J 4 3

♠ Q J 10 8
♡ J 9
◇ Q 10 8 2
♣ A K 9

♠ 4
♡ Q 10 7 4 3
◇ J 5 4
♣ Q 7 5 2

♠ K 7 6 3 2
♡ K 8 6
◇ 9 6
♣ 10 8 6

Trump Reduction

One of the requirements for a successful *coup en passant*, and indeed for any trump coup, is that at the moment when the critical lead is made from dummy the declarer must hold no more trumps than the defender on his right. If he has too many trumps to begin with, as is usually the case, the declarer must take steps to reduce his trump length by ruffing dummy's side suits at every opportunity. This will be possible only if there are enough entries in dummy – one for each ruff plus one for the final lead that activates the coup. A fine sense of anticipation is called for, because the need to reduce trump length may have to be foreseen before the bad trump break is revealed.

Try your hand at this six diamond contract.

♠ A K 6
♡ J 7 6 3
♢ Q 4
♣ A Q 7 3

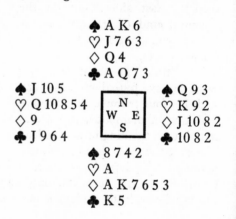

♠ 8 7 4 2
♡ A
♢ A K 7 6 5 3
♣ K 5

West leads the jack of spades to dummy's ace. What do you play at trick two?

It seems natural to test the trumps by cashing the queen of diamonds and continuing with a diamond to the ace or king, but to play in this manner diminishes your chance of success.

Clearly there will be no problem if the trumps break evenly. If either defender has four trumps, however, you will need to score your small trumps separately, and that means planning to reduce your trump length from the beginning. The queen of diamonds is needed as an entry and must not be wasted at trick two. The proper play is a diamond to your ace, the ace of hearts, and a diamond back to the queen. Now if someone shows out you are in a position to do something about it. Let us fill in the defenders' hands and see one of the distributions we are guarding against.

After winning the queen of diamonds, you ruff a heart, play three rounds of clubs discarding a spade from hand, ruff another heart, and return to dummy with the king of spades. Now your trumps have been reduced to the same length East's, and the lead of either the heart or the club from the table gains you a twelfth trick in the ending shown below.

♠ A K 6
♡ J 7 6 3
♢ Q 4
♣ A Q 7 3

♠ J 10 5
♡ Q 10 8 5 4
♢ 9
♣ J 9 6 4

♠ Q 9 3
♡ K 9 2
♢ J 10 8 2
♣ 10 8 2

♠ 8 7 4 2
♡ A
♢ A K 7 6 5 3
♣ K 5

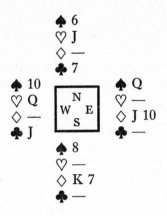

If East discards the queen of spades, you score the twelfth trick at once with the seven of diamonds. If East ruffs, you discard your spade and claim the last two tricks.

The main feature of the *coup en passant* is that you have an inescapable trump loser, but that is not the case in most trump coups. The usual position is that you have a major tenace over the defender on your right and could pick up his trumps by finessing but for the fact that dummy has no trump to lead for the finesse.

West leads the king of spades against your contract of four hearts. He continues with the ace of spades and then switches to the jack of clubs. You win with the king and play the ace and king of hearts, learning the bad news that East has the guarded jack. However, your contract is secure provided that East has at least three clubs.

You continue with the queen of clubs, lead your third club to the ace, and ruff a spade in hand. A diamond to dummy's ace is followed by a further spade ruff. Now, having reduced to trump parity with East, you simply exit with your diamond and claim the last two tricks with the queen and ten of hearts.

Here your trump reduction play prepared the ground for a throw-in, which is quite a common ending in such situations. No special foresight was needed, for the trump break revealed itself before you were called upon to make use of dummy's entries.

Suppose, however, that after cashing his two top spades West switches to a diamond instead of a club. Now, in order to succeed, you must go up with the ace of diamonds and ruff a spade before testing the trumps.

Finally, suppose that West switches to a diamond after cashing *one* top spade. This is the killing defence, for at this stage there is nothing for you to ruff to start your trump reduction. True, you can hold up the ace of diamonds, but East will then play a second spade, removing your last exit card and your chance of a throw-in ending. A switch back to diamonds or

[203]

to clubs will then defeat the contract (barring a double-dummy trump finesse), for you are short of an entry in dummy to achieve your trump coup. You may shorten your trumps twice, but you have no further entry for the final lead through East's trump holding.

It is often a good idea in defence to attack one of dummy's entries at a point in time when the declarer has no opportunity of reducing his trump length by ruffing.

We shall be looking more closely into the subject of trump coup defence in the latter part of this chapter. Meanwhile, back to the problems of the declarer.

♠ Q J
♡ A 9 4
♢ 10 6 5 2
♣ A 8 7 2

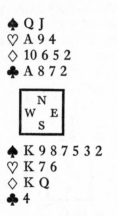

♠ K 9 8 7 5 3 2
♡ K 7 6
♢ K Q
♣ 4

You play in four spades after East has opened the bidding with a strong (15–17) no trump. West leads the queen of clubs to dummy's ace. How should you continue?

It looks like ten easy tricks, but there can be no excuse for carelessness. It is not impossible for East to hold all four missing trumps, and the correct technique is to anticipate the need for a trump reduction by ruffing a club at trick two.

Then lead a spade to dummy's jack, and your heart need not sink when West shows out. You can win the heart return in hand and lead the king of diamonds to East's ace. Win the next heart with the ace, ruff a club, cash the queen of diamonds, lead a spade to the queen and ruff another club. Now you are reduced to K 9 in trumps, and by exiting with your losing heart you can make sure of the last two tricks.

The full hand:

This time the initial lead of a heart would have frustrated your efforts, but it is hard to blame West for not finding it.

It is sometimes possible to achieve a trump throw-in when the trumps are held behind you, but only if the need for trump-reducing play is spotted in good time.

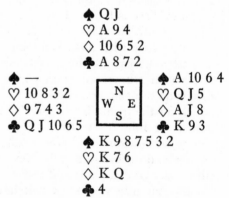

♠ 7 5
♡ A Q 7 6 2
◇ 9 6 4
♣ 8 5 4

♠ A K 9
♡ 4
◇ A K Q
♣ A K 10 9 3 2

West leads the jack of hearts against your contract of six clubs, and you win the first trick with dummy's ace. What now?

There will be thirteen tricks if the trumps break 2–2, and no trouble in making twelve tricks if they break 3–1. All that you have to worry about, therefore, is the possibility of a 4–0 break. If East has four trumps, you will still succeed when he also has at least three spades. But if West has all four trumps your only chance will be to find him with a 3–3–3–4 distribution, and you should prepare for this contingency by ruffing a heart at trick two.

If East shows out on your next play of the ace of clubs, you can continue with three rounds of diamonds, three rounds of spades, ruffing in dummy, and a further heart ruff. You are now down to K 10 9 in trumps, and the lead of the ten or nine throws West in to give you the last two tricks. The full hand:

More difficult to handle are those trump coups where the declarer can afford to lose no more tricks. There is then no question of a throw-in, and the declarer has to arrange to lead from dummy when his trump reduction has been completed.

♠ 7 5
♡ A Q 7 6 2
◇ 9 6 4
♣ 8 5 4

♠ Q 8 4
♡ J 10 8
◇ 10 7 2
♣ Q J 7 6

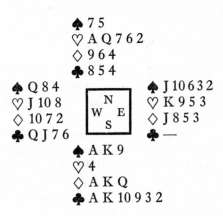

♠ J 10 6 3 2
♡ K 9 5 3
◇ J 8 5 3
♣ —

♠ A K 9
♡ 4
◇ A K Q
♣ A K 10 9 3 2

West opens with a weak two bid in spades, and you eventually play in six hearts. East overtakes the opening lead of the king of spades with his ace and returns a spade, forcing dummy to ruff.

Clearly the best chance is to finesse in trumps, and the only question is whether or not to cash the king of hearts first. Cashing the king will bring in the points when West has a singleton queen, but if West has a singleton it is four times

♠ 5
♡ K 6 3
◇ A K Q 8 7 2
♣ A 8 5

♠ K Q J 9 6 2
♡ 4
◇ 10 5
♣ J 10 9 2

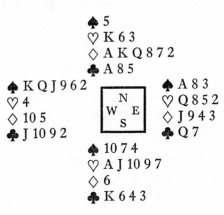

♠ A 8 3
♡ Q 8 5 2
◇ J 9 4 3
♣ Q 7

♠ 10 7 4
♡ A J 10 9 7
◇ 6
♣ K 6 4 3

as likely to be a small card. In that case you will have to coup East's trumps, and you cannot afford to cash the king of hearts which will be needed as an entry to dummy at a later stage.

The correct play at trick three is a low heart for a finesse of the nine. When the finesse succeeds you can continue with a diamond to the ace and a diamond ruff. This serves the dual purpose of establishing the diamond suit and reducing your trumps to parity with East's hypothetical four. Now a trump to dummy's king will reveal the position. If both defenders follow, you can ruff a diamond, draw the last trump and claim the remainder.

On the actual lie of the cards West shows out, and now you play the diamonds from the top, discarding a spade and two clubs from your hand. If East ruffs the fifth diamond, you can over-ruff, draw the last trump and claim. If East discards on the fifth diamond, you can cash the ace of clubs before playing the sixth diamond from dummy. No matter what East does, the rest of the tricks are yours.

The Grand Coup

A coup in which trump reduction is achieved by ruffing winners rather than losers is designated a Grand Coup. It hardly deserves this lofty title, for the mechanics of the play are exactly the same as in a normal coup. Here is an example.

You play in seven clubs, and West leads the eight of spades to your queen. All looks well until West discards a heart on the second round of clubs. Now you must plan to reduce your trumps twice, and your first move is to play three rounds of hearts, ruffing the third heart in hand. The fact that you are ruffing a winner rather than a loser is neither here nor there.

Having ruffed a heart, you revert to spades, discarding two diamonds from hand when East refuses to ruff.

	♠ A K J 10 5	
	♡ K Q 3	
	◇ A Q 5	
	♣ 7 3	
♠ 8 7 3		♠ 9 6 4
♡ J 9 6 5 4	N	♡ 10 8 2
◇ J 8 6 2	W E	◇ K 9 4
♣ 4	S	♣ J 8 5 2
	♠ Q 2	
	♡ A 7	
	◇ 10 7 3	
	♣ A K Q 10 9 6	

Then you complete your trump reduction by ruffing the fifth spade (another winner) in hand as East discards a second diamond. Finally, a diamond to the ace puts the lead in the right place at the right time, and East's J 8 of trumps are trapped ahead of your Q 10.

It is worth noting that a diamond lead would in practice defeat the contract irrespective of the position of the king. With so many other chances, declarer would hardly rely on an immediate diamond finesse, and as soon as the ace of diamonds has gone dummy is an entry short for the trump coup.

The Devil's Coup

This is a rare situation in which an apparently certain defensive trump trick is made to disappear as though by black magic.

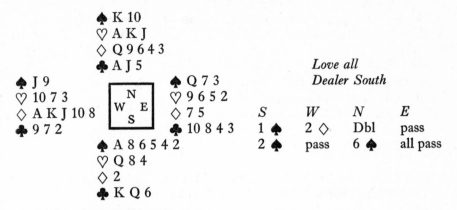

```
                    ♠ K 10
                    ♡ A K J
                    ◇ Q 9 6 4 3
                    ♣ A J 5
♠ J 9                              ♠ Q 7 3
♡ 10 7 3            N               ♡ 9 6 5 2
◇ A K J 10 8    W     E             ◇ 7 5
♣ 9 7 2            S               ♣ 10 8 4 3
                    ♠ A 8 6 5 4 2
                    ♡ Q 8 4
                    ◇ 2
                    ♣ K Q 6
```

Love all
Dealer South

S	W	N	E
1 ♠	2 ◇	Dbl	pass
2 ♠	pass	6 ♠	all pass

Annoyed at having his double of two diamonds removed, North raises to six spades 'to teach you a lesson'.

West leads the king of diamonds and switches to a heart, and the sight of dummy brings you little joy. At first glance there appears to be no way of avoiding a trump loser. Even Q J doubleton does not help, for the other defender will score a trick with his 9 x x.

Still, if you have seen this sort of situation before, and perhaps even if you haven't, you may decide to proceed as far as possible with a trump reduction. Winning the heart switch with the jack, you ruff a diamond, return to the jack of clubs, and ruff another diamond. Suppose that East discards a club on the third diamond. You do not want to give him the chance to discard again in that suit, so you play the king of clubs and continue with the queen of clubs to the ace. A further diamond ruff is followed by the ace and king of hearts, and the position has been reduced to the following cards.

When the last diamond is led from dummy the defenders are caught in a truly fiendish coup. If East ruffs low, you can over-ruff and score the last two tricks with the top trumps. If East ruffs with the queen he fares no better. You over-ruff with the ace and finesse against the jack on the next round to land your slam. The defenders' 'sure' trump trick has melted away.

Most players manage to get through a lifetime at the bridge table without encountering a Devil's Coup, and the same can be said of the next variation.

```
              ♠ K 10
              ♡ —
              ◇ Q
              ♣ —
♠ J 9                      ♠ Q 7 3
♡ —        ┌─────┐        ♡ —
◇ A        │ N   │        ◇ —
♣ —        │W   E│        ♣ —
           │  S  │
           └─────┘
              ♠ A 8 6
              ♡ —
              ◇ —
              ♣ —
```

The Smother Play

This is another type of 'vanishing trump' trick which makes more appearances in bridge columns than at the card table.

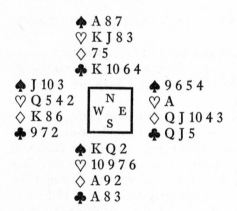

```
              ♠ A 8 7
              ♡ K J 8 3
              ◇ 7 5
              ♣ K 10 6 4
♠ J 10 3                    ♠ 9 6 5 4
♡ Q 5 4 2    ┌─────┐        ♡ A
◇ K 8 6      │ N   │        ◇ Q J 10 4 3
♣ 9 7 2      │W   E│        ♣ Q J 5
             │  S  │
             └─────┘
              ♠ K Q 2
              ♡ 10 9 7 6
              ◇ A 9 2
              ♣ A 8 3
```

The contract is four hearts, and West leads the jack of spades to your king. When you run the six of hearts, East wins with the ace and switches to the queen of diamonds. You let him hold this trick, but win the next diamond and run the ten of hearts. Annoyingly, East discards a diamond.

Now the contract looks impossible, for if you draw the rest of the trumps you will score only nine tricks before you have to let the defenders in to make hay with their diamonds. And if you duck a club before drawing trumps, a further diamond lead will force you to ruff in dummy, establishing a sure trick for West's queen of hearts.

Your only chance, in fact, is to ruff the third diamond yourself. Then cash ace and queen of spades, ace and king of clubs, and exit with a third club, hoping that East has to win.

This is the position when you lead the third club:

East wins with the queen of clubs and has the choice of returning a diamond or a spade. It makes no difference which he chooses, for you ruff in hand and West's queen is smothered between the weight of your trumps and the singleton king in dummy.

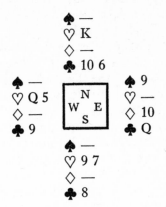

DEFENCE AGAINST TRUMP COUPS

The first line of defence, when a trump coup appears to be in the offing, lies in refusing to offer gratuitous aid to the declarer. A forcing defence is taboo, for declarer will be only too happy to have a chance of shortening his trump length.

If there is no obvious way of launching a direct attack on dummy's entries, make a passive switch rather than risk giving the declarer a chance to ruff. These are much the same defensive tactics as those recommended against throw-in play, although the hazards are different. In throw-in positions a ruff may help declarer to eliminate a side suit; in coup endings it will help him to shorten his trumps.

Here is a common defensive situation:

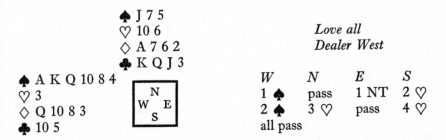

You lead the king of spades on which partner plays the nine. When you continue with the ace of spades, both East and South follow suit. Now what?

It is not too hard to visualize that partner may have four hearts, and that declarer may be unable to pick them up except by trump coup. At all costs you must keep your thumb away from the queen of spades. A diamond switch, attacking the entry in dummy, is the best shot.

The hidden hands:

As it happens either a diamond or a club switch will serve to defeat the contract, for the declarer is short of an entry in dummy to bring off his coup. After a spade continuation at trick three, however, South has an easy time. He ruffs, leads a club to the king and ace, wins the club return on the table and finesses twice in trumps.

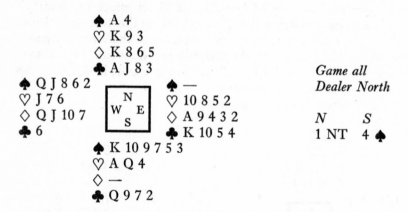

♠ 9 3
♡ K 8 5 4
◇ J 9 4
♣ A 9 8 2

♠ 6 2
♡ A Q J 9 7 2
◇ K 5
♣ 7 6 4

When you show out on the second round, all that he has to do to achieve trump parity with East is to cross to dummy in clubs and ruff the fourth club. The king of diamonds is then followed by a diamond to the ace, and East's trumps are picked up on the way back.

A defender holding a stack of trumps behind the declarer will normally expect to defeat the contract, but he may be disappointed if he fails to guide the defence along the right lines. The opening lead can be of crucial importance in such situations.

```
                    ♠ A 4
                    ♡ K 9 3
                    ◇ K 8 6 5
                    ♣ A J 8 3
  ♠ Q J 8 6 2               ♠ —                Game all
  ♡ J 7 6          N        ♡ 10 8 5 2         Dealer North
  ◇ Q J 10 7    W     E     ◇ A 9 4 3 2
  ♣ 6              S        ♣ K 10 5 4         N       S
                    ♠ K 10 9 7 5 3             1 NT    4 ♠
                    ♡ A Q 4
                    ◇ —
                    ♣ Q 9 7 2
```

Given the bidding and shown only the West cards, nine players out of ten would pick the automatic and 'safe' lead of the queen of diamonds. But that is quite the wrong defence in view of West's trump holding. From the start West should be concerned with reducing his *own* trump length, and to that end he should lead his singleton club.

Observe what will happen on a diamond lead. The declarer will ruff and lead a spade to dummy's ace. On discovering the bad news, he will ruff another diamond, play three rounds of hearts ending in dummy, and ruff a third diamond. A club to the ace will enable him to ruff a fourth diamond with the ten of spades, and the king of spades will be his tenth trick.

On a club lead South has no chance. Even if he goes up with the ace and ruffs a diamond immediately, he can make no more than nine tricks.

A surfeit of trumps can be a great embarrassment to a defender, for there is always a danger of being thrown in to make a fatal return.

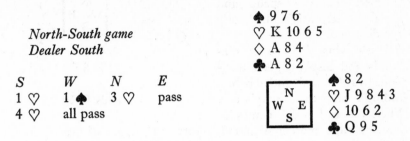

North-South game
Dealer South

♠ 9 7 6
♡ K 10 6 5
◇ A 8 4
♣ A 8 2

♠ 8 2
♡ J 9 8 4 3
◇ 10 6 2
♣ Q 9 5

S	W	N	E
1 ♡	1 ♠	3 ♡	pass
4 ♡	all pass		

West leads the queen of spades to the declarer's ace. South plays the ace of hearts, wincing when West discards a diamond, and continues with the king of diamonds, a diamond to the ace, and a diamond ruff in hand. Then he plays the king of spades followed by a small spade, which West covers with the ten. How do you play?

It seems natural to discard a club, but that defence cannot defeat the contract. Think about it. You need four tricks, which can only be two clubs and two trumps, so partner's clubs will have to be at least as good as K 10 x. If you discard a club on this trick, West will no doubt switch to clubs, and you may discard your queen under dummy's ace. But you will be forced to ruff the third round of clubs and return a trump into dummy's tenace, giving South his tenth trick.

♠ Q J 10 4 3
♡ —
◇ Q J 9 7 3
♣ K J 10

♠ A K 5
♡ A Q 7 2
◇ K 5
♣ 7 6 4 3

You must therefore ruff your partner's winning spade and switch to clubs yourself. Partner will be able to win the third round, and you will score a further trick in trumps. You can call this a defensive Grand Coup if you like, but it is really just a matter of common sense to avoid a throw-in by reducing your trumps to parity with dummy.

Sometimes the only way a defender can shorten his trump holding is by under-ruffing.

North opens one diamond, East overcalls one spade, and South eventually buys the contract in three clubs. You lead the seven of spades to your partner's king. East continues with the ace and then the three of spades, and you ruff and switch obediently to a diamond.

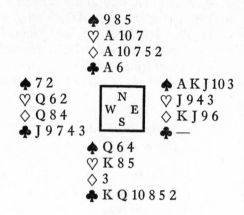

♠ 9 8 5
♡ A 10 7
◇ A 10 7 5 2
♣ A 6

♠ 7 2
♡ Q 6 2
◇ Q 8 4
♣ J 9 7 4 3

♠ A K J 10 3
♡ J 9 4 3
◇ K J 9 6
♣ —

♠ Q 6 4
♡ K 8 5
◇ 3
♣ K Q 10 8 5 2

South wins the ace of diamonds and displays good technique by ruffing a diamond before leading a club to dummy's ace. When the bad break comes to light, he ruffs another diamond, returns to the ace of hearts, and ruffs a further diamond with the queen of clubs. With you still to find a discard from the West hand, the position is as shown.

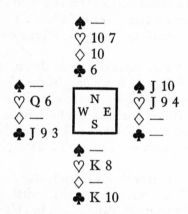

♠ —
♡ 10 7
◇ 10
♣ 6

♠ —
♡ Q 6
◇ —
♣ J 9 3

♠ J 10
♡ J 9 4
◇ —
♣ —

♠ —
♡ K 8
◇ —
♣ K 10

It is not hard to see what will happen if you discard a heart. The play of the king and another heart will force you to ruff, and you will have to return a trump into South's tenace. To avoid the throw-in you must discard a trump on this trick. By under-ruffing, you retain trump parity with South, and when he continues with the king of hearts you can keep up the good work by unblocking your queen. Partner is then able to win the third round of hearts, and the lead comes through the declarer's trump tenace at the end to put the contract one down.

Finally, the defenders should bear in mind that it usually takes a plentiful supply of entries in dummy to bring off a trump coup. The chance to kill one of those entries should not be allowed to slip.

South plays in a shaky contract of six hearts, and West leads the ten of spades which runs to the king. The heart finesse loses and East returns a heart to the ace.

♠ A J 5
♡ A Q
◇ A J 9
♣ J 10 9 4 3

♠ 10 9 8 4   ♠ Q 6 2
♡ 3   ♡ K 10 6 2
◇ Q 10 8 5 3   ◇ 7 6 4
♣ 7 6 5   ♣ K 8 2

```
        N
   W         E
        S
```

♠ K 7 3
♡ J 9 8 7 5 4
◇ K 2
♣ A Q

The declarer finesses the queen of clubs successfully, cashes the ace of clubs, and then leads the two of diamonds. When West plays low, he finesses the jack of diamonds, ruffs out the king of clubs, and plays his king of diamonds to dummy's ace. An established club is then played from the table. East cannot afford to ruff, and therefore discards a spade or a diamond. The declarer discards a spade, ruffs the nine of diamonds, and returns to dummy with the ace of spades to pick up East's trumps.

Very pretty, but at the point where South led the two of diamonds West should have asked himself what was going on. Why should declarer play on diamonds instead of drawing the outstanding trumps? There could be only one logical answer. The declarer must be unable to draw the trumps without loss and must be planning a trump coup against East. If West had reached that conclusion, he might have found the killing play of the queen of diamonds on declarer's two. This denies South two diamond entries in dummy and makes the coup unworkable.

It must also be said that East, who knew the position rather better, could have helped his partner out by returning a low diamond instead of a heart at trick three. It would then have been easier for West to find the play of the queen of diamonds.

15

Squeeze Play

Squeeze card – menaces – entries – timing – positional and automatic squeezes – isolating the menace – a split two-card menace – inversion – the double squeeze – squeeze variations – squeeze defence – attacking an entry – rubbing out a menace – upsetting the timing – discarding technique

You may not yet have experienced the thrill of inflicting a squeeze on your opponents, but I expect you know what it feels like to be on the receiving end. It is rather like being put through a giant mangle. You have to watch in helpless agony as your apparently sure tricks vanish in front of your eyes.

What is a squeeze? The only accurate definition is the broadest one possible. A squeeze at bridge occurs when a player is forced to make a discard that is disadvantageous to his side.

Squeeze play is made possible by the fact that the declarer and dummy between them hold twice as many cards as any one opponent. A defender who is saddled with the task of keeping winners or stoppers in more than one suit may therefore find himself unable to cope. Outflanked and outnumbered by the menaces around him, he is compelled to release a vital card. Consider this diagram:

West has the job of protecting both hearts and spades, but when South leads the ace of clubs he has to surrender. Pressure of space squeezes either the ace of hearts or a spade out of his hand, and the declarer makes all three tricks.

In this diagram all the essential features of the squeeze can be seen. Let us examine them one by one.

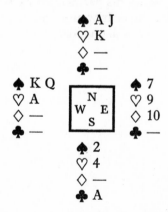

Squeeze Card. This is the card that applies the lethal pressure. Very often

the squeeze card is the declarer's last trump, or the last of a string of winners at no trumps.

Menaces. These are cards which may be promoted to winning rank by the forced discard of the defender. There are three points to remember about menaces:
1. The same defender must be threatened in two suits, and one of the menaces must be accompanied by a card of winning rank. In the diagram West's ace of hearts is threatened by the king, and his king and queen of spades are threatened by the ace and jack. The heart king is a one-card menace, and the ace and jack of spades a two-card menace. Note that a two-card menace consists of a winner and a loser in the same suit.
2. At least one of the menaces must lie 'over' the defender to be squeezed. If West is to be squeezed one of the menaces must be in the North hand, while if East is to be squeezed one of the menaces must be in the South hand.
3. The two-card menace must lie in the hand opposite the squeeze card. The reason for this becomes clear when we examine the next requirement for the squeeze.

Entries. It is no use forcing a defender to discard a winner unless there is some means of access to the established menace card. The master card of the two-card menace provides the required entry. In order to complete the link, of course, you must also have a small card of this suit in the hand containing the squeeze card.

Timing. If you look at West's cards in the diagram you will see that they are all performing a vital role at the time when the squeeze card is led. They are what we term 'busy' cards. This is necessary if the squeeze is to succeed, for by our definition the forced discard must damage the defender's hand.

Turn your attention to the North and South cards and you will see that the declarer has two winners and only one loser. In all basic squeezes this is an essential feature of the timing. **At the point when the squeeze card is led, declarer must be in a position to win all the remaining tricks except one.** In other words, he must not have more than one loser when he leads his squeeze card. For this reason the basic squeezes are sometimes referred to as one-loser squeezes.

Let us alter the diagram by adding a small diamond to each hand.

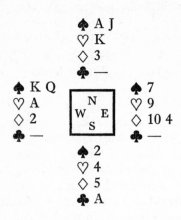

♠ A J
♡ K
◇ 3
♣ —

♠ K Q   ♠ 7
♡ A   ♡ 9
◇ 2   ◇ 10 4
♣ —   ♣ —

♠ 2
♡ 4
◇ 5
♣ A

In this four-card ending South still has two winners, but he also has two losers and it is clear that the squeeze does not work. The presence of the extra loser creates space for an 'idle' card in the defender's hand, and West escapes the pressure by discarding the two of diamonds on the ace of clubs.

When planning a squeeze, therefore, you must time the play carefully in the early stages, conceding the required number of tricks to the defenders in order to bring your loser count down to one. This process is known as 'rectifying the count'.

Positional and Automatic Squeezes

Before leaving our formal examination of how the squeeze machinery works and getting to grips with some practical examples, we must take note of the effect of re-aligning the menaces. Let us have another look at our original diagram:

(a)

♠ A J
♡ K
◇ —
♣ —

♠ K Q   ♠ 7
♡ A   ♡ 9
◇ —   ◇ 10
♣ —   ♣ —

♠ 2
♡ 4
◇ —
♣ A

(b)

♠ A J
♡ K
◇ —
♣ —

♠ 7   ♠ K Q
♡ 9   ♡ A
◇ 10   ◇ —
♣ —   ♣ —

♠ 2
♡ 4
◇ —
♣ A

In (a) it is clear that the squeeze succeeds by virtue of the position of the enemy high cards, trapped between the squeeze card and the menaces. Playing after West, dummy can keep the menace card that has been promoted and discard the other one.

This type of squeeze, where both menaces lie opposite the squeeze card, is termed a positional squeeze. Just like a finesse, it depends on finding the enemy honours favourably placed.

Interchange the East and West cards, as in diagram (b), and the squeeze fails, for dummy has to play ahead of East and one of the menaces has to be discarded. In fact we can forecast the failure of this squeeze by observing that neither of the menaces lies 'over' East.

The value of the positional squeeze is therefore limited by the fact that it is effective only against the defender on the left of the squeeze card.

When discussing menaces earlier, we noted that the two-card menace must lie in the hand opposite the squeeze card. There is no reason why the one-card menace should do so, however. If we bring the one-card menace into the same hand as the squeeze card, we create an entirely new situation.

On the lead of the ace of clubs, the four of hearts is thrown from dummy and East is squeezed. There is no positional factor in this squeeze, which works equally well if the East and West cards are interchanged. This is known as an automatic squeeze. Either defender is squeezed if he holds all the key cards, since one of the menaces lies over each defender.

The main difference between the two types of squeeze can be summed up as follows: in a positional squeeze, where both menaces lie in the same hand, one of these menaces must always be discarded on the squeeze card. The choice depends on the discard of the defender.

	♠ A J	
	♡ 4	
	◇ —	
	♣ —	
♠ 7	N	♠ K Q
♡ 9	W E	♡ A
◇ 10	S	◇ —
♣ —		♣ —
	♠ 2	
	♡ K	
	◇ —	
	♣ A	

In an automatic squeeze, the hand opposite the squeeze card is relieved of the burden of holding both menaces. Consequently, it always contains an idle card that can be thrown on the squeeze card irrespective of the card played by the defender. It is this fact that permits the squeeze to operate against either defender.

Clearly the automatic squeeze is the less restricted form, and one would expect its frequency of success to be roughly twice that of the positional squeeze. This is borne out in practice, and if a player has a choice between positional and automatic he should usually opt for the more flexible automatic form by trying to arrange for the menaces to be divided between the two hands.

Enough of theory for the moment. Let us have a look at some example hands.

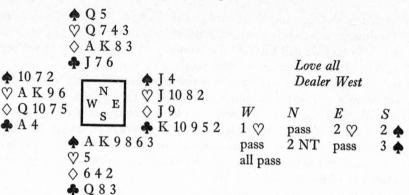

♠ Q 5
♡ Q 7 4 3
◇ A K 8 3
♣ J 7 6

♠ 10 7 2   ♠ J 4
♡ A K 9 6   ♡ J 10 8 2
◇ Q 10 7 5   ◇ J 9
♣ A 4   ♣ K 10 9 5 2

♠ A K 9 8 6 3
♡ 5
◇ 6 4 2
♣ Q 8 3

Love all
Dealer West

W	N	E	S
1 ♡	pass	2 ♡	2 ♠
pass	2 NT	pass	3 ♠
all pass			

West leads the king of hearts and switches to the ace and another club. East wins the second club with the king and plays another club for his partner to ruff, and West then leads the five of diamonds to dummy's ace. How should you proceed?

The first step, naturally, is to count your winners. Six trumps and two diamonds give you a total of eight tricks, and the ninth can come only from a squeeze. The timing is right at this stage, for the defenders have already taken their four tricks and you have only one remaining loser.

Can you identify the menaces? Dummy's queen of hearts will serve as a one-card menace, and the king and eight of diamonds will have to be the two-card menace. With both menaces in dummy only a positional squeeze is available, but the opening lead makes it certain that the ace of hearts is in the right place. There is no guarantee that West has four diamonds, but you must assume this to be the case since there is nothing else to play for.

The two-card menace is opposite the squeeze card (your last trump), making the entry position satisfactory. Just run the trumps and reduce to the three-card ending shown here.

The play of the last trump forces West to surrender.

Many players are deterred from making any serious attempt to master squeeze play by the idea that it involves watching each discard with the eyes of a lynx and performing prodigious feats of memory in counting every suit. Nothing could be further from the truth. Once you have learned

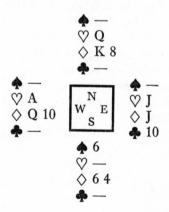

♠ —
♡ Q
◇ K 8
♣ —

♠ —   ♠ —
♡ A   ♡ J
◇ Q 10   ◇ J
♣ —   ♣ 10

♠ 6
♡ —
◇ 6 4
♣ —

the basic forms of the squeeze, the demands on your concentration are minimal.

In this hand, for instance, there is no need to watch the discards in the diamond suit, no need to count diamonds at all. The only card you have to look out for is the ace of hearts, and it would take a very short-sighted or inattentive declarer to fail to notice that card. After West has played to the last trump, if the ace of hearts has not popped out, you simply discard the queen of hearts from the table and play diamonds, hoping for the best.

This is the correct procedure in all basic squeeze play. Watch only for the card or cards that can beat your one-card menace and leave the long menace to look after itself. Remember that in a positional squeeze the one-card menace is always discarded on the squeeze card unless it has been promoted to winning rank.

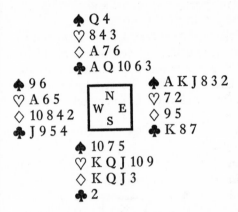

East opens with a bid of one spade and you eventually play in four hearts. West leads the nine of spades to his partner's jack. A trump comes back and your king is allowed to hold the trick. You play a spade to the queen and king, and East produces his second trump. West wins and plays a third round of trumps, putting paid to your plan of ruffing the third spade in dummy. What do you do now?

The club finesse is one way of trying for the tenth trick, and the alternative is a squeeze. The long menace in clubs is opposite the squeeze card (your last trump) and the spade menace is in your own hand, so the squeeze will function automatically if East has the king of clubs. Often the choice between finesse and squeeze is a hard one, but here it is clear-cut since bidding marks the club king with East. Just play off your red winners to apply pressure in the ending shown here.

East has no answer when the heart nine is led. If the spade ace does not appear, lead the club to dummy's ace and the king must fall.

```
              ♠ —
              ♡ —
              ◇ —
              ♣ A Q 10
    ♠ —                      ♠ A
    ♡ —         N            ♡ —
    ◇ —      W     E         ◇ —
    ♣ J 9 5     S            ♣ K 8
              ♠ 10
              ♡ 9
              ◇ —
              ♣ 2
```

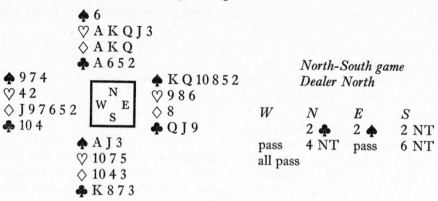

West leads the nine of spades to his partner's queen, and you see that North's eccentric bidding has landed you in the wrong contract.

Your only chance is to play for a black suit squeeze against East, but the timing needs adjusting. At the moment you have eleven winners and two losers, and you know that the squeeze will operate only when you are in a position to take all the remaining tricks but one. To rectify the count, therefore, you permit East to win the first trick with the queen of spades. He promptly switches to the queen of clubs.

The squeeze card will be in dummy this time, so you must arrange for the two-card menace in clubs to be in your own hand. Accordingly, you win in dummy with the ace, come to hand with the ten of hearts, cash the ace of spades for a club discard, and run the red suits to inflict the agony.

Be sure that you appreciate that the squeeze does not work if you win the first trick with the ace of spades. Play it over and check for yourself.

Isolating the Menace

The menaces needed for a squeeze are not always sitting there waiting to be used. Often it takes a little preparatory work to establish a menace against a particular defender.

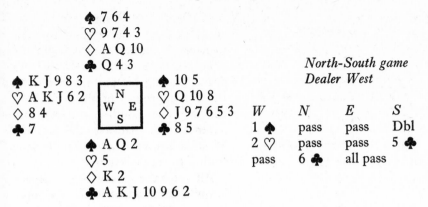

North-South game
Dealer West

W	N	E	S
1 ♠	pass	pass	Dbl
2 ♡	pass	pass	5 ♣
pass	6 ♣	all pass	

West leads the king of hearts and then switches to the seven of clubs. How should you play?

There are eleven top tricks and, since the spade finesse is sure to be wrong, the twelfth can come only from a squeeze. With heart and spade menaces in opposite hands, you should be able to set up an automatic squeeze position if West has a five-card heart suit.

There are a couple of points to watch, however. Firstly, the two-card spade menace is in your own hand, which means that the squeeze card must lie in dummy. In other words, the trumps will have to be run before the diamonds. Secondly, you do not have an effective heart menace against West at the moment, for it is likely that East will have at least one heart higher than the nine. But it should be possible to ruff out East's stoppers in the suit, thus establishing the nine as a real threat to West. This process is known as *isolating the menace.*

Two entries to dummy are needed for the two heart ruffs, and since you cannot touch the diamond entry until later both of these entries must be found in trumps. Win the first trump with the queen, taking care to unblock the six from your hand. Ruff a heart high, cash the trump ace, lead the two of trumps to dummy's four, ruff another heart high, and play the remaining trumps, discarding two spades from dummy.

Now three rounds of diamonds will make West unhappy. If he retains a master heart you will know that he has bared his spade king.

A Split Two-Card Menace

In a positional squeeze it is permissible for the elements of the two-card menace to be divided between the two hands, provided that the winner is still in the hand opposite the squeeze card.

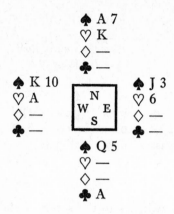

♠ A 7
♡ K
◇ —
♣ —

♠ K 10   ♠ J 3
♡ A   ♡ 6
◇ —   ◇ —
♣ —   ♣ —

♠ Q 5
♡ —
◇ —
♣ A

If South had a singleton or two small cards in spades, the two-card menace in dummy would not be effective. West could safely throw a spade, leaving his partner to control the second round of the suit. It is the fact that South has queen and another spade that saves the day, and West is squeezed as before on the lead of the ace of clubs.

Although the split two-card menace is quite common, it is effective only in positional squeezes which limits its value somewhat.

You play in six diamonds after West has opened with a bid of one heart. The king of hearts is led to dummy's ace. Plan the play.

Again you are a trick short of your contract, and you must aim to squeeze West using the split two-card menace in clubs. The heart menace can be isolated by ruffing out East's stopper, and you should start the process by ruffing a heart at trick two. Continue with the queen of diamonds, for the diamond ace must be smoked out be-

♠ 9 4
♡ A 7 5 4
◇ K 8 3
♣ A 9 5 2

♠ 10 6 3   ♠ 8 7 5 2
♡ K Q 10 9 3   ♡ J 8 2
◇ A 4   ◇ 9 5
♣ K 10 6   ♣ J 8 7 3

♠ A K Q J
♡ 6
◇ Q J 10 7 6 2
♣ Q 4

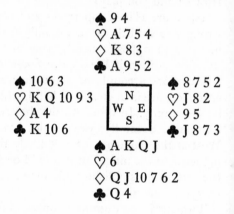

fore you ruff another heart. Suppose that West takes his ace and returns a trump. You win in dummy, ruff another heart, and play out your trumps and spades to squeeze West into submission.

In automatic squeeze play a split two-card menace is not only useless but positively dangerous. Consider the following diagram.

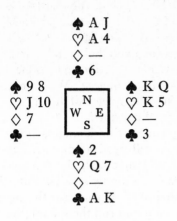

♠ A J
♡ A 4
◇ —
♣ 6

♠ 9 8
♡ J 10
◇ 7
♣ —

♠ K Q
♡ K 5
◇ —
♣ 3

♠ 2
♡ Q 7
◇ —
♣ A K

Observe what happens if South plays off the ace and king of clubs. Dummy has no idle card to play on the second club. If the four of hearts is discarded, the heart suit is blocked and East escapes the squeeze by baring his king of hearts.

To inflict the squeeze in this five-card ending, South must first unblock by cashing the master card of the split two-card menace. After a heart to the ace and a club return, the menaces are properly arranged for the automatic squeeze. This simple unblocking play has the grandiose title of the Vienna Coup.

West leads the queen of hearts against your contract of four spades. East captures the king with his ace and returns the two of hearts to his partner's jack. West switches to the nine of diamonds. When you play low from the table, East wins with the queen and returns a trump. Take it from there.

East is marked with the king of diamonds, and if the clubs do not break you must hope that it is East who has the length, for then you will have a minor suit squeeze. But be careful! There is a split two-card menace in diamonds, and that is a

♠ K 10 7
♡ K 6
◇ A J 8 4
♣ A K Q 3

♠ 9 8 5 2
♡ Q J 9 5 4
◇ 9 3
♣ J 5

♠ 6
♡ A 8 3 2
◇ K Q 7 2
♣ 10 9 6 4

♠ A Q J 4 3
♡ 10 7
◇ 10 6 5
♣ 8 7 2

treacherous sort of thing to possess when you are planning an automatic squeeze.

You must employ the Vienna Coup to overcome the blockage in diamonds. After two rounds of trumps lead the six of diamonds to dummy's ace. Then finish the trumps and watch East squirm.

When there is a choice between a positional and an automatic squeeze, it is almost always right to prefer the automatic form.

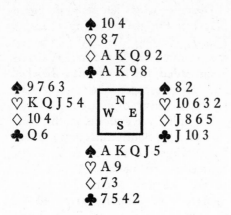

```
        ♠ 10 4
        ♡ 8 7
        ◇ A K Q 9 2
        ♣ A K 9 8
♠ 9 7 6 3            ♠ 8 2
♡ K Q J 5 4    N    ♡ 10 6 3 2
◇ 10 4      W   E   ◇ J 8 6 5
♣ Q 6          S    ♣ J 10 3
        ♠ A K Q J 5
        ♡ A 9
        ◇ 7 3
        ♣ 7 5 4 2
```

You land in the third-best contract of six no trumps and West leads the king of hearts. Not being greedy, you hold up your ace in order to rectify the count for a possible squeeze. West continues with the queen of hearts to your ace. What now?

Unless the diamonds break 3–3 you will need a squeeze, and you should first cash the top cards in one of dummy's suits. But which one? Well, if you cash the top diamonds and run the spades, the only squeeze available will be a positional one against West, since both menaces will be in dummy. Cashing the top clubs, on the other hand, will effect a Vienna Coup, permitting you to hold the club menace in your own hand. You will then have an automatic squeeze which will succeed when *either* defender has length in both minors.

East has no answer when the last spade is led in the following ending:

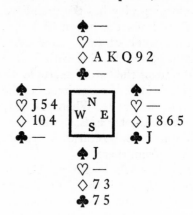

```
          ♠ —
          ♡ —
          ◇ A K Q 9 2
          ♣ —
♠ —                 ♠ —
♡ J 5 4    N        ♡ —
◇ 10 4   W   E      ◇ J 8 6 5
♣ —         S       ♣ J
          ♠ J
          ♡ —
          ◇ 7 3
          ♣ 7 5
```

Inversion

In all the squeezes we have looked at so far the long menace has been opposite the squeeze card. That is the normal rule, but it has exceptions. When the long menace lies in the same hand as the squeeze card, we have what is called the inverted form of the automatic squeeze.

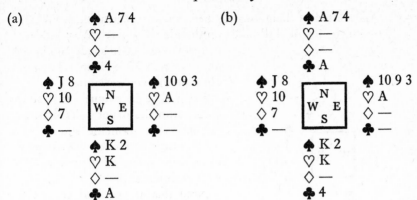

The spade menace above is a split three-card menace. Note that both hands contain a master card in the suit. There is nothing very unusual about the position in diagram (a). If the king of spades is played off, we are left with a normal automatic squeeze. But see what happens when the club holdings are interchanged as in diagram (b). Now the squeeze card is in the same hand as the long menace, yet the inverted squeeze works just as well. That is the special property of the split three-card menace; it permits the squeeze card to lie in either hand.

There may be three cards in each part of the split menace.

♠ K 9 4
♡ K
♢ —
♣ —

♠ Q 7 6   ♠ J 3
♡ A   ♡ 5 3
♢ —   W E   ♢ —
♣ —   ♣ —

♠ A 8 2
♡ —
♢ —
♣ A

Such menaces are common in practical play and should be preserved when possible. The split three-card menace is highly flexible, for you can arrange to have the squeeze card in your hand and the one-card menace in dummy, or vice versa according to the needs of the situation.

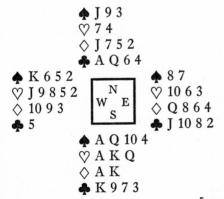

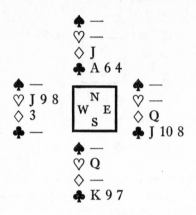

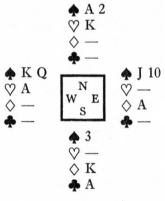

West leads the ten of diamonds against your contract of six no trumps. You cross to the queen of clubs and run the nine of spades. West holds off, but wins the second spade and knocks out your remaining diamond stopper. How should you continue?

Do not be in a hurry to test the clubs. Run the major suits first, and the inverted automatic squeeze will pinch either defender who happens to hold the queen of diamonds along with club length.

Note that if you had cashed the king of clubs earlier 'to test the position', you would have had nothing left but a positional squeeze, which fails on the lie of the cards.

The Double Squeeze

A double squeeze is just a combination of two single squeezes, one against each defender. Three menaces are required altogether – a one-card menace against each defender and a two-card or longer menace against them both. Here is a standard position.

When the ace of clubs is played, West must part with a spade in order to keep his ace of hearts. The king of hearts, having done its job, is discarded from dummy, and East is squeezed in diamonds and spades. Clearly this is a positional squeeze, for it does not work if the East and West cards are interchanged. In this form, the one-card menaces must lie over the defenders they threaten.

Both one-card menaces may lie opposite the squeeze card when the long menace is a split three-card menace.

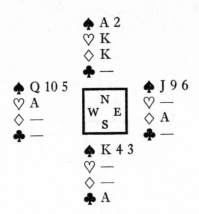

```
          ♠ A 2
          ♡ K
          ◇ K
          ♣ —
♠ Q 10 5          ♠ J 9 6
♡ A      N        ♡ —
◇ —   W     E     ◇ A
♣ —      S        ♣ —
          ♠ K 4 3
          ♡ —
          ◇ —
          ♣ A
```

This is the inverted form, more flexible in that it will still operate if the East and West hands are interchanged. But for all that it is still a positional squeeze. The declarer needs to know which of the red suits is controlled by West; otherwise he may discard the wrong king from dummy on the ace of clubs.

To set out an automatic double squeeze, we need to put both one-card menaces with the squeeze card and have a three-card menace in the opposite hand.

Here South has no worries about discards, and the play of the ace of clubs squeezes both defenders automatically.

Note that in all these positions both defenders are squeezed on the same trick. For that reason they are sometimes called simultaneous double squeezes. With a more complex arrangement of menaces it is possible to squeeze the defenders on successive tricks, but such situations are rare and beyond the scope of this chapter.

As it is, double squeezes are not too common in practical play, but it is useful to be able to recognize these positions when an opportunity presents itself.

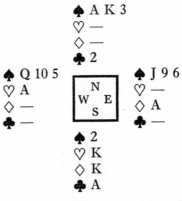

```
          ♠ A K 3
          ♡ —
          ◇ 2
          ♣ 2
♠ Q 10 5          ♠ J 9 6
♡ A      N        ♡ —
◇ —   W     E     ◇ A
♣ —      S        ♣ —
          ♠ 2
          ♡ K
          ◇ K
          ♣ A
```

You play in an adventurous contract of six hearts and West finds the best lead of a trump. Winning with the ace, you lead a club from the table. East takes his ace and returns a second trump, thereby denying you the chance of ruffing two clubs in dummy. That leaves you with only eleven tricks, but there are still chances in the spade suit.

After the ace of spades, the king of clubs and a club ruff, you

```
          ♠ K J 10 7 3
          ♡ A K J
          ◇ A 9 5
          ♣ 9 6
♠ Q 9 6 5 2        ♠ 8 4
♡ 7 2      N       ♡ 8 6 3
◇ J 8 2  W     E   ◇ Q 10 6 3
♣ 8 7 4    S       ♣ A Q J 5
          ♠ A
          ♡ Q 10 9 5 4
          ◇ K 7 4
          ♣ K 10 3 2
```

[227]

cash the king of spades and discard a diamond. When East shows out on the next spade, you ruff and draw the outstanding trump. The only remaining chance is a squeeze. West is known to have the spades, and if East has the master club a double squeeze with diamonds as the long menace is sure to work. Cash the diamond king and play your last trump.

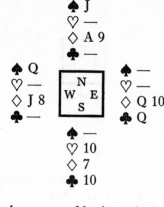

♠ J
♡ —
♢ A 9
♣ —

♠ Q   ♠ —
♡ —   ♡ —
♢ J 8   ♢ Q 10
♣ —   ♣ Q

♠ —
♡ 10
♢ 7
♣ 10

When the ten of hearts is led, West has to part with a diamond in order to keep his queen of spades. You discard the jack of spades from dummy and East has to bow the knee.

Normally when the queen of a suit is missing you have to choose between finessing and playing for the drop. But sometimes it is possible to enjoy the advantages of both methods.

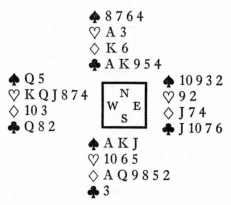

♠ 8 7 6 4
♡ A 3
♢ K 6
♣ A K 9 5 4

♠ Q 5   ♠ 10 9 3 2
♡ K Q J 8 7 4 ♡ 9 2
♢ 10 3   ♢ J 7 4
♣ Q 8 2   ♣ J 10 7 6

♠ A K J
♡ 10 6 5
♢ A Q 9 8 5 2
♣ 3

You play in six diamonds after West has made an overcall of one heart. West leads the king of hearts and you decide to let him hold the trick. If he switches you will have a chance of establishing the clubs, and in any case it is good technique to rectify the count for a possible squeeze. In fact West continues with a second heart to knock out dummy's ace.

Now a straightforward method of play would be to draw trumps, discard the losing heart on a club winner, and try the spade finesse for the twelfth trick. But no player with a knowledge of squeeze technique would dream of finessing in spades. If the spade finesse is working there is no need to take it, for you have an automatic double squeeze position with the ten of hearts menacing West, the jack of spades menacing East, and with clubs as the long menace.

Once trumps have been drawn, therefore, the correct procedure is to play the ace and king of spades. On the actual lie of the cards all your problems are solved by the fall of the queen. But if the queen of spades had been guarded in the East hand, you would simply have played off the rest of your trumps to reach this ending.

When you play the last diamond, neither defender can keep three clubs.

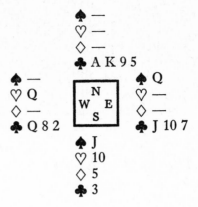

Squeeze Variations

There are so many variations on the squeeze theme that it would be possible to fill several large volumes on the subject. Lack of space in this chapter has precluded any discussion of the large family of strip-squeezes in which one trick or more is given up after the squeeze has taken place. Criss-cross, ruffing and trump squeezes make up another significant group. Irregular arrangements of entries and menaces can give rise to mutations of all kinds. There are complex variations such as guard, triple, progressive, compound and backwash squeezes. And there are some squeezes so obscure that names have yet to be found for them. Experts frequently lose their way in the maze of squeeze possibilities.

Fortunately the exotic flowers do not bloom very often. The squeezes you are most likely to encounter in practical play are the ones we have examined here, and an understanding of these basic forms will provide a sound foundation on which to build.

SQUEEZE DEFENCE

The player who has learned to recognize and execute a squeeze at the table is well equipped to deal with the problems of squeeze defence. Mind you, it is not so easy to recognize a squeeze from the defender's viewpoint. Accurate card-reading is the key. A count of the declarer's tricks will often warn you of impending danger. When it appears that straightforward play will leave declarer a trick short, it is time to take a long, hard look at the squeeze possibilities.

The chance to nip a developing squeeze in the bud usually comes at an early stage in the play. There are certain well-established lines of defence, each aimed at destroying one of the essential features without which a squeeze cannot function. It may be possible, for instance, to launch an early

[229]

attack on the vital entry that forms part of the long menace. Alternatively you may be able to break up the squeeze by obliterating one of the menaces altogether. Or you may be in a position to control the declarer's loser count. It is often a mistake to tighten up the position for declarer by taking your winners too soon. If you refuse to rectify the count, the timing will be upset and the squeeze will founder. Finally, when all else fails and the squeeze is upon you, something may yet be achieved by deceptive discarding.

Let us examine each form of defence in turn.

Attacking an Entry

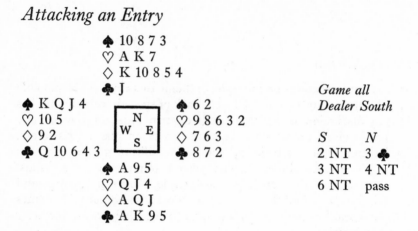

```
              ♠ 10 8 7 3
              ♡ A K 7
              ◇ K 10 8 5 4                 Game all
              ♣ J                          Dealer South
♠ K Q J 4              ♠ 6 2
♡ 10 5          N      ♡ 9 8 6 3 2
◇ 9 2        W   E     ◇ 7 6 3             S      N
♣ Q 10 6 4 3    S      ♣ 8 7 2             2 NT   3 ♣
              ♠ A 9 5                      3 NT   4 NT
              ♡ Q J 4                      6 NT   pass
              ◇ A Q J
              ♣ A K 9 5
```

Your lead of the king of spades is permitted to hold the first trick. How should you continue?

Look into your crystal ball and see what the future will hold if you continue with the queen of spades to knock out the ace. South will run three hearts and five diamonds, the last of which will squeeze you automatically in the black suits.

Actually you should get there without the crystal ball. You can count South's tricks as five diamonds, only three hearts (since he did not bid the suit), two clubs and one spade, making eleven altogether. The only danger is from a squeeze, and you should therefore examine the entry position. Dummy has no winner in either of the menace suits, so the squeeze card would need to be on the table. That means it would take an automatic squeeze to damage you, and since dummy holds a menace only in spades the long menace would have to be in clubs.

Once you reach this point in your deliberations, it is but a short step to find the killing switch to the queen of clubs. With the entry to the long menace removed, no squeeze is possible.

Rubbing Out a Menace

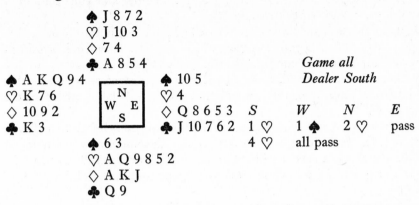

<pre>
              ♠ J 8 7 2
              ♥ J 10 3
              ◇ 7 4
              ♣ A 8 5 4   Game all
♠ A K Q 9 4   ♠ 10 5   Dealer South
♥ K 7 6   ♥ 4
◇ 10 9 2   ◇ Q 8 6 5 3   S   W   N   E
♣ K 3   ♣ J 10 7 6 2   1 ♥   1 ♠   2 ♥   pass
              ♠ 6 3   4 ♥   all pass
              ♥ A Q 9 8 5 2
              ◇ A K J
              ♣ Q 9
</pre>

You win the first two tricks with top spades. How should you continue?

The king of hearts will provide a third defensive trick, and you will have to rely on the king of clubs for the fourth. But there is a danger, if South has the queen of clubs without the jack, that you will be subjected to a black suit squeeze on the run of the trumps. How can you prevent this squeeze from maturing? An attack on the entry is not possible in this case, for you cannot lead clubs without giving declarer his tenth trick immediately.

The attack must be directed against the spade menace with a view to wiping it out completely. Continue at trick three with a small spade, for it is essential to make use of partner's trump while he still has it. South will over-ruff, ruff his third diamond in dummy and play trumps. When in with the king of hearts, you can eliminate the threat of the jack of spades by playing the queen. And, with his squeeze chances gone, South will have to lose a club trick at the end.

Upsetting the Timing

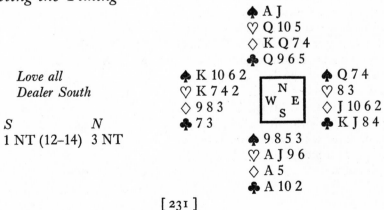

<pre>
                                   ♠ A J
                                   ♥ Q 10 5
                                   ◇ K Q 7 4
                                   ♣ Q 9 6 5
    Love all   ♠ K 10 6 2   ♠ Q 7 4
    Dealer South   ♥ K 7 4 2   ♥ 8 3
                          ◇ 9 8 3   ◇ J 10 6 2
                          ♣ 7 3   ♣ K J 8 4
    S   N   ♠ 9 8 5 3
    1 NT (12–14) 3 NT   ♥ A J 9 6
                                     ◇ A 5
                                     ♣ A 10 2
</pre>

Your lead of the two of spades goes to the jack and queen, and partner returns the seven of spades to dummy's ace. The declarer runs the ten of hearts to your king. How do you defend?

This is more difficult, for it is your partner's hand, not your own, that you have to protect. If you cash your winning spades at this point you will be unable to defeat the contract. The declarer will throw clubs from dummy win the next lead in hand, and run the hearts. Another club will be discarded from dummy on the last heart, and East will be squeezed in the minor suits.

You must avoid rectifying the count for this squeeze. Switch to a club at trick four. On the bidding partner is marked with something good in one of the minors. If it is an ace it will not matter how you defend. But when East has the king and jack of clubs plus a diamond stopper, a club switch is essential.

Sometimes the moment of truth arrives early.

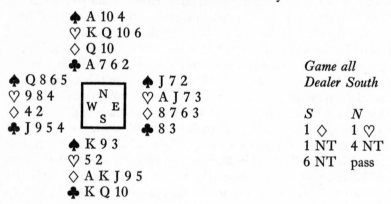

♠ A 10 4
♡ K Q 10 6
◇ Q 10
♣ A 7 6 2

♠ Q 8 6 5   ♠ J 7 2
♡ 9 8 4   ♡ A J 7 3
◇ 4 2   ◇ 8 7 6 3
♣ J 9 5 4   ♣ 8 3

♠ K 9 3
♡ 5 2
◇ A K J 9 5
♣ K Q 10

Game all
Dealer South

S	N
1 ◇	1 ♡
1 NT	4 NT
6 NT	pass

West leads the nine of hearts which is covered by the king, and the fate of the contract is in East's hands. If East takes his ace there will be no further defence. South will win the club or diamond return and cash the queen of hearts, three clubs and five diamonds to produce the following ending.

The play of the last diamond inflicts the double squeeze.

To defeat the contract, all East has to do is refuse the first trick, leaving the declarer with two losers. With its timing disrupted, the double squeeze fizzles out.

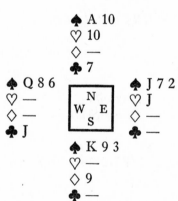

♠ A 10
♡ 10
◇ —
♣ 7

♠ Q 8 6   ♠ J 7 2
♡ —   ♡ J
◇ —   ◇ —
♣ J   ♣ —

♠ K 9 3
♡ —
◇ 9
♣ —

Discarding Technique

When you are forced to unguard your winners under pressure, it is important to do so smoothly and naturally, without showing any sign of discomfort. If the declarer has a guess to make in the ending, there is then a fair chance that he will get it wrong.

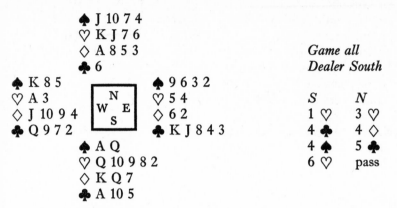

```
              ♠ J 10 7 4
              ♡ K J 7 6
              ◇ A 8 5 3                Game all
              ♣ 6                       Dealer South
♠ K 8 5              ♠ 9 6 3 2
♡ A 3        N       ♡ 5 4            S        N
◇ J 10 9 4  W   E    ◇ 6 2            1 ♡      3 ♡
♣ Q 9 7 2     S      ♣ K J 8 4 3      4 ♣      4 ◇
              ♠ A Q                    4 ♠      5 ♣
              ♡ Q 10 9 8 2             6 ♡      pass
              ◇ K Q 7
              ♣ A 10 5
```

Your opening lead of the jack of diamonds is won by the king. South cashes the ace of clubs, ruffs a club in dummy, and leads a heart to his eight. You take the ace and return your remaining heart. South wins in hand, ruffs his third club in dummy, returns to hand with the queen of diamonds and plays out the rest of the trumps.

You can count eleven tricks and you know that South will be able to make twelve if he has the queen of spades, as seems likely. Meanwhile you have to find three discards on the trumps. To part with a diamond would be to throw in the towel, so your discards must be the fourth club and the two small spades. However, if you sit and stew for a minute before baring the king of spades, you will surely alert the declarer to the fact that you are in trouble. You must steel yourself to part with those small spades calmly and without any fuss. The three-card ending will be as follows.

When a diamond is led to the ace and East shows out, South will have to decide whether you have, in fact, been squeezed on the run of the trumps, or whether the king of spades has been nestling in the East hand all along. Without any clues from your manner, South may well take the finesse and go two down.

It is surprising how often an honour card will fulfil its normal function whether it is guarded or not, particularly if its owner behaves as though he has not a care in the world.

	♠ J	
	♡ —	
	◇ A 8	
	♣ —	
♠ K		♠ 9 6 3
♡ —	N	♡ —
◇ 10 9	W E	◇ —
♣ —	S	♣ —
	♠ A Q	
	♡ —	
	◇ 7	
	♣ —	

No declarer is able to see through the backs of the cards, which is perhaps just as well for the future of the game.